"We...have a beautiful view of Perdido Bay, but miss seeing commercial crab trappers harvesting their catch, shrimpers going up the bay and boats with sightseers ...We no longer see crabs and other sea life in the rocks under our boathouse.

Dr. Lane's book, *Perdido Bay Blues,* traces an environmental movement against the pollution of Perdido Bay. Five hundred people met at the Community Club in Lillian on January 22, 1987 and organized to fight the paper company polluting Perdido Bay, along with the creeks and rivers feeding into it. She exposes the land owners, timber industry and politicians who colluded in making it happen. Her book is interesting, well-written and thoroughly referenced."

Harold B. Hayes, BA, MS, PhD

"This is an extremely interesting, readable account of the efforts of the author, who has lived on the shore of Perdido Bay for many years, to counter the polluting effects of a colossus to the north: a huge paper mill. It is a detailed personal record of an individual who became aware of the deterioration of the bay from the effluents from the mill and a record of attempts by her and others to cope with the situation. As such, it is a historical document and a classic account of the conflict between industry and those it affects."

John Lawrence, PhD Professor Emeritus, University of South Florida

1

Perdido Bay Blues
The Struggle to Save Perdido Bay

Jacqueline Lane, PhD

Black and White edition

Perdido Bay Blues

Copyright ©2017 by Jacqueline Lane, PhD

Acknowledgements

I wish to thank my late husband, Jim, whom I am sure is still fighting by my side; our children, whom I am sure are tired of hearing the stories; and all the Friends of Perdido Bay who stuck around all these years.

I would also like to thank and acknowledge the work of my editors, K & K Manuscript Editing in Pensacola. These two ladies, Katherine Nelson-Born and Katheryn (Ryn) Holmes, took a rough manuscript and turned it into a readable book.

PERDIDO BAY BLUES

APPENDIX

PROLOGUE

Driving west along U.S. 98 in Alabama on this pleasant backroad to Florida, you will approach the Lillian Bridge crossing Perdido Bay that marks the state line between Alabama and Florida. On a warm summer day, when the famous Florida sunshine lights up the bay, you might see sparkling emerald green waters gently lapping sandy shores dotted with single family homes and boat docks. The bay is small and the only high density development you see is in the distance at the beach along the Gulf of Mexico. You might feel a tinge of envy for the people who live where others want to vacation. As you drive across Perdido Bay, you might think to yourself how wonderful it would be to live on this beautiful bay with year-round swimming and fishing available in your backyard. And you would almost be right. Almost. But what you don't see is what's lurking beneath the surface. What you don't see is the growing dioxin-infested dead zone that has killed marine life and infected human swimmers. What you don't see is the effluent from the local paper mill poisoning the water.

The idyllic scene sparkling before your eyes as you drive cross Perdido Bay does not reveal the stories hidden in the bay's waters; stories of dioxin produced by bleaching chemicals; stories of oxygen-depleting replacement bleaching chemicals which are toxic and herbicidal joining the mix; biased studies downplaying the pollution; government entities denying the problems; and local citizens trying desperately to save their beloved bay as it dies. Because of its natural and previously unspoiled beauty, the bay has attracted generations of loyal supporters. Children grew up with happy memories of

7

swimming in its warm shallow waters. For over 30 years, I have fought to save Perdido Bay, with small victories here and there, but it is still dying.

I wonder if I would have spent so much effort and time fighting the paper mill if I had known from the beginning what I know today - the power of the paper industry. The supporters of paper mills are timber growers, large and small, who plant trees to sell to the paper industry, "environmentalists" who support forests and planting trees over using land for development, the chemical industry who manufactures tons of chemicals for pulping trees into paper, labor unions who preserve jobs in the paper industry, and all the politicians elected with the money from the paper mill supporters. If I had known before I got started just how weak and misguided environmental laws would be for my cause, would I have spent so much effort fighting this massive polluter? I cannot say for sure, but I did put up a fight. Currently, however, the bay is still polluted, perhaps worse than ever. I am hoping that with these words documenting the heroic efforts of this David against the Goliath of the local paper mill, others will take up the fight. My Perdido Bay Blues song is a sad one that is being repeated across the nation and across the world without being sufficiently heard. Our local efforts kept the paper mill from getting a valid permit, but did not stop the pollution from happening. Even without a permit, the paper mill can continue its operations for many years. Perhaps in 2019, when the Consent Order expires, the paper mill will finally be held accountable, but I would not bet on it. Nevertheless, I will continue to fight, and I hope others will join me.

I have been doing this so long. I cannot quit now, but the paper mill may outlive *me*. This is my story and the story of others, some still living and others who have died, including my husband. I hope it brings about the changes needed to save our waters from continued paper mill pollution.

LANE FAMILY – PERDIDO BAY, 1980s

9

CHAPTER 1 ~The Area

After my husband and I were married, we moved to his family's homestead along the shores of scenic upper Perdido Bay in 1975. Most of the land had been purchased in 1940. This is a place he had talked about for years. The rituals of lunch and dinner. A swim before lunch, a swim before dinner. At first, I was not particularly impressed. It was rural and unkempt - dirt roads full of holes, a swamp full of mosquitos when it rained, yellow flies in the spring, black flies in late summer. The weather did not seem as nice as the Florida from which I had come, St. Petersburg. Sometimes in summer, it would rain for a week with over cast skies hovering over Perdido Bay. Humidity was high nearly all the time. In the winter, it could be a bone-chilling, wet cold. In the summer, of course, it was hot and humid. But Perdido Bay is a place that grows on you, like the mildew covering your shoes in the closet and ruining the lenses of your cameras. The stately live oak trees with Spanish moss hanging from their limbs tower over the Bay. The Magnolia trees with their big, white, lemon-scented flowers burst open every spring. It is a Southern place out of the past that seems lost in time. The family's twenty-acre homestead had been allowed to grow wild, so the woods were everywhere and home was private. The neighbors were friendly but not too close. The bay was beautiful…most of the time.

Perdido Bay. On the map, you can hardly see it, covering just 50 square miles running in a southwest-northeastern direction. It is just a slight enlargement of the state line between Florida and Alabama. It is really the enlarged mouth of the river which feeds it - the Perdido River. The length of the bay is 17 miles and the width varies from 2 to 4 miles. The shoreline is lined with narrow beaches of tan, coarse sand. Some say the sand was white before the paper mill defiled the waters. My father-in-law spent his retirement from the Marine Corps building groins out from the beach to keep the beach from washing away. It worked, but the groins are beginning to crumble now. The cement-block walls which had been built in terraces up the 8 - 9 ft. banks beyond the beach are also beginning to topple over. Some neighbors have fortified their beaches using rocks and rip-rap. They also have built docks that extend into the bay, occasionally with boat houses and decks at the end. We never built a dock.

As you stand on our beach and look out over the upper bay, you are struck by the lack of development. Across the bay is the mouth of the Perdido River and Alabama. Just a little to the south is the great expanse of land known as the Lillian Swamp. It was used primarily by various entities to grow pine trees in Silviculture operations. Attempts to sell the swamp have been unsuccessful. The state of Alabama has bought parts of it[1]. Just south of the Lillian Swamp, more recent developments have begun to spring up with a few homes on the bay. This area is known as Lillian, Alabama, a small un-incorporated community composed of long time locals and Northern retirees. To the east of our beach, there are a string of docks and single family homes, many built in the 1940's. Absent are condominiums and apartments. Further to the east of our beach, not visible from our beach, is a low area with pilings jutting up out of the water. These pilings are the remains of a thriving lumber business and its town, Millview, built in the mid 1800's. Virgin southern pine had been cut and floated down the Perdido River to these docks. Some timber was cut into boards, and loaded onto a little railroad which connected to the docks in the city of Pensacola. After all the virgin pine had been cut down at the turn of the century, the little town of Millview and the railroad ceased to exist.

Beyond the pilings is a housing development known as La Paz. It is built on a small strip of land which faces the bay on one side and a canal on the other. The area is low and houses not built on pilings will flood with high water events. Further is a wooded area now owned by the local utility, Escambia County Utilities Authority (ECUA). Intersected by Bayou Marcus Creek, one thousand acres are used to "polish" domestic wastewater.

This is Florida's new approach to disposal of domestic wastewater - discharge to wetlands. Later, this discharge would be misrepresented as a culprit for deterioration of the bay by Dr. Livingston, a scientist hired by the paper mill to deflect criticism. The density of human population is low and impact nominal.

On the most northerly side of the bay is land owned by the Navy, called Saufley Field, where potential Naval aviators practiced their landings and take-offs. It is currently used as a federal prison, an educational facility, and a photography school by the Navy. You can hardly get together with Perdido Bay residents without hearing a story or two about flying out of Saufley Field. My husband had his share of stories.

The next landmark is Elevenmile Creek. This was a crystal- clear, spring-fed creek where people would go to enjoy a day in the country…a long time ago. In 1941, the paper mill began dumping into this creek, turning the clear water into a foul-smelling black mess - until 2013. A restaurant which served chicken dinners on Sunday soon closed after the paper mill began operations; no one would dream of using this creek for recreation to the current day. The people who owned property along the creek sold permanent easements to the paper company for very little money. The State of Florida deemed it an industrial river until the early 1980's when its classification was changed to Class III, a recreational designation! Despite its recreational designation, it is not a place one would want to swim because of its dark color and nasty smell. Locals named it "stink creek." A few ill-advised fishermen may fish there but people bathe their dogs in the creek to cure them of mange. The sulfur in the effluent kills the mange parasites.

Going northwest from Elevenmile Creek is the opening to marsh lakes known as Tee and Wicker Lakes. At one time these were beautiful wild lakes lined with the marsh grass *Spartina* and *Juncus*. Once the paper mill started dumping into Elevenmile Creek, tidal action carried the effluent into the lakes.

At some point, a cut was made between the lower part of the creek and the upper lake, so that paper mill effluent enters both lakes at this point as well. The land above the lakes was owned by one of the local timber barons, Mr. Rainwater. In addition to using the land for harvesting timber, sheep were also reported to have been raised there. The property had a large stream, Wicker Creek, which flowed into Wicker Lake. There were other smaller feeder streams on the property as well. In the 1980's, the owners of the paper mill, Champion International, bought this property from Mr. Rainwater. Exactly what they were going to do with it I do not know, but it was being considered for the Florida's land purchase program. This land is now the property where International Paper Company, the new owners of the paper mill, discharges their effluent. The streams have been completely obliterated by International Paper Company and the property has been extensively reworked. The paper mill effluent flows over this property and out into the bay. The once beautiful lakes are now settling ponds for paper mill sludges.

Going northwest from the entrance to Tee and Wicker Lakes is the mouth of Perdido River, the main source of water for Perdido Bay. The Perdido River is considered to be the "highest quality free-flowing black-water river of the southeastern Coastal Plain"[2]. The river is fed by groundwater from the sand and gravel aquifer. The water is "soft" with low pH. Generally, the water quality of the river is excellent. It was designated a "Florida Outstanding Water" in 1979. The water is tea colored and fairly clear. To try and "explain" the dark water in Perdido Bay, government agencies called the river a "black-water river," or river with a lot of tannic acid. It is not really. There are some wetlands along the river, but not as many as in other local rivers[3]. The lack of wetlands makes the Perdido River less productive than the rest which have more nutrients. Bass fishermen still ply its water for bass. The river water is fresh, except where salt water enters from the bay.

As the river twists and turns its way south, many small streams enter on the Florida side. Two main tributaries enter on the Alabama side, the Styx and the Blackwater. The Styx River drains forest land in mid Baldwin County, Alabama and is used as a canoe and float stream. The Blackwater is further south and drains farmland in Baldwin County, Alabama. The Blackwater, as its name implies, is darker and deeper and probably is the source of nutrient pollution into the main Perdido River. The entire watershed of the Perdido River is 70% forested land[4] which at one time had been owned by the major paper companies in Pensacola, Florida, and Mobile, Alabama. The paper companies paid very low property taxes because of agricultural tax exemptions. The taxes were a little more than $1.00 per acre. The paper companies would then rent tracts of forest lands to hunt clubs who paid about $2.00 per acre for the right to hunt on the property. The hunt clubs also maintained vigilance over the property and make sure no one dumped trash on the property. I remember beaching our boat along the banks of the Perdido River in this wild area. To my surprise, a person appeared out of the woods and told me the property was private. Because so much of the land along the Perdido River was private, there was very limited access to it. Today, both the states of Florida and Alabama have bought land along the river from the paper and timber companies to preserve the wildness of the river. Access to the river has been increased but the usual management problems have arisen. On summer weekends, locals go out to the river and cool off. People sitting in lawn chairs in the shallow areas of the river while drinking beer is a common sight. But many times, the garbage from these summer outings is left at the site. Instead of cooling off, drinking may lead to heated arguments and fights. One private landowner who allowed access to the river at one of the bridges, had to withdraw the public's access privileges due to garbage and rowdiness. The few developments along the river are small and found mainly in the upper parts of the river. One Alabama town, Bay Minette, discharges domestic wastewater into the river but its impact is limited. There are several Alabama municipalities

14

in its watershed but none along the river. Their discharges have minimal impact on the water quality in the river[5].

Pilings of old bridges which once traversed the river are still present in the river today. They are remains of a once flourishing timber trade along the river. The town of Muscogee, Florida which had been located along the banks of the Perdido River had about 1,000 residents in 1857. The town disappeared once the virgin pine had been cut. Today Atlantic white cedar, red bay, sweet gum and swamp maple dot the white sandy banks of the river. Further from the banks are plantations of pine interspersed with live oak. Folks say the pine plantations are on the fourth and fifth cuttings. It takes about 17 years for pine trees to grow to a size able to be harvested for pulp wood; longer for timber. Several endangered plants and animals are found in the watershed, most notably, the carnivorous pitcher plants which have a special protected designation.

Several miles before the river empties into Perdido Bay, it widens into a multitude of small islands and bays. Even today, after many trips up the river, I still worry about getting lost. The river is also deeper. During heavy rains, flow of the river increases and gouges out holes. Some of them are 35 to 40 feet deep. Perdido Bay is also a tidal bay where salt water and fresh water mix. When the flow of the river is low, salt water from the Gulf of Mexico comes all the way up the bay and enters the river. Because salt water is usually heavier than freshwater, the salt water in the river is found on the bottom. This is called the "salt wedge" and can extend seven miles up the river. The deep holes in the river usually have salt water in them. Some scientists who have studied the Perdido River have postulated that the salt water in these holes may be very old.

It takes a lot of flow to drive this salt water from these holes. Because the river is affected by the tidal flow from the bay, the dark smelly water from the paper mill has also been carried into the river. The black organic ooze which is characteristic of the bottom of the river is partially natural deposits from the river and partially sludges from the paper mill. These sludges use up the oxygen in the bottom water and very little life is left to be found in deeper parts of the Perdido River.

The upper part of Perdido Bay is a wider extension of the river. The bay is shaped like an hourglass. The upper part of the bay may be defined (although it has not been standardized) as the upper bowl of the hour glass. The deepest part of the upper bay is considered fairly shallow, averaging 9ft. deep. All around the edge of the upper bay is a very shallow sandy shelf which may only be 2 to 3 feet deep. The distance this shallow shelf extends out into the bay depends, in part, on storms. Recently, a very heavy rain storm in April, 2014 increased the flow of the river nearly 10-fold. Our beach, across from the mouth of the river, was greatly enlarged from sand washing out of the river. You can walk out for 5 minutes before ever getting into waist deep water. In addition, large trees still with their roots were washed out of the river during that storm and are now "caught" in the shallow bottom. The folks here call them "snags." These snags will be here until another storm with high water dislodges and carries them away. This shallow shelf was great for children playing in the warm summer water. Our children learned to swim early with no fear of the water. We were unaware of the dangerous chemicals in the water during the time our children were growing up.

The deeper parts of Perdido Bay are sediment traps for the organic material washed out of the river and also for the sludges from the paper mill. As with the deeper parts of the river, there is very little oxygen in the deeper parts of Perdido Bay. As a result, very little bottom life exists.

At the waist of the hour glass, Perdido Bay is traversed by the only bridge across the bay. U.S. Highway 98 connects Florida and Alabama. Because the bay narrows abruptly at this point, it is deeper here (10 to 20') and the currents that run through the pilings of the bridge are strong. Underground springs well up from the bottom and bring freshwater into the

16

bay at the constriction. It was said that when contractors were driving piles for the new bridge built in the late 1970's and early 1980's, they had not anticipated those springs being present. Piles sank a lot further than planned; consequently, the bridge took longer to be built.

The bottom, or southern part of the hourglass is the middle section of Perdido Bay. It is much like the upper, only a little wider and deeper. The deepest is toward the western side. There is also a shallow shelf which runs along the edge. The edge of the middle bay is dotted with residences: single family homes. There is an occasional open space. On the Florida side, Pensacola Christian College has a recreational facility, where small sailboats are launched. Next to that facility is a Navy recreational park. Named Bronson Field, this park was built during World War II as a sea plane base and the concrete ramps are still there. Next to Bronson Field is a Florida State preserve - the Tarkiln Bayou Pitcher Plant preserve. A spit of land juts out into Perdido Bay and forms a small peninsula that is defined by two points - to the north, DuPont Point and to the south Tarkiln Point. A bay is formed on the southern side of this peninsula - Tarkiln Bay. At its northern end, Tarkiln Bay, is nearly cut off from Perdido Bay, and forms an enclosed pond. At low tide, it is nearly impossible to access this pond by boat and the county has deemed it a non-motorized area.

South of Tarkiln Bayou, Perdido Bay widens and the shoreline is low. Single family residences are dotted along the shore. As you head toward the Gulf of Mexico, the sand becomes whiter and finer like the sand of the Gulf of Mexico, and one finds various small communities like Perdido Beach. The density of people increases. It is on the barrier islands, protecting the inland bays, that the condominiums begin appearing. This part of the bay has cleaner water coming from the Gulf - at least until heavy rainfall washes the polluted water from upper Perdido Bay into the lower bay. Continued paper mill pollution and increased rainfall make potentially deadly partners.

VIEW OF PERDIDO BAY NOT SHOWING POLLUTION

CHAPTER 2 ~ The Mass Mortality of Clams

After moving to Perdido Bay in 1975, I grew to love the place where my husband and I began our family. I thought Perdido Bay would be a great place to raise children - lots of woods and water to play in. By 1982, we had five children - three girls and two boys. My mother and father-in-law gave us some land and we started building our house on the bay. My husband, Jim, a civil engineer, designed our house, and it is truly unique. One building inspector said it looked like a Frank Lloyd Wright house. It took us three years to get it built. While my husband and I would work on the house, the children would play around and "help" us. Jim was working as a civil engineer in Pensacola at the time, then took a job teaching civil engineering at the University of South Alabama. It was a long drive - three hours round trip - but he had summers off, which was nice. By the time the house was completed in 1982, it was already too small. With five children, three bedrooms and two baths made for a pretty tight squeeze. But of course, once they were grown, the stories about how their parents squeezed five children into two bedrooms made for a few laughs.

We built our bay house without air-conditioning, putting in lots of sliding glass doors which we opened wide in summer. Although the house is situated on the bay, we are surrounded by trees. Not only do they obscure our view of the water, they also block the breeze off the bay. This is a good thing in the winter when the wind comes roaring out of the north at 30 miles per hour, but in the summer it is hot and humid. Luckily, we thought, we had the bay out back beckoning us to swim. We kept to my husband's routine of swimming in the bay twice a day – once before lunch and again before dinner. After swimming, we would shower off in an outdoor shower built soon after we completed our house. And yes, it did keep us cool ... for at least 30 minutes. It was clear that the bay was an integral part of our lives. The children grew up swimming and fishing in its waters. The little Rangia marsh clams which once covered the bottom of the bay, made great bait for pinfish. They also made great weapons to throw if you happened to get mad at your brother or sister. The consequences of throwing clams, however, were severe: they were opened by throwing them hard on the cement groins. The many pinfish which lived in the bay would gladly bite. They were usually too small to eat although occasionally we caught several and would fry them up. Our early years on Perdido Bay were basically good, but we were blissfully unaware of what was entering the bay from the local paper mill.

The bay once held lots of fish. Wading out from our beach with a shrimp on the line would usually produce a "bite". If it wasn't a catfish, and there were plenty of them, it could be a speckled sea trout or a redfish. On weekends, we would put the runabout boat in the water and motor up to the old pilings. Fishing was always better at the pilings than at our beach and we would usually be able to catch a few trout or redfish. We could always catch croakers. Redfish were tricky because as soon as you caught them, they would head for a submerged piling with sharp barnacles. When you felt your line go limp, you knew it had been cut. My husband decided that it would be neat to fly fish for speckled trout. For years, you would see him "looping" his line out into the water with a floating popping bug. He may have gotten a bite, but I never once saw him catch a fish, even while the fish were still plentiful.

Summers were always characterized by seeing many schools of menhaden swimming near the surface of the water. Menhaden are fish which feed on plankton (small plants in the water). There were so many fish that the ripples were visible from the Lillian Bridge and our beach on calm days. Today, the schools of menhaden have vanished.

At night in the summer, one of our favorite pastimes was floundering. You usually had a floundering set-up: a small boat which held a battery that ran an underwater light. You would push the boat along in the water quietly without the motor. The smaller children would sit in the boat. Only two to three feet deep, the water was usually clear and calm enough to spot the outline of the flounder in the sand. We then aimed for the spot between the two eyes and stabbed it with the sharp point of the gig then removed it while the flounder was still in the small boat and look for the next one. Sometimes we could get four or five flounder in one night. Of course, the children were always pushing ahead trying to be the first to spot a fish. I think quite a few flounder were probably pre-warned and swam off before they were spotted. The floundering was especially good around the cement breakwaters or groins which my father-in-law had built out into the water. Often, we were not alone when we were out there at night. Even when we were not out in the bay, we still heard other people floundering around the groins at night. The practice has since disappeared along with the fish.

Another night time activity was setting our gill net back in the days when gill nets were still legal. We would set the gill net perpendicular to our beach at sunset. Two or three hours later we would pull it in. Most of the children were in bed by the time we began pulling in the gill net, so many times it was just me and Jim. Our goal was to catch mullet but catfish sometimes got tangled up in the net as well. Their sharp fins always managed to catch two or three loops of the net and make a mess. Sometimes, we had to cut the fins to get them out. Mullet were easier to get out of the net. If their gills hadn't been caught too badly, you could just push the fish through the net. We always ate the mullet, very seldom the catfish. Jim liked to smoke mullet using fresh bay wood cut from a tree at the end of our driveway. Fresh-caught fish is a delicacy I miss. Like most responsible bay dwellers, we let little go to waste. The fish heads from the cleaned mullet would either go one or two places - into the garden or into the crab traps…when there were crabs to be caught. If planted in the garden, the fish heads had to be dug deep enough to keep wild animals from uncovering them. Fish heads that went into the crab traps were always successful in catching three or four blue crabs. After baiting the crab traps with fish heads, the traps usually had to be checked within two or three days. Blue crabs will start attacking and eating each other if left too long in the trap. Blue crab meat is good; however, cleaning the meat from the body and claws is hard work. Serving boiled blue crabs and allowing our family to clean and eat them at the table was fun but a big mess, so we did not put out crab traps often. Today, crabs have become nearly extinct in the upper bay.

Another night time activity on our little bay no longer available to the casual fisherman is shrimping. It seemed like everyone who owned a boat also owned a shrimp net. These were not the big nets of the shrimp trawlers, but smaller nets which could be pulled behind a runabout with a 40hp engine. Because Perdido Bay is interstate water with a state line running down the middle, the size of mesh allowed in the net depended on which state waters you were in. Once shrimping season opened in Alabama, the size of the shrimp you were allowed to catch was smaller than that allowed in Florida. So, all Florida shrimpers had "Alabama" sleeves that could be put in the Florida net when shrimping in Alabama. When you were out there at night it was hard to tell exactly in what state you were. Several hours at night usually yielded 3 or 4 pounds of bay shrimp. These were not the pink shrimp of the Gulf, but the brown shrimp that lived near the muddy bottom of the bay. Today you must have a commercial license to shrimp in the Bay. Although a few shrimp can still be caught, shrimping, in the upper and mid-bay has gone the way of the shrimp – disappeared.

It was always pretty dark in the bay at night so in order to work the net, you had to take your lantern. Still, what you could see at night was amazing. The phosphorescence in the water would illuminate the tract of a dragged net or the path of a big fish. One night, I remember being approached by a boat with a bright light. Two guys, so drunk they could hardly stand up, were looking for Rose's Marine which was about four miles to

22

the north. I often wondered if they ever found the marina or just beached the boat and passed out. Even sober it was easy to lose your bearings in the bay at night.

The only shellfish available to eat out of the upper bay were the little marsh clams the kids liked to throw at each other, despite parental warnings not to do so. These clams once covered the bottom of the bay even though attempts to eat them were unpleasant. They had a metallic taste and imparted it to any chowder. I always thought that oysters should be present in the bay. There were historic accounts of oyster beds in the bay, but since we have lived here, none grew. I know several people who unsuccessfully tried to grow their own oysters in Perdido Bay by using various contraptions. People living in the lower parts of the Bay would report that they had oysters growing on pilings or rocks at their beaches, but they would disappear, usually after heavy rains when water from the upper bay washed into the lower bay.

I remember grass beds would begin to grow at our beach and then disappear. We had extremely lush grass beds growing at our beach as late as the late 1990's. They were so vibrant that several times I even saw them flowering. There were permanent grass beds in the bayou just around the corner from our beach. It is still there today, but the fronds are red. This is abnormal. A big permanent grass bed existed across the bay from us along the shore of the Lillian Swamp. I always figured that the name "Grassy Point" came from the presence of this large and healthy grass bed, having fronds 1½ feet long. This grass bed was just outside the mouth of the Perdido River and was flushed by its clean water. The grass bed had been there as long as anyone could remember and were still there until 2000 when everything in the bay died. The introduction of a different habitat to the otherwise plain sand bottom allowed a different type of fauna to develop. Grass shrimp, pipefish, sculpin fish and snails made the grass fronds their permanent homes. Baby fish and crabs would take advantage of the protection of the fronds. Grass beds provided additional entertainment for the family. It was always fun to drag a net through the grass beds and see what you found. That's all gone now.

Not only did the bay provide recreation and food in the early years, but it was also a place to socialize. Any time a family member came to our homestead for a visit we would end up sitting in the bay talking. It was shallow; it was warm; and it provided a comfortable place to just sit and chat, especially since we did not have air conditioning. It was cooler than sitting on land if you went later in the day to avoid getting sunburnt. We would see our neighbors also out enjoying the water and wave at them. Many people told me sitting in the bay was how neighbors used to chat with one another. I also heard stories about floating saunas and wild parties. While we never saw any of these where we lived, summer visitors in the lower bay had some tantalizing stories to tell.

The water was never crystal-clear in the summer, even before it became polluted. Perdido Bay waters were clear enough to see to your toes in knee deep water, but Caribbean-clear water - No. The color of the water was slightly brown, like Southern sweet tea. You could tell when the water from Elevenmile Creek and the paper mill were flowing by your beach. The water grew darker, smelling and looking nasty. In the winter, it was usually clear because phytoplankton and bacteria didn't grow when the water temperature dropped below 70° F. Storms sometimes churned up the bay and made it turbid. Then there were days when the foam on top of the water was bad and you would want to avoid the big patches fouling your beach. We knew the foam came from the paper mill despite the paper mill telling us the foam was "natural." Well, it may have been natural, but it was too much of a natural thing.
Paper mills actually make soap[1]. The fatty acids in the pine wood combine with the lye of the pulping process and make soap. There were days when I came out of the water from my daily swim and my skin would sting or my body hairs would

have small fibers, like dirt caught in them. A shower after swimming became necessary. Sometimes I am amazed at how naïve I was at first about the pollution going on in my little bay. The water wasn't great, but it seemed passable. My husband and his older sister told stories about how much clearer the bay had been in the 1960's, recalling how the family would come down and spend their summers on Perdido Bay. Jim's family had been doing this since the property was purchased in 1940.

Since I am a biologist with a PhD in marine biology, I couldn't help but eventually get around to doing some research on Perdido Bay in my spare time when I wasn't chasing after my five children. I conducted my first research project on the bay in September 1979. The most obvious thing to study was the Rangia paving the bottom of the bay. I went to the University of West Florida library to find out what research had been done on these clams. There were some papers, but certainly more could be learned. I started doing monthly surveys. The little snails crawling on the cement groins at our beach also caught my interest. They ate the microscopic scum alga growing on the groins. There were hundreds of these little snails. Sometimes they were above the high tide line; sometimes they were submerged in the water. I would later do more studies on the factors which affected the position of the snails. As I look back, I remember the bay having an abundance of life in the early 1980's. I saw things not seen since - like little jelly fish.

The clams died in 1986. Before they died, I had only a rather vague idea about the pollution of the bay by the paper mill. I knew the foam and the dark water which intermittently came to our beach was caused by the paper mill, but other than that, I didn't have any idea about how pervasive the pollution was or what a damaging impact it was having on the bay. At first, we were unconcerned, about swimming in the bay twice a day. No one had said swimming in it was dangerous. It may have been a little unpleasant from time to time, but mostly we enjoyed our daily swims. Our children spent most of their

25

childhoods playing in the waters of Perdido Bay. I look back on those years with some alarm now. We were innocent and ignorant. We knew nothing about the permitting process or what was happening at the paper mill. From time to time we would read a news article about the paper mill in Cantonment Florida. We vaguely knew that the St. Regis Company had recently sold the paper mill to Champion International. But we were not paying attention to what was going on behind our little house on Perdido Bay. The clam kill changed all that, and it changed my life.

On Saturday, October 4, 1986, we had planned to have a picnic at our beach with another family. It was warm for early fall. We planned to have lunch and then spend the rest of the day playing in the bay. We were going to put the boat in the water, and when we went down to look at the bay, we were shocked. Thick foam and scum extended from our beach 40 feet into the water. A few dead fish floated in the foam, but even worse was the color of the water. It was black and oily-looking. Our friends had put their boat in at a public boat ramp around the corner from our beach. They reported coming through a sea of dead fish on their way. Looking back, I am amazed that we decided to continue with our party anyway. We rode the bumper inner tube around behind the boat in the foamy water. The foam slowly dissipated as the day went by. Within a few days, it was gone and the water seemed to have returned to normal. But the clams had all died. I didn't know they were dead at first. Then they all came up out of the bottom sand in the bay. Since they were so numerous and paved the bottom of the bay, walking on objects sticking up 1 to 2" was nearly impossible. A few days after the clams had all come out of the bottom, they opened up and I realized they were dead. At this point I didn't know what to do, so I called the local office of the Florida Department of Environmental Regulation (FL DER). They said they would send out a biologist to inspect. An article appeared in the local newspaper about the death of the clams.

I spent the days after the clam kill trying to find a few living clams. All the clams I had marked with numbers in my earlier research were dead. From time to time, the water was dark and nasty. I did take pictures of the dead clams. There were just a few remaining alive in the bayou around the corner from our beach, and a few further down the bay as well. But at our beach, the mortality was 100%.

From that time on, the deluge of public interest began. We began to get phone calls from people all over the bay and from interested parties. We had people offer suggestions about what may have killed the clams. One man told us they were painting the bridges on the Perdido River. One of the people calling was Jo Ann Allen, a person like me who would end up spending the rest of her life working to clean up Perdido Bay. With her husband, Harry, a former naval aviator, Jo Ann was a realtor in Lillian, Alabama. She told us about a group of people, including herself, who had been active in the 1960's in fighting the paper mill. Jo Ann and her husband lived on Soldier's Creek in the Lower Bay. She told us that there had been two lawsuits in the 1970's against the paper mill, but that they had been dismissed. She told us that the groups had never really gotten organized. She said the paper mill had been ordered to go to a "closed loop" or zero discharge of pollutants in the early 1970's. She suggested calling a meeting and organizing an environmental group. We did just that. We also began writing letters to the EPA, our congressmen, and our local officials. There was a lot of interest generated. We began to learn about our bay, the environmental permitting process, and the paper mill. There was no bringing the clams back, but the fight to save the rest of Perdido Bay had begun.

CHAPTER 3 ~ Beginning of the Environmental Groups

The 100% clam mortality at my little beach had been a real wake-up call. Joining forces with Jo Ann Allen, the realtor from Lillian, Alabama, I became committed to saving Perdido Bay. Public interest in our bay after the clam kill still ran pretty high. Our first environmental meeting was January 22, 1987 in Lillian, Alabama. It was held at the former (a new one has since been built) Lillian Community Club. Five hundred people showed up; four hundred signed in. The place was packed. We invited one of the local EPA scientists involved in an EPA study to address the group. The EPA had begun a comprehensive study of Perdido Bay in the fall of 1986 in preparation for the renewal of the paper mill permit. Dr. Bill Kruczynski described the study the EPA was doing. He declared the bottom of the upper bay dead. There were no longer worms or other small animals on the bottom sand. These animals are usually present, even in much polluted waters. Dr. Kruczynski said the EPA was going to place more stringent limits than those currently required. Jo Ann also addressed the crowded house and gave a small history of the 1960's and 1970's fight against the paper mill. I also spoke to the group, discussing my expertise as a marine biologist and my studies of the bay since 1979 and ended my presentation saying that I suspected Champion, the local paper mill, was responsible for the clam kill. A year later I came across a letter in the files of DER(P)[1] that confirmed my conclusion was correct. At the time, however, I did not want to shut down the mill. I just wanted the paper mill to address the preventable problems it was causing. We adjourned the January 1987 meeting with plans to hold another in February and formally set up a new environmental group to fight the local paper mill's pollution of Perdido Bay. Thirty years later, the paper mill is still actively polluting our little bay.

The environmental group was incorporated in Alabama as a nonprofit corporation on February 9, 1987 as the Perdido Bay Environmental Association, Inc. At the incorporation

28

signing, I, along with Jo Ann Allen and Larry Sutley, a lawyer from Foley, AL, comprised the major officers of the corporation. The official election of officers would wait for the next general meeting. I realized early the need for communicating our actions and concerns with the larger general membership, so I began writing a short newsletter called "Baywatch." The newsletter went out to all the people who had signed up at the first meeting in January 1987. We also had to develop organizational goals, a constitution, and bylaws. Besides the general officers of the association, it was Larry Sutley's idea to elect representatives from the various districts around the bay and to set up working committees. That meeting was set for February 19, 1987. Unfortunately, my husband, Jim, and I were not able to attend due to an unexpected mechanical problem. Jo Ann Allen was elected president; Vice-presidents were Joe Trapp, Martin Fink, Thorton Garth, and Bob Small; Secretary, Dr. Jim Law; Treasurer, Fred Garth. At that meeting, Jo Ann presented to new members a passionate petition advocating the paper mill go to a "closed system." It was to be signed by all the members of the newly formed Perdido Bay Environment Association and sent to all the local elected officials:

"CRIME AGAINST HUMANITY - A SILENT DEATH"
I know that for me to keep your attention I must keep this short and to the point, therefore:
Perdido Bay is near death! Alabama and Florida waters and those contiguous to Perdido Bay are being strangled by apparent toxins and other latent pollutants. It is my understanding, there are three known industrial dischargers and ten known municipal dischargers to the Perdido Bay Basin; there may be more of less today.
We know these industries provide jobs and dollars to the local economy, but it does not license them to commit unbridled devastation of our waters and set the stage for potential illnesses. Clams have been killed in upper parts of the bay, fish are diseased with cancerous-like lesions and we can no longer enjoy other recreational uses of these waters. The stench is

becoming unbearable and the water surface bears evidence of human waste being discharged into some waters. A neglected environment will precipitate economic decline. Be warned!

Alabama and Florida residents have joined forces to protect and demand that corrective action be taken to stop this unmitigated assault on our rights of free choice of life styles.

We have not yet heard your voice in this matter. As a representative of the peoples of the States of Alabama and Florida, we demand your response to this signed petition along with publication of your response and intended action via local news medias.

The cost of effective "CLOSED SYSTEMS" for the above should be of little consequence.

Board of Directors
Perdido Bay Environmental Association, Inc.

The closed system referred to in Jo Ann's 1987 letter was the solution that had been recommended by the EPA for the paper mill in the early 1970's but was never installed.

The letters to the public officials did get their attention in 1987. We were getting calls almost daily from various people in environmental agencies, from many outside agencies, and other environmental groups. The news media also began covering our story. One reporter from the Associated Press, Bill Kaczor, wrote a story which appeared in the *Tallahassee Democrat* on Feb. 16, 1987. He had covered the original meeting in January, and had also gotten comments from the EPA concerning the study they were doing on Perdido Bay. One comment attributed to Jim Greenfield, the EPA's head engineer in Atlanta, was the same comment he had given to us over the phone in January 1987. He said his agency had not "dealt with a bay like Perdido before." Jim Greenfield admitted Perdido Bay was "a non-flushing bay," and that anything going in there stayed in there despite the hurricanes we had a couple years ago. Mr. Kaczor also interviewed Bob Kriegel, district director of Florida's DER, about the clam kill. Kriegel claimed there was no reason to connect the paper mill with the clam kill. Champion officials did admit that they had spilled solids from their ponds on October 7, 1986, but conveniently this was after the clam kill and the bay of dead fish that had set off local alarm on Saturday October 4, 1986. The officials at DER were never helpful despite their assertions to the contrary; on the other hand, some of the permitting engineers and the biologists were.

In its efforts to fight Perdido Bay pollution, bi-monthly meetings of the Perdido Bay Environmental Association (PBEA) continued throughout 1987. Speakers were usually biologists with the Federal and State agencies. Most of these biologists pointed out that Perdido Bay had been polluted in the past by St. Regis, the old owners of the mill, but that things supposedly were getting better. Our speakers also liked to point out other potential sources of pollution - septic tanks, wastewater treatment systems, storm water, leaking landfills, etc. Interestingly, no speaker since January's first speaker, EPA scientist Dr. Bill Kruczynski, admitted the bay was dead. An Alabama fisheries biologist reported that Alabama had tagged striped bass in the Perdido System and were getting returns in live fish caught, indicating the bay was not dead. There were also reports of diseased fish being caught in the Upper Bay. State biologists tried to down play the polluted nature of the bay.

The Perdido Bay Environmental Association stayed very busy in 1987. Besides the general membership and committee bi-monthly meetings, the Board of Directors of the Perdido Bay Environmental Association also held meetings. Unfortunately, I had to resign from the Board because it was too much for me to leave my family to attend so many meetings at night. My husband, Jim, continued on the Board and served as Secretary. I continued to write the newsletter for a while; but eventually Jo Ann Allen, the president, reassigned it to fellow member Fred Garth.

31

I still have the minutes from those early meetings. Looking through them, I am moved by how much effort the group put in getting organized and fighting for our little bay. The Board meetings were supposed to be held once a month but ended up being held almost weekly to get things done. When all the representatives from all the different areas of the bay were included, the number was about 12 or 13. It seemed there were too many people with too many different ideas to get much done. Everybody had good ideas, but putting those ideas into action was a different story. The meetings grew contentious with different members wanting to pursue different courses of action. Jo Ann Allen, the elected president, was a tireless worker and campaigned with all the local politicians for help. The Board called Florida DER anytime we saw a problem. Besides opposing the proposed, new state permit to Champion which had supposedly expired in 1986, a wastewater treatment plant on the Florida side was seeking to increase its discharge by one million gallons a day (MGD). We had to oppose this increase. Someone wanted to put a hazardous waste landfill along the Perdido River. We had to oppose this. The problems with closed landfills on the Florida side being deemed superfund sites also caught the interest of the Board. There were so many battles to fight, it was hard to keep up with what I had thought was the primary purpose, fighting the paper mill.

Although we all knew that the DER was going to issue the paper mill a new permit, we still were shocked when it finally came out. On September 26, 1987, a legal notice appeared in the *Pensacola News Journal* announcing that the Florida DER intended to issue an operation permit for five years to Champion International, our local nemesis. Variances from water quality criteria for iron, transparency, zinc and specific conductance (saltiness in fresh water) were also proposed. It was apparent to us that the Florida environmental agency had not waited for the EPA to complete its study or for its recommendations before issuing the Florida DER permit. A trip to the Pensacola office showed us the proposed permit was no more stringent than the past permit, and if possible, even more lax. More Biological Oxygen Demand (BOD)[2] was allowed; the Total Suspended Solids allowed slightly lower than the past permit yet were still extremely high. All our letters from citizens to DER seemed to have no effect. The reports written by DER's own biologists had no effect. Early data from the EPA studies had no effect. We decided to challenge this permit in the Florida Administrative Hearing process.

Despite its other flaws, Florida has a very good rule which allows "affected" citizens to challenge their government's actions. Jim and I had attended a weekend seminar about this Administrative Rule presented by the very law firm that we were going to oppose. So, we were more or less versed in how this process operated. We had to determine what state rules were being violated that would prevent issuance of the permit. It wasn't too hard. DER records were full of violations of water quality standards caused by Champion's discharge from its paper mill. In a compliance monitoring report issued by a DER inspector dated September 21, 1987, monthly violations of BOD limit, ammonia, saltiness, and iron were all listed, just five days prior to the legal notice announcing Champion's five-year permit.

My husband and I wrote identical requests for administrative hearings on both the issuance of Champion's permit and on the issuance of variances. In our requests for hearings, we said the DER "...had ignored the recommendations of their own biologists concerning the welfare of Perdido Bay...In addition, biological studies provided by Champion consultants clearly indicate the condition of Perdido Bay is getting worse."[3]. We mentioned that they had just installed a new bleaching technology and very little was known of the harmful products to be released. Accumulation of dioxin was a concern, especially since Champion was going to 100% bleached paper. In the request for relief, we asked that Champion be given three years to look for alternate methods of effluent disposal. If after three years, Champion was still in Elevenmile Creek and Perdido

Bay, they should be fined (or shut down) if still non-compliant. Champion could have sent its effluent to a domestic wastewater treatment plant for treatment at a cost of over $10,000 a day. Champion didn't want to pay this. The petitions for hearings were sent by certified mail on October 2, 1987.

Because there was a 14-day deadline after publication of the Legal Notice in which to file requests for hearings, we quickly notified Jo Ann Allen and the others on the Perdido Bay Environmental Association (PBEA) Board. Nelson Bethune, a local realtor, drafted a petition which PBEA joined. A concerned citizen and fisherman on Perdido Bay, Alfred Powell, also sent in a petition for a hearing although I am not sure it conformed to the legal standards of the state. A general meeting of PBEA was set for October 22, 1987 to talk about the hearing and to set up a defense fund. We began the task of looking for attorneys.

Shortly after everyone had filed their petitions for an administrative hearing, we were contacted by a Champion representative, Victoria Tschinkel. She was the ex-secretary of DER and had been hired by Champion as a consultant. She most likely had been involved in giving Champion the O.K. to go to 100% bleached paper. She called and said she would like to meet with my husband and me. We agreed. She told us during our meeting that Champion had been caught by surprise upon learning of our petitions for an administrative hearing. She said Champion wanted to do what was right. It was going to do more than simply adhere to the letter of the law; they were going to conform to the spirit of the law. Later, I wondered what the spirit of the law was, but it sounded good at the time.

We met again with Ms. Tschinkel and she addressed the whole group at PBEA. On November 19, 1987, she came to Lillian, Alabama, for an evening meeting with the PBEA Board, assuring us that she had been hired by Champion but was able to speak freely. She said she had the commitment of Champion to correct any problems uncovered. She said it was committed to spending up to $200,000 on a study to uncover all the problems if PBEA would not pursue a hearing for two years. She also indicated that we would not be giving up our rights to a hearing, only putting off the plans for a hearing for two years. Most PBEA people were suspicious, thinking it was "a snow job," including Jo Ann and her husband, Harry. They thought we should not have allowed Ms. Tschinkel to address the Board. We had already held a symposium where many of the problems of Perdido Bay had been discussed. Some board members thought that another study was just a way of pointing the finger away from Champion. Ms. Tschinkel gave the impression that she was on our side. She indicated that Champion would look at land disposal. After many questions, the meeting was adjourned. We told Ms. Tschinkel we would think about her proposal and discuss it before making a decision.

At the time, I recall thinking it rather strange that Champion was not aware of the problems the paper mill caused. The St. Regis consultants had done previous studies on the bay. Although they were panned by the DER biologists, there appeared to be plenty of other studies confirming obvious problems. I was afraid that no matter how much the paper mill was harming the bay, the environmental rules were still weak allowing Champion to get off the hook and continue its pollution. Despite its harm to our little bay, the paper mill was doing better than the designated, technology-based limits in the Clean Water Act. All the environmental rules have the statement - it must be in the public interest[4]. But in whose public interest? Champion's or ours? At the time, Champion employed 1200 people. The problem remained that Perdido Bay was a little bay which did not flush. I was leaning toward letting Champion have the requested two years' time to figure out what to do. My husband and I naively trusted what Champion was saying. We met with the mill's environmental supervisor, the Vice-President for Environmental Affairs, the mill manager, and the public relations guy. Everyone seemed so nice and so sincere.

While considering Champion's request, the PBEA board meetings and general meetings followed in quick succession. Jo Ann became dissatisfied with the endless discussions. She and her husband opposed Champion's two-year study proposal. Several board members stopped coming to meetings. In the December 2, 1987, Board meeting, a motion was made to remove JoAnn as the President of PBEA because some board members felt she was not following the Board's policy. She was making statements and communicating to people without getting the Board's approval first. The motion failed. Larry Sutley, the attorney who had incorporated PBEA, suggested making the Board smaller. It was decided to allow the general membership to vote on Champion's proposal at the general meeting the following evening. The vote in the general membership meeting was 70 to accept Champion's proposal and 44 not to accept. It was also decided that the Board hire an attorney. Some people who had sent in money for the defense fund did not agree with the vote to accept Champion's proposal and asked for their money back. PBEA ended 1987 very divided and disbanded with contention over conceding to Champion's proposed two-year study.

As PBEA entered 1988, the search for an attorney to represent the organization and its battle against Champion continued. Because the hearings are legal proceedings, time became a factor. A hearing officer (Judge) was assigned to the case and he began setting dates for answering motions and hearings. We had to find an attorney fast. My husband, Jim, did most of the searching. We had several recommendations - one being the attorneys who eventually represented Champion. Jim and I personally settled on J. Alan Cox, a former attorney for the DER who had set up a private, environmental practice in Tallahassee, FL. He usually represented people who had violated Florida law, not environmentalists. We sent him a retainer fee. Jo Ann Allen as the PBEA president, however, did not like Mr. Cox. He came over to meet with PBEA representatives, but Jo Ann liked another environmental attorney from Tallahassee, Randi Denker, and PBEA eventually hired Ms. Denker. Our attorney, Mr. Cox, filed a motion, tolling (extending) the time for us to answer the papers Champion had filed. We had until February 22, 1988.

In the meantime, PBEA sent out a brochure to general members explaining the issues. A billboard was purchased. Jo Ann continued to visit DER offices and made copies of studies and interoffice comments. She was aided in her work by a small group of women, Ester Johnson and Lilian and Betty Davidson. Her copying charge was $700. PBEA held elections at a general meeting on February 17, 1988. At that meeting, there was again discussion about the Champion proposal. Jo Ann was adamant about going to a hearing. Many were on her side. Champion sent us several different versions of the 2-year settlement agreement. Various people could not agree on the language for the agreement. Champion's proposal had split the group into two camps - those who were going to a hearing, and those who wanted to wait. At this point, I decided to form yet a third group - a group who would wait and work with Champion on its study. I called this group the Friends of Perdido Bay. It was formally incorporated June 24, 1988. Brad Durling, a former PBEA Board member, my husband, Jim, and I were the original officers. We decided to make the Board much smaller. We had 9 officers at the beginning - some from Florida, some from Alabama. The Board was much more congenial since these were the people who had agreed to work with Champion.

Our "Memorandum of Agreement" to work with Champion was officially signed July 29, 1988. Champion agreed to budget $200,000 for a study on Perdido Bay and to share all its data. My husband Jim, myself, along with Friends of Perdido Bay, agreed to withdraw our pending petitions and refrain from litigation of both the state permit and the federal permit for three years, or until the completion of the study and final report - whichever came sooner. Our agreement with Champion caused a lot of hard feelings with members of the

PBEA. People said we had been "bought off," although Champion never gave us any money. We spent nearly $1,000 of our own money on legal fees. The order formally dismissing our petitions was signed by Judge Michael Ruff on August 29, 1988. Champion continued to try and get PBEA to drop its legal action, even to the extent of offering money to the Association. PBEA decided to go to hearings scheduled for November 14 through 18, 1988, in Tallahassee, FL; November 21 through 29, 1988; and December 5, 1988 in Pensacola.

The discovery process began. PBEA had hired Randi Denker and a local attorney from Foley, Alabama, Tommy Bear. Since we were not a part of this hearing, most of the information about what occurred came to me from others who had attended the hearing. During the discovery process, the three biologists who worked for the local DER office in Pensacola were interviewed. Don Ray, Glen Butts, and Lawrence Donenlon testified that Champion's effluent was causing low dissolved oxygen and damaging the life in Elevenmile Creek. The EPA also forwarded on to DER the results of its studies on Perdido Bay. In a letter to Jo Ann Allen dated September 9, 1988, EPA outlined the results of its water quality model in Elevenmile Creek. The EPA had determined that in order for Champion to meet the State requirements of 5 mg/l of dissolved oxygen in the creek, Champion's BOD would have to be 3 mg/l. At the time, the BOD concentration was running between 17 and 55 mg/l. Obviously, Champion was not going to meet standards in Elevenmile Creek without significant changes.

On October 19, 1988, roughly one year after the first posting of the legal notice had of its intended five-year operating permit, Champion modified its request to a Temporary Operating Permit and a Consent Order. A Consent Order was a legal agreement between DER and Champion that certain actions had to be undertaken and completed during defined[5] time periods. It was an admission that Champion could not meet the water quality standards of the state. It was a major victory for PBEA.

They had stopped the issuance of a faulty permit. The variances which were sought remained in the permit. The Consent Order required that Champion improve the dissolved oxygen in the creek immediately and then study treatment alternatives "…to determine the most environmentally sound and practicable means to correct identified water quality violations caused by Champion."[6]. Besides dissolved oxygen, biological integrity, transparency (effluent color), un-ionized ammonia, and dioxin were identified problems to be addressed. All studies and corrective actions were supposed to be completed by expiration of the permit in 1994. Dr. Robert Livingston, a biology professor from Florida State, was named as the head researcher in Champion's studies on Elevenmile Creek and Perdido Bay. Jim, and I along with Friends of Perdido Bay, had previously agreed with Champion that Livingston was probably the best biologist to do the research since he had studied many other bays in North Florida. We had no reason to doubt that his research would be anything but honest. We learned much later we were wrong.

Meanwhile, the Florida DER gave notice of its intent to issue a Temporary Operating Permit and Consent Order to Champion on October 24, 1988. PBEA was not satisfied that they had caused a major industry to admit they were causing water quality problems in a creek and bay. They continued to press for a hearing on the temporary operating permit, Consent Order and Variances. The hearings were held over a two-week period in November 1988. The first week of the hearing was held in Tallahassee where many of the expert witnesses gave testimony. Mr. James Pitts, PBEA's economics expert, said that he had researched Champion's files and that the company had the funds to install pollution abatement equipment. Dr. Robert Livingston, Champion's expert biological witness, testified that the saltiness in Champion's effluent would not cause undo harm to the organisms in the creek. Bob Kriegel, district director of DER, lied under oath when he testified that DEP had just discovered Champion violations in the Creek since EPA had just forwarded their result to DER. Before the permit was issued, DER's own engineers wrote memos about the violations. The three biologists from the Pensacola DER office testified about the violations to state standards Champion's effluent was causing in Elevenmile Creek. They would later be reprimanded for their factual testimony.

The last week of the November 1988 hearing was held in Pensacola at the city hall where local citizens could give their testimony. Everybody had their "due process", Constitutional right to be heard. The hearing room was packed with citizens from Perdido Bay as well as Champion employees. One life-long resident of Perdido Bay, Mr. David Resmondo, age 91, sat on the stand and recounted how Perdido Bay had once been a beautiful body of water so clear he could see 15 feet to the bottom. He described how there were oysters once thriving in the bay - all before the paper mill in Cantonment began in 1941. They had mysteriously died after the mill began its operations, and are still absent. The mayor of Pensacola at the time, Vince Whibbs, spoke on behalf of Champion. He said they were a good corporate citizen who spent $50 million annually on payroll to improve the quality of life in Pensacola, apparently ignoring the deteriorating quality of life in Perdido Bay. The Champion supporters applauded; Perdido Bay supporters booed. On the Perdido Bay side was David Whetstone, District Attorney for Baldwin County, Alabama. "I beg to differ with the good mayor," Whetstone said. "The quality of life in our county is based on good clean water. We're a tourist county." Steve McMillan, an Alabama representative who accompanied Whetstone to the hearing, did not comment. The McMillian family was heavily involved in forestry and owned large tracts of forest land used by the paper mill. The Executive Vice President of the Pensacola Chamber of Commerce, Joe Ragland, testified that he hoped a compromise between the mill and the environmentalists could be reached[7].

At the termination of the November 1988 hearing, PBEA members were very hopeful. They expected to win. They anticipated that the hearing officer would deny the variances, and that he would order Champion to install pollution abatement equipment to come into compliance with Florida Laws. As many members of PBEA kept saying, a permit should not have been issued until it was known if the new bleaching technology would work. PBEA was also left with some big legal bills. The lawyer cost $25,000 and the experts cost another $26,000. The transcripts of the hearings cost another $15,000. At the beginning of January 1989, the association had only paid $20,000 and needed another $31,000. They hoped to raise the additional money through donations and fund raisers. It was a lot of work. Champion continued to try and get PBEA to "settle" before the hearing officer made his recommendations. The citizens declined. They expected the hearing officer's decision in March 1989.

On September 28, 1989, Michael Ruff, the hearing officer, finally rendered his decision. Unfortunately, he recommended giving Champion the Temporary Operating Permit, Consent Order and Variances. He said that Champion needed time to find the correct technologies and come into compliance with state laws. In regards to the variances, the hearing officer wrote: "In resolving those issues, it must be determined whether the phrases "there is no practicable means known or available for adequate control of the pollution involved" means no "possible" means known or available, or no "reasonable" means known or available."

The Judge's Recommended Order contained an obvious error that, unfortunately, the PBEA attorney, Randi Denker did not catch. The Judge's Order also included some interesting points. An important mathematical error in the calculation of the total amounts of chlorine used prior to conversion to 100% bleached paper and post conversion (Finding of Fact 18 and 19) gave the impression that the total use of chlorine had actually decreased when the mill converted to 100% bleached paper over the previous unbleached condition. In reality, the use of chlorine, even with the new oxygen delignification (removal of structural polymer, lignin from plant material) technology, had increased - 36,000 pounds of chlorine/ day pre-conversion and 56,000 pounds per day post-conversion. This is a significant amount.

It was a shame Ms. Denker did not catch the error. The Hearing Officer also said that the Temporary Operating Permit and Consent Order required Champion to "complete corrective actions and be in compliance with all applicable standards prior to the five-year expiration of the TOP "unless otherwise agreed."" The underlining was Mr. Ruff's and it came with a footnote. The footnote said the "language "unless otherwise agreed" "would seem to indicate the contemplated possibility of a change or permitting modification." Mr. Ruff also noted in Finding of Fact 47 that it seemed more than a little odd that Champion and the regulating authorities "...*after years of mill operation, and after the 1986 permit proceeding, and related investigations, to purportedly not have more knowledge of the chemical constituencies of the discharge and the receiving water, and some inkling of the effect of it on the Creek and Bay system.*" [8]. Exactly! Nevertheless, Champion must have given Mr. Ruff as hearing officer, the impression that it was going to correct whatever problems it caused to our local waterways. I had to admit that I had been fooled as well.

Following the hearing, per the Recommended Final Order, PBEA's counsel, Randi Denker, did not submit the required "Proposed Finding of Fact and Conclusions of Law" but only a letter which was her closing argument. She also sought leave to withdraw as PBEA's counsel before completion of the proceedings and this likely affected the outcome. There was quite a lengthy delay in the proceedings while Ms. Denker obtained an opinion from the Florida Bar supporting her withdrawal. I suspect that PBEA was not able to obtain

42

sufficient funds to pay her and was having internal debates about who would pay the legal fees incurred. Jo Ann, PBEA's president, told me that she personally had paid $60,000 of the legal fees. For several months after the hearing, Jo Ann and her friends held bake sales in Lillian, Alabama to be reimbursed for the legal defense of Perdido Bay.

Based on the Hearing officer' s Recommended order, the Secretary of the DER, Dale Twachtmann, issued the Temporary Operating Permit, Consent Order and Variances that went into effect December 1, 1989 and were set to expire in five years - December 1, 1994. The last docket entry in this case was October 18, 1999. I had written to Michael Ruff complaining that Champion still had not come into compliance after the expiration of the "Temporary" Operating Permit. He wrote back that there was nothing he could do. It was in the jurisdiction of DER (now Department of Environmental Protection - DEP). Although PBEA lost the 1988 hearing, the organization won an award from the Alabama Wildlife Association as environmental group of the year in 1988. Unfortunately, despite the gargantuan grassroots efforts of the PBEA watchdog, Champion waited for the citizens to disappear and continued its on-going pollution of Perdido Bay.

CHAPTER 4 ~The Mill and the Permits

Once Jim and I had challenged the proposed permit for Champion in 1987, we decided we had better find out how paper mills operated and how they were permitted. We began learning about the history of the mill and environmental permitting. Throughout 1987 and 1988, we made many trips to the local DER (the name would later be changed to Department of Environmental Protection - DEP) office in downtown Pensacola and talked with many of the permitting engineers and biologists who studied the bay.

We learned that there were studies on the bay that had been done when the paper mill was owned by St. Regis, in the late 1970's, and also by the DER biologists. We found that Champion International Corp. had merged with St. Regis in 1984 and acquired much of the St. Regis forestlands. A construction permit had been issued in January 1986 to convert the mill from a brown paper bag plant to 100% bleached paper. If we had been aware of the conversion and the increased threat of dioxin and chemicals from the bleaching operation, I am sure we would have challenged this permit, as well. But we were unaware of the history, dangerous chemicals and problems at the mill until Jim and I began to study the files in 1987 and 1988. When Champion bought the mill in 1984, two operating permits were required - one state and one federal. The federal permit created under the Clean Water Act is called NPDES, which stands for National Pollution Discharge Elimination Systems. The NPDES permit was up for renewal in January 1988. Florida's state permit was expiring July 1, 1987 (this was the permit which was challenged in Chapter 3). The EPA was doing extensive studies on Perdido Bay beginning in Fall 1986, in preparation for issuing a new permit. The permitting engineer at Florida's Department of Environmental Regulation said he hoped to have EPA's data available before he had to issue the new state permit, indicating that he that would have a difficult time telling Champion to stop

44

dumping unless he had definite proof that their current dumping in 1987 (and not past dumping) was hurting the bay [1].

The paper mill, which was officially located in Cantonment, Florida, had been built in 1941 as an integrated type, which meant they made pulp from wood and then made paper from the pulp. The mill made mostly brown paper until Champion took over and was converting the mill to making 100% bleached white paper. The mill used mainly pine trees which were grown in vast pine plantations in the area. After treatment, the effluent was discharged into the headwaters of a small creek, Elevenmile Creek, and then Perdido Bay. Paper mills treat their wastes in large aerated ponds using microorganisms to degrade the wastes. In 1986, Champion was constructing a new, larger aeration pond to accommodate the increased pollution from going to 100 % bleached paper. It was large enough to hold the effluent for 7 to 9 days. Many (16 to 20) giant mixers agitate and add air to the effluent to keep the microorganisms alive. Nutrients, nitrogen and phosphorous must be added to the aerated basin to get the maximum number of microorganisms to grow. The greater the number of organisms and the longer the liquid effluent is held in these ponds, the better the treatment. There were four ponds at the Champion mill; two were treatment ponds, and two were settling ponds.[2] Once the micro-organisms degraded the organic material in the effluent, then those microorganisms had to settle out. While pine trees contain many chemicals, the applicable microorganisms mainly degrade tree sugars and other chemicals. Certain chemicals in pine trees such as resin acids and wood fibers not caught on screens in the making of pulp are not easily broken down and released to the environment in the treatment process.

Besides the material which can be broken down by microorganisms, called organic material, there are also salts which cannot be broken down. The paper mill in Cantonment, Florida, uses wood chips which are cooked under pressure, in a very alkaline solution of sodium sulfate. This is called the Kraft process, and has not basically changed in 100 years. The cooking chemicals are recaptured, along with some of the organic material in giant recovery furnaces. But the recapture process is not 100%. The paper mills lose some of their cooking chemicals. I saw figures which showed the paper mill lost approximately 60,000 pounds a day of sodium. The cooking chemicals, sodium, chloride, and sulfates, and other salts from the trees, end up being discharged to the environment. This gives paper mill effluent a slight saltiness. Over the years, paper mills have become more efficient at recapturing their cooking chemicals. It takes a lot of water and rinsing to get the cooking chemicals out of the paper pulp. The mill in Cantonment Florida used 28 million gallons of water a day which it got from wells pumping the sand and gravel aquifer. This mill was considered water -saving; others are not so economical (50 million gallons of water a day). Paper mills use a lot of water for rinsing, so that many mills are located on rivers.

While paper mill engineers use rules of thumb to design and operate their treatment ponds, it isn't always predictable. Some upset or spill in the making of the pulp can disrupt the micro-organisms which are breaking down the organic material. These "upsets" may occur frequently resulting in less treatment. Spill catching devices are considered environmentally necessary. Cold weather generally slows down the treatment. Rain storms falling on these large ponds (6 acres and larger) can add a lot of water, which then lessens treatment. Lessened treatment usually means more organic matter flowing out into the environment, in this case into Perdido Bay. This usually causes the formation of more foam and can have serious environmental consequences. Very seldom do paper mills stop operations. It is a 24 hour, year-round business, although production may increase or decrease from time to time.

As indicated earlier, paper mills produce foam. Pine trees are sappy and produce various oils, fats and other chemicals. Some of these materials, such as tall oil, are removed to make other industrial products. But the removal process is not 100% and these materials get into the treatment ponds. Lignin from the pine trees is also a foam causing chemical. In the treatment ponds, the alkali salts combine with the fats to make soap or foam. The agitators in the ponds make foam which can be a serious problem. Defoamers are used to keep it under control. But once the soap gets into the environment, it re-forms. Foaming is "natural," as the paper industry keeps saying, but the quantities of fatty acids from trees are more than natural.

The Champion Paper mill in Cantonment was considered a large mill. In 1986, it had a permit to make 1600 tons per day of air-dried pulp. It turned this pulp into paper on one of the largest paper-making machines in the world. It consumed a lot of pine trees. Generally, it takes four tons of pine trees to make one ton of air-dried pulp.

In 1987, when I first saw the permit limits for the paper mill in Cantonment, I could hardly believe my eyes. The numbers were huge. In April, 1982, the St. Regis Corporation got an operational permit for the mill. The amount of oxygen-consuming material (Biological Oxygen Demand) they were legally allowed to discharge to the Elevenmile Creek and Perdido Bay was 2313 pounds per day. Biological Oxygen Demand (BOD) is a standard test which is used for both domestic and industrial wastes to measure the organic material broken down by microorganisms. This process consumes oxygen. In standard practice, the amount of oxygen consumed after five days is the BOD number. Five days was chosen as the end point because organic wastes in most domestic wastewater are completely broken down within that time period. Unfortunately, paper mill wastes require longer than five days to completely break down the organic material. The tests which the EPA was doing in Perdido Bay in 1986 showed that after five days, paper mill wastes had only been degraded about a fourth of the total amount. EPA ran the oxygen consumption tests for 120 days to get the true BOD of paper mill effluent. So, to calculate the true oxygen consuming capacity of the effluent, one had to multiply 2313 pounds per day and multiply by 4 resulting in 9,232. This is a huge amount. It didn't take me long to realize that the BOD released by the paper mill was going to use up the oxygen in the Elevenmile Creek and Perdido Bay. Perdido Bay was little more than a treatment pond for the paper mill, and bound to become oxygen depleted, thus a dead body of water.

Even worse were the permit limits for Total Suspended Solids (TSS). The 1982 permit allowed the paper mill to discharge 9942 pounds of solids a day (dry weight) into the environment, meaning Perdido Bay, a non-flushing body of water. That is more than 4 tons. The one day maximum was even worse - 21,820 pounds per day. These solids are composed of small wood fibers which require a long time to degrade and do not settle out in the settling ponds. The microorganisms may also be part of the solids component. Various chemicals can be used to help the solids settle. Those solids released into the environment are food for bacteria and still consume oxygen. They are a component of the BOD. These are the sludges for which paper mills are famous (or infamous). It is one thing to discharge these sludges into large fast flowing rivers, or into the Baltic Sea as do the Scandinavian paper mills which do not have oxygen depletion problems. But to discharge these oxygen consuming solids into a small creek or bay is sure to cause problems. Nevertheless, that was exactly what was happening on Perdido Bay. I recalled the fibers which we had washed off our bodies after swimming in the bay. They were suspended solids from the paper mill! I was disgusted. I had seen much lower limits for Total Suspended Solids for domestic wastewater. It turns out that the local domestic wastewater treatment plants run their effluents through sand filters to remove the suspended solids. Paper mills, on the other hand, do not. As one paper mill vice president told me "It's too expensive"[3] - not cost effective.

The permitting engineers at the DER office assured me, however, that the limits applied to the local paper mill in the 1987 permit were very stringent. I wondered how they could be considered "stringent." I looked more closely at the Clean Water Act. Yes, under the section of the Clean Water Act which dealt with technology-based limits (40 CFR 430), the BOD and TSS permit limits for this paper mill were lower than the enforceable technology-based limits in the Clean Water Act. I could see the problem clearly now. These technology-based limits, which had been established in 1978, were based on technology available at that time - called best available technology (BAT) or Best Practical Technology (BPT) in the paper industry for different paper-making methods. What self-respecting paper mill would want to do more than is required to meet the prescribed BPT? It cost money, after all, to treat wastes. And what paper mill would want to install a more advanced technology and be way ahead of the group? A paper mill flaunting expenditures on what sounded like non-necessary costs to exceed required "best practices," would be excoriated by board members and stock holders. Such a paper mill would not be welcome in the papermaking industry. But the Clean Water Act also has another set of limits, called the Water Quality Based Effluent Limits (WQBEL's). To paraphrase the Clean Water Act, if the technology-based limits are not adequate to protect water quality standards in the Clean Water Act, then Water Quality Based Effluent limits must be set. This is usually done by modeling. This is what we had to make sure was being done on Perdido Bay - a good water quality-based effluent model. The EPA studies of 1986 and 1987 were supposed to establish such water quality based limits, or at least that should have been a goal.

In 1987, I was pretty sure that any water quality model would point to a zero discharge for the paper mill. This was especially true once we found out that Perdido Bay was "stratified" with fresh water on top and the heavier salt water on the bottom, as shown by the 1986 and 1987 EPA studies. Perdido Bay was an estuary, where freshwater from the Perdido

River and salt water from the Gulf of Mexico meet. The mixing of fresh and salt waters does not occur instantly, especially in Perdido Bay, which is long and narrow. Much of the mixing is caused by wind. The freshwater is lighter (it does not contain salts) and tends to float on the denser salt water. A situation with the heavier salt water on the bottom tends to create a barrier for oxygen that is there. Water holds much less oxygen than does air. The oxygen is quickly used up when not mixed with air. When you combine the barrier to oxygen with the oxygen-consuming solids of the paper mill, the deeper, saltier parts of Perdido Bay would certainly have little oxygen, resulting in a "dead" bay. I was relatively certain that the environmental agencies would tell Champion that they would have to dispose of their effluent in some other way - close loop. This had been the technology proposed for the mill in the 1970's.

Prior to the 1986 clam kill, I had visited the paper mill twice. From 1982 to 1995, I taught as an adjunct professor at Pensacola Junior College (now Pensacola State College). While teaching a botany course, I took students for tours at the mill. The last visit I had made to the mill was in 1983 while it was still owned by St. Regis, and even then I noted that the mill had become run down. The salts used for cooking are very corrosive. Many metal ladders were eaten away at the bottom. I did not yet realize in 1983 the severity of the economic conditions at the mill. As the story later was told to me by a Champion employee, St. Regis had pinned its economic hopes on a new, heavy-duty brown paper bag which it hoped to market. It was bad timing because plastic bags were just making their appearance in grocery stores. The result was that the St. Regis bags just couldn't compete. This is when Champion stepped in and bought the mill in 1984, sort of as a "white knight." Those were the days of "white knights" (the good guys) and "black knights" (the bad guys). Champion took over St. Regis including its assets and liabilities vowing to keep the mill open. They also agreed to spend millions of dollars to renew the mill. Champion agreed to modernize it and not shut it down, which

50

made them a "white knight" in the eyes of St. Regis and in the eyes of the local community afraid of losing jobs. A Champion engineer told me that Champion was aware of the environmental problems at the mill it was assuming from St. Regis, but it was confident the problems could be solved. There probably were a few agreements made between local politicians, DER, EPA, and Champion officials of which the public was not aware. The governor of Florida at the time was Bob Graham and coincidentally Victoria Tschinkel, later hired by Champion as a consultant, was Bob Graham's Secretary of Environmental Regulation.

In 1986, Champion started making only white paper. All the additional color created more pollution, hence the need for a larger treatment pond. The saltiness of the effluent also increased. At the time, Jim and I didn't know anything about dioxin and the dangers of chlorinated byproducts. We were told that Champion had invented a new bleaching technology called oxygen-delignification which they were going to install at the mill. According to Champion, this new technology would reduce the use of chlorine and all its harmful products. This was going to be state of the art, the new "Best Available Technology" for Bleached Kraft Paper mills. According to a DER engineer, installation of this new technology was one of the main reasons DER agreed to the construction permit granted to Champion in 1986. All other mills would have to follow suit, or that was the plan as we were told. Champion went to pulp and paper meetings extolling the virtues of their new technology. The end result, however, was that Champion was still using more chlorine than St. Regis ever had, only Champion had allegedly installed a new technology to address the added chlorine. According to documents found in DER files in 1987 and 1988, St. Regis had been using 37,200 pounds per day of chlorine. Champion was going to be using 71, 400 pounds per day of chlorine, nearly double. This was a huge increase. As years went by, the demand for white paper grew less. The computer age began to have an effect on the white paper market. Champion's main product, white paper, became less profitable.

Since the clam kill in 1986, we still hadn't found what had killed the clams. In 1987 and 1988 meetings with Bob Kriegel, the district director for DER, he said he just didn't know. He said he had checked the records and Champion was well within their permit limits set by the state - as if this should have been sufficient. His agency indicated it had no reason to connect the paper mill to the clam kill. I began to go through the DER files, utilizing Florida's Sunshine Law, the law that gives the public access to all government records. The answer to the clam kill happened to be in the records, specifically in a letter dated October 7, 1986 from Champion engineer, David Arceneaux to Steve Baisden, a DER engineer. The letter describes how on October 1, 1986, the "gates were pulled on Pond II and Pond III to lower the level in these ponds five feet. This was done to repair the effluent weirs and to remove accumulated sludge."[4] It just so happens to take approximately three days for material released at the mill to reach Perdido Bay, and the clam kill took place on October 4, 1986. The black oily water we saw that awful day in October 1986 was the sludge-laden effluent from Champion, and it had chemicals that killed the clams. It was amazing to me that an industry could do this without regard to the environment and avoid repercussions. At the minimum, they should have warned people. After I swam in this effluent, trying to determine what was wrong with the clams, I also developed a bad case of acne and facial hair. For the next year, I had to see a dermatologist for my skin problems. Also, a cut on my finger became inexplicably infected and would not heal, and I eventually had to go to another doctor besides the dermatologist. My wound ended up being operated on, and I had to take tuberculosis medicine for several months. The bacterium was identified as a *Mycobacterium marinum*. Although it was the cold months of the year, I wondered how many other people had been affected similarly by this careless industrial action.

52

Other papers from DER records revealed many more problems. In *A Review of Champion (St Regis) Paper Company's Discharge Impacts on Waters of the Perdido Basin* by Bill Young, head of the biology section at DER, Pensacola, written in May 8, 1985, the problems were laid out. He summarized the condition of the receiving water of Elevenmile Creek as degraded although still somewhat improved over the 1960's:

"Since the required receiving water monitoring was initiated by St. Regis in 1978, degradation of Elevenmile Creek, lower Perdido River and Perdido Bay has been repeatedly documented in benthic macroinvertebrates and plankton data of St. Regis and DER surveys and monitoring."… "Quiet waters of the tidal portion of the Creek and shallow adjacent Perdido Bay provide the initial repository for accumulated paper mill wastes. Settling of the suspended organics and adsorbed chemical creates deep sludge deposits. Depletion of dissolved oxygen is chronic. Aquatic vegetation consists of large patches of pollution-tolerant alligator weed. The macroinvertebrate fauna is further reduced to 7% of natural species diversity."

As for his summary of Perdido Bay, Bill Young writes:
"Conspicuous degradation of Perdido Bay includes – (1) brown discoloration of the water, (2) paper mill odor, (3) foam, (4) the absence of submerged and intertidal vegetation, and (5) noxious black sludge-muck. Dissolved oxygen depletion occurs through the water column near Elevenmile Creek and in the lower water column in other Bay areas. The muck substrate that covers most of the Bay produces approximately 5% of a natural bottom life species composition and approximately 2% of the natural standing crop. Recent analyses of the sediments and clams from upper Perdido Bay revealed substantial levels of heavy metals. The usual phytoplanktons produced are blue-green, non-food chain species. Most of Perdido Bay is essentially not producing organisms that are necessary for maintaining a healthy ecological and fish population balance."

With this review, I felt certain the state of Florida could not issue a permit to Champion in 1987 without substantial improvement. I was wrong!

Besides the documented damage to the fauna in Elevenmile Creek and Perdido Bay, the mill's effluent could not meet water standards of the Clean Water Act long before our permit fight with Champion in 1988-1989, after which Champion was granted a permit anyway. In an interoffice memorandum dated December 20, 1985 from Abdul Khatri, a permitting engineer at DER, to Robert Kriegel, the problems of Champion's effluent not meeting standards is laid out. (Kriegel testified at the 1988 administrative hearings on Champion's permit that he was unaware of the permit violations until the EPA study in 1988!). Variances for iron and specific conductance (saltiness) were discussed. There were no practicable means (key word here is practicable) known or available for adequate control of these parameters. The state grants variances (or exemptions from the rules) when such language is used. The list of problems and standards the mill could not meet goes on. Storm water, unionized ammonia, cyanide, zinc, chloroform, phenol, color were all areas of concern. In 1988, it seemed to me that Champion had many more problems than they could easily address. In some cases, technology was available to correct the problems but it was too expensive and not economically feasible.

Throughout 1987 and 1988, we contacted some of the EPA scientists who were doing the study on Perdido Bay. Jim Greenfield, the EPA's lead engineer in Atlanta, sent us some preliminary data on dye studies which had been taken in December 1986. All the data was stamped with "preliminary - subject to revision". The data showed that dye which had been injected at the mouth of Elevenmile Creek, headed for our side (the Florida side) of the bay. Mr. Greenfield also told us that EPA hadn't dealt with a bay like Perdido before. "It's just a non-flushing bay," he said, a matter that was quite important since we had heard this before but it did not seem to stop or change the pollution being poured into it by Champion. "Anything that goes in stays there, even with the hurricanes we had a couple of years ago," Mr. Greenfield also said that Champion's permit would be more stringent and would be based on how much pollution the bay could stand. His comments were heartening to me because I figured that the bay, since it couldn't flush, could take zero pollution. EPA said the study should be done by the later part of 1987 in time for the renewal of the NPDES permit which expired January 3, 1988. Deadlines for permit renewals and expirations did seem to concern the environmental agencies very much, as time would show.

FOAM AND ALGAE AT SEAWALL

CHAPTER 5 ~ THE STUDIES

The 1986 clam kill and citizen fury over the poor health of Perdido Bay did get the politicians' attention, at least for a little while. Their response was to spend money for studies and conduct meetings to keep the public distracted. It seems that when politicians are confronted with a dilemma, they dodge making any kind of decision by coughing up money for a study, usually conducted by one of their own governmental agencies. A study will always postpone any requirement for action, and the politicians will be off the hook for a while. They can always hope that the study will show different results from previous studies. Or better yet, that citizens will lose interest and disappear. As Ms. Tschinkel, the ex-DER Secretary and Champion consultant told me several years later, grass-roots environmental groups are only known to last an average of three years. So, I am sure the politicians, along with the paper company and their allies were hoping that citizen interest would wain and the problem would be over, returning to the collusion between government and industry.

EPA 1986/1987 Study of Perdido Bay
The EPA study of Perdido Bay was begun almost simultaneously with the beginning of environmental groups in 1986. It was actually started to help the EPA set limits on the paper mill for the new NPDES permit which the federal government was going to issue in 1988. As we knew from going through DER(P) files, my husband and I were expecting the study to show that Champion should go to zero discharge, because their discharges were causing chronically low-dissolved oxygen in the deeper parts of Perdido Bay. The study was supposed to be finished in 1987, but citizens waited in vain because it never came out in final form. On July 2, 1987, several citizens, including the Friends of Perdido Bay, got a packet of data stamped, "Preliminary - Subject to Revision," along with a statement that a formal report would be issued when the entire project was complete. That report never came out. In summer

of 1988, I did get a modeling analysis from the EPA showing the amount of oxygen-consuming material Champion could put in Elevenmile Creek without violating water quality standards. Champion had to decrease the biological oxygen demand (BOD) in their discharges by about eight-fold. PBEA was awaiting the start of their administrative hearing on the Champion state permit challenge and could probably use this information at their hearing. The deadline for the renewal of the federal NPDES permit scheduled to expire, January 3 1988, had passed. From the preliminary data the EPA did send, I could see how effluent flowed out of Elevenmile Creek and headed for our beach. To say the least, this was not reassuring. The 1986/1987 EPA study also found that 60% of the oxygen-consuming carbon compounds entering the bay came from the paper mill. We continued to wait for the written analysis. From calls to the local EPA office, I learned that the local scientist who had worked on the project and had declared the Bay dead at our first PBEA meeting, Dr. Bill Kruczynski, had been transferred.

NOAA Near Coastal Water Study – Joint Florida/Alabama Report

While waiting for the results of the 1986/1987 EPA study, I was surprised to learn Perdido Bay had been chosen for a Joint Florida/Alabama 309 NOAA grant, *Near Coastal Waters Initiative*. It would be a cooperative effort between Florida and Alabama environmental agencies attempting to pinpoint all the sources of pollution entering the entirety of Perdido Bay. A Florida scientist, Dr. Steve Schropp, was the head DER scientist coordinating the studies. He was also a favorite speaker at our environmental meetings. This study did produce final reports. The first interim report came out September, 1989, giving the provisional results from March, 1988, to February, 1989, and was titled *A Report on Physical and Chemical Processes Affecting the Management of Perdido Bay*. This report was detailed and difficult for a non-scientific person to understand; however, I thought it gave an accurate picture of what was happening in Perdido Bay. As for the oxygen-consuming material (BOD) brought into the bay, about half was coming down the Perdido River and half was coming from Champion. The BOD coming from the paper mill was a little less than EPA had calculated. As the scientists calculated, the level of BOD found was going to create an oxygen deficient in the bay. They identified the major problem in Perdido Bay as an excess of carbon causing oxygen depletion in the lower waters. For nutrients nitrogen and phosphorus, Champion was delivering about 30 % of those to the bay. All other sources - septic tanks, other smaller streams - had a negligible contribution. The conclusion of the joint Florida/Alabama report quieted for a while, all the people who kept pointing to other sources of pollution, like septic tanks, runoff from agriculture etc. If those sources of pollution were present, they were not significant in causing low-dissolved oxygen in the bay. One of the scientists who participated in the study told me that the pollution of Perdido Bay by the paper mill was the worst case of pollution he had ever seen. The Final report came out in January, 1991 as well as a prediction of the water quality in Perdido Bay using a simple model[1]. It looked at the transport of material in the bay and used some of the data that the EPA had taken previously. The results of the model reinforced the conclusion that Perdido Bay was a poorly-flushing bay and material deposited in the bay remained there. (Many years later we would get Dr. Schropp to be an expert witness at an administrative hearing.) This was basically the last biological study on Perdido Bay paid for by public funds. After this study (1991), all large studies would be funded by Champion and following those, by the next owners of the mill, International Paper.

Perdido Bay Cooperative Management Project
    In September, 1988, while we were waiting on the NOAA Interstate Study, the EPA announced yet another grant for Perdido Bay. It was called the *Perdido Bay Cooperative Management Project*. Friends of Perdido Bay was selected to administrator part of the grant. We were going to get $50,000 to do a public outreach project. Another $250,000 was going to the

58

Fish and Wildlife Service in Panama City, Florida. October 1, 1988, was the official start of the program. The EPA in Atlanta was to be the administrator of the program with Bob Lord as the contact person. According to our agreement with the EPA, Friends of Perdido Bay was supposed to establish a public outreach program, set up a public location to deposit studies and information about Perdido Bay, establish a coalition of environmental groups, and set up a Citizen's Monitoring Network. The Fish and Wildlife Service was going to review the data and hold public meetings, check on toxins and pathogens, identify land use practices around the bay, and develop a management plan. At Friends of Perdido Bay's meeting on October 25, 1988, Bob Lord outlined various aspects of EPA's management grant for Perdido Bay. On December 7, 1988, the EPA, Fish and Wildlife and Friends of Perdido Bay held a workshop for the public and government officials on the Perdido Bay Management Grant. Workshops such as these would be held every three or four months.

We did what the EPA asked us to do. We had plenty of people who wanted to help monitor Perdido Bay for turbidity, salinity, and foam. We had two boat monitors who took salinity and dissolved oxygen readings. We bought two remote weather stations to assist in Champion's study of the Bay and established a small information center at Pensacola Junior College Library which would later be transferred to University of West Florida. We established a coalition of environmental groups called the E.C.C.C.O. (Environmental Coalition of Concerned Citizens' Organization). Jack Starbuck of Lillian, Alabama, was our Executive Director. Best of all, we had a summer science camp for sixth graders going into seventh grade that ran for two weeks. We hired a high school science teacher, and we made sure to have plenty of field trips. I am certain that most of the students that attended will never forget that camp. As I look back, we really kept busy trying to save Perdido Bay. Maybe that was the point of the grant. We got a lot of goodwill, but I am not sure it helped Perdido Bay get cleaned up. Once the grant monies ran out in 1991, our initiatives stopped, including the ECCCO group and the citizen monitoring. Later, the *Mobile Bay Estuarine Program* would begin a citizen monitoring program like ours and include lower Perdido Bay.

Fish and Wildlife studies were not designed to look at the overall health of the bay or to point fingers at any particular discharger, but look at historical changes in the bay and its environs. Land-use, changes in fish diversity over a period of time, sea grasses and sediments in Perdido Bay were the focus of the Fish and Wildlife monies. This data was to be used in developing a management plan. According to the 1988 land-use survey, growing of trees (*silviculture*) comprised 60% of the acreage within the basin's watershed; cropland, nursey and orchard, 30%; urban uses, 8%. The land uses had not changed much from the mid-1970. Silviculture was a little higher and cropland was a little lower then. Because of the large amount of forested land in the Perdido watershed, it was difficult for people to point their finger at septic tanks and non-point source runoff as causes of the deteriorating water quality in the bay. This bay was not an urbanized watershed. There were localized problems in some of the smaller tributaries. The various studies which were taking place on Perdido Bay did not coordinate results.

The Fish and Wildlife studies looked at historical records of fish diversity and abundance but could not draw any definite conclusions bay-wide. The analyses went back to 1967 and analyzed fish abundance from old trawls done by the St. Regis biologists, by the Alabama Department of Natural Resources, and by fish landings reported to the National Marine Fisheries Service. In Elevenmile Creek, fish diversity definitely had declined. The low fish diversity in Elevenmile Creek also "...confirmed the preliminary findings of an ongoing study by the Florida Game and Fresh Water Fish Commission, in which entire taxonomic families were absent from the Creek...." Fish and Wildlife also concluded that "...the frequently low, sometimes very low diversity of finfish collected by trawling in the upper bay during both the winter and summer suggests that environmental conditions at or near the upper bay bottom may be degraded...."[2]. But for the other parts of the bay, the results were inconclusive. There seemed to be a decline in fish during the summer months from 1983 to 1989 bay-wide. There were some good years and some bad years. As the study report concludes, the data only went back to 1967 and the changes in the fish populations may have occurred before that time.

One of the more useful reports from the Fish and Wildlife Service was the compilation of changes in submerged, aquatic vegetation (seagrasses) from 1940 to 1987 in Perdido Bay using aerial photos. Grass beds are important because they are one indicator of the health of the bay. They provide habitat for juvenile animals and only grow where they can get sufficient light. In the upper bay and middle parts of the bay, changes in sea grasses "...consisted mainly of shifts in the locations of small submerged vegetation areas, with only minor changes in extent....".[3] All of the grass beds visible in the aerial photographs from the upper bay were on the Alabama side. The small patches of grass beds which would appear and then disappear at our beach in the upper bay were apparently not large enough (larger than ½ acre) to be visible in aerial photographs. Along the western (Alabama) side of the upper bay, 3 acres of grass beds were seen in 1940-41 and 12 acres in 1987. In the lower bay, the grass beds did not fare as well with time. In the lower bay, mainly along Innerarity Island, 793 acres were present in 1940-41 and 534 acres in 1987[4]. As far as I know, the final report never came out with only a draft form seen. A report written on Perdido Bay to justify nutrient limits in Perdido Bay would say that no grass beds ever existed in Upper Perdido Bay[5] - an obvious lie.

The toxics report from Fish and Wildlife was finally published in 1993. The EPA supervisor, Bob Lord, had moved to another section of EPA and was no longer overseeing the project. The report contained a summary of some past studies and some new data which Fish and Wildlife collected mostly in 1989. In the abstract of the report, Fish and Wildlife found that field toxicity tests "...suggest that the water and sediments tested are not acutely toxic, ...but there appears to be reduced water quality at some locations...." Also at some locations, they found that sediments were contaminated. "...Contaminates of concern at some sediment sites include: mercury, silver and dioxin compounds.... Samples of some species of fishes in the Perdido River contain undesirable concentrations of mercury. In the past, fish from Elevenmile Creek have contained quantities of dioxin.... Fish collected from Elevenmile Creek, and analyzed within the last three years, contained minimal or non-detectable concentrations of dioxin compounds.... However, significant concentrations of dioxin have been found in two turtles collected from the Creek"[6]. Years later we asked Mike Brimm, the lead author on these studies, to testify for us in various hearings. He refused. His data was published in a 1996 textbook[7] about paper mill effluents and their environmental fate.

Draft Gulf of Mexico Toxic Substances and Pesticides Characterization Report[8]

One of the studies mentioned in the Fish and Wildlife report was a report which was being compiled by the EPA and the technical steering committee of the Gulf of Mexico program. The sediment inventory report consisted of quality data which had been collected by federal, state and private agencies from 1980 through 1992. The draft *Gulf of Mexico Toxic Substances and Pesticides Characterization Report* came out in 1993. The report was produced by Science Applications International Corporation of Chicago, IL. Of all the estuaries in the Gulf of Mexico which were examined, Perdido Bay ranked number 1 in toxic contamination of sediments. The top five toxic compounds were ammonia, catechol, chloroform and acetone. Of the five, four could be traced back to the paper mill and the bleaching process. Perdido Bay ranked ahead of Galveston Bay. This was a shocking piece of information which we attempted to introduce into later legal hearings. Unfortunately, the report never came out in any other than as a draft. When we contacted the EPA about this report, they said there had been an error and the data was being re-analyzed. We never saw the re-analyzed data as it never was published.

Masculinization of Mosquitofish in Elevenmile Creek

Early research by a professor at University of West Florida in a peer-reviewed journal had uncovered unusual phenomena; the masculinization of female mosquito fish in streams containing Kraft paper mill effluent. This was found in only three streams throughout the world, one being Elevenmile Creek. In 1989, the professor and his graduate students examined the data in more detail [9]. They found that a phytosterol (a plant hormone) from pine trees was the likely culprit. In high enough concentrations, that plant hormone will cause masculinization. I began to wonder if this was why I had developed facial hair after swimming in the bay water after the clam kill.

The Livingston Study

The report which all parties, environmentalists, government officials, and even paper mill people waited for, the Livingston study, came out in 1992. It was titled *Ecological Study of the Perdido Bay Drainage system*. Champion was true to its word as far as involving us in the studies. We got draft copies and were allowed to critique the studies. Dr. Livingston was a frequent speaker at our environmental meetings. We could see immediately that the study was going to produce a lot of paper. It was difficult to review because it contained no page numbers, some graphs had no legends, or if they had legends they were too small and impossible to read. The 1992 Livingston study comprised twelve volumes and forty appendices totaling 15,000 pages.

Even before the report officially came out, I could see it was going to exonerate Champion. In February 1991 I wrote to Bob Kriegel, District Director of DER telling him of my concerns. The Livingston study completely ignored the organic carbon which Champion was putting into the bay, which the earlier government studies had pointed to as the problem [10]. My early criticisms of the Livingston study were ignored.

The results of the study were not surprising since Champion had paid for the report. One doesn't pay for a report that was going to be incriminating, something my husband and I painfully learned. Ms. Tschinkel tried to make it seem like Dr. Robert Livingston was completely independent. The name of his consulting business made it appear independent: "E P & A - Environmental Planning and Analysis" (like "EPA"). He was not independent of industries influence. The 1992 Livingston report found that Champion was damaging life in Elevenmile Creek and a small part of Perdido Bay around the mouth of the creek. Other than that, Champion's effluent seemed to not affect Perdido Bay. His studies also found that the deeper waters in Perdido Bay had low-dissolved oxygen and blamed this on salinity stratification. According to the Livingston study, this was caused by opening of the mouth of the bay at the turn of the 19th century, allowing the entrance of salt water from the Gulf. This was true. There is some historical evidence to suggest that Perdido Bay was nearly fresh water at the turn of the 19th century. The flow from the Perdido River was not sufficient to keep a permanent mouth into the Gulf of Mexico open hence the name "Lost Bay". But of course if that was true, the bay certainly could not have handled the oxygen-consuming sludges from the paper mill. It would have been just a treatment pond for the paper mill, which in all practicality, it was anyhow. The dredging of the permanent mouth to the bay allowed salt water to enter. But Dr. Livingston totally downplayed or ignored the 10,000 pounds or more of oxygen-consuming solids (carbon) which the mill put into the bay daily. This "ignoring" of paper mill solids would later become part of EPA policy allowing large amounts of paper mill solids in permits for paper mills, claiming it was not cost-effective to clean them up.

64

Part of his study involved hiring other consultants. I thought one piece of research especially interesting because it demonstrated how data could be skewed by selection of sampling sites. The researchers looked at different isotopes of carbon. They identified the particular variety which came from the paper mill. They then looked for this isotope in the bottom sediments of Perdido Bay. They found this isotope in sediments of the upper bay and to a lesser extent in the lower bay, but not in the mid-bay. They took their mid-bay sample at the Lillian Bridge. This is the area which narrows and gives Perdido Bay its hour-glass appearance. This area of the bay at Lillian Bridge is narrow and deep. Water flows very fast and very little deposition goes on in this area. In addition, people have reported that springs well-up from the ground. It was in the sediments of this area that the researchers did not find carbon isotopes from the paper mill. Because there was no nice progression of carbon isotopes from the paper mill, the carbon which was on the bottom of lower Perdido Bay could not be attributed to the paper mill according to the researchers. Later modeling studies[11] would find that the lower bay, especially on the Florida side, was where much of the paper mill solids settled.

Livingston also found that there was a very productive area full of fish and crabs at the mouth of Elevenmile Creek. When I went up to see the area, it was a shallow bar just at the mouth of the creek. This shallow bar had been formed by the erosion of the creek bed and because it was shallow, did not suffer the problem of low-dissolved oxygen as had all the areas on either side of the bar. The choice of sampling site was one way of skewing data.

The 1992 Livingston Report concluded that it was the development in the lower part of Perdido Bay around the beaches which cause most of the environmental deterioration of Perdido Bay. Champion was only responsible for the deterioration of Elevenmile Creek and a small part around the mouth.

When the conclusions of the report came out, we all "rolled our eyes." We had somehow trusted Champion and Livingston. After all, my husband and I were the ones who had helped choose Dr. Livingston as a consultant. We wrote letters to DER and called them. DER hired a reviewer for the Livingston Report, Dr. Jack Taylor. He was a good biologist whom I knew from graduate school. In a kind way, Jack panned the report and pointed out various problems. Where was the pollution coming from? At the southern end near the Gulf as postulated by Livingston or the northern end of the bay, from the paper-mill? DER biologists took water samples to find where the oxygen-consuming material (BOD) originated. There was a nice progression of increasingly higher BOD's as you went from the Gulf north into Perdido Bay. The problem was coming from the north end of the bay, according to the DER biologists, not from the Gulf.

Livingston would continue studying the bay for the next 15 years, always working for the paper mill as a contractor. During the 1990's, Champion did produce a variety of reports on alternative treatment technologies. They looked at groundwater discharge, surface water discharge and constructed wetlands. Several in-mill technologies were considered. One technology, Bleach-filtrate Recycle, which would have eliminated the harmful bleaching products, was installed at another mill in North Carolina. Why they did not install it at the mill in Cantonment, Florida, I do not know. Champion constructed a pilot wetland project at the Cantonment mill. CH2MHill were the engineers. The first report came out in 1990. This was the technology my husband and I favored. We had read a lot about the inexpensive and effective removal of pollutants from effluents by wetlands. We had even gone on a tour of DeGusa Chemical's rock and reed wetland, in Mobile, Alabama, with some Champion personnel. After Champion built their pilot wetland, Friends of Perdido Bay's Board of Directors was invited to the mill to tour the wetlands in 1992. We did,

66

congratulating Champion on their experiment and trying to encourage them to install this treatment. They also built a small activated-sludge, pilot treatment project and there was talk (a threat) about building a pipeline directly to Perdido Bay and getting special variations from the permit for Champion's problem with low-dissolved oxygen in the creek.

State Monitoring and Federal Studies

Other than the special grant funded studies in 1987 and 1988 and studies in Elevenmile Creek, the local Pensacola office of DER stopped doing any type of regular field sampling or testing in Perdido Bay in 1988. It was obvious; the local (and maybe national) politicians had put a lid on using public funds that incriminate industry. There was to be NO independent verification of industry's environmental compliance in Perdido Bay. The Florida environmental agency was still testing Elevenmile Creek and finding violations. A bacteriological report done by the Tallahassee DER (DEP) office, of the coliform bacteria in Elevenmile Creek in 1999 (The sampling took place in 1996) found very high levels *of E. coli* bacteria and *Klebsiella sp.* in Elevenmile Creek [12], especially after rainfalls. Both bacteria are considered coliform bacteria and live in organically rich, low dissolved oxygen environments, much like our intestines and paper mill ponds. *Klebsiella* is implicated in different types of infections. High levels of bacteria had not been mentioned as a possible problem in Elevenmile Creek previously, and Champion wanted to correct all problems. There was also some sampling done by DER biologists for the Total Maximum Daily Load Program (TMDL) in 2005. Much of this data was never put into report form but only put into a computerized data base and some of which disappeared (See TMDL chapter). But by 1999, it was obvious that the environmental agency in Florida, DEP and maybe even EPA, was pushing the paper mill to get their discharge out of Elevenmile Creek because it could not meet state water quality standards.

After 1998, Friends of Perdido Bay would also run various tests, including bacteriologic counts in Perdido Bay and Elevenmile Creek. There were many violations of state standards. Toxicity tests in Elevenmile Creek showed that paper mill effluent was not acutely toxic *most* of the time (organisms did not die within 96-hours) but the effluent had chronic effects on growth and reproduction of water fleas and minnow larvae after 7 days. Certain heavy metals and dioxin testing in Perdido Bay sediments (see dioxin days chapter) demonstrated unsafe levels. When Friends of Perdido Bay pointed this out to Florida DEP, we were told that Florida did not have "sediment standards." Friends of Perdido Bay also did nutrient testing at various sites in the bay. We would use some of these data in future administrative hearings. Although we used certified labs to analyze our samples, our data did not seem to carry much weight with the environmental agencies. They were not interested in implicating paper mills in environmental problems. The government focus turned to non-point (unpermitted) sources of pollution, like storm water runoff.

CHAPTER 6 ~ WAITING

After Florida DER issued the Temporary Operating Permit and Consent Order for Champion in 1989, Friends of Perdido Bay began working on many different issues confronting the environment on Perdido Bay. My husband, Jim, and I were especially interested in land-use issues in our Florida county, Escambia County. Florida was experiencing explosive growth which was putting a strain on all infrastructures. In response to this growth, the Florida legislature enacted a particularly strong growth management law with enforceable rules in 1985. We were especially interested in getting a strong wetland ordinance passed for Escambia county. In the summer of 1988, Jim and I attended many county commission land-use meetings where people would come and asked that their property be re-zoned, mostly always to a higher density. Commissioners nearly always granted everyone's request, no matter what the location or the presence of wetlands, etc. This disregard for the state comprehensive plan caused the Florida Department of Community Affairs, the state agency overseeing guidance of the law, to ask Escambia County to come up with a better wetland ordinance. Escambia County did eventually write a special wetland ordinance and a growth management plan in 1990; unfortunately, Escambia County's plan did not comply with the plan the state had developed as a model for counties to follow. As a result, the state Department of Community Affairs declared its plan "not in compliance". Escambia County and the state went to hearings starting September 11, 1991. We participated in this hearing along with the League of Women Voters on the side of the state. Eventually, the county did adopt a fairly decent wetland ordinance which used the federal manual for identifying wetlands. Afterwards, I realized this aggressive approach turned many people off. From the comments made to us and from the increasing use of private property rights' arguments, I realized we had made many enemies, especially among the land developers. Many of the new developments which were constructed during that time were built in filled wetlands. It would be better to try to educate people about the importance of wetlands rather than fight them in court. Florida also developed a wetland banking system giving value to wetlands. This helped as well. The aggressive enforcement of the growth management plan also spelled the demise for the state agency which enforced the plan. Over the next several years, the Florida legislature totally dismantled the Department of Community Affairs.

In 1988, domestic wastewater treatment plants discharging to Perdido Bay were also coming under our review, especially that closest to our property, Avondale. In Fall of 1988, we learned that the Florida DER and EPA had allowed this small wastewater treatment plant to increase its discharge from 0.8 million gallons a day to 2 million gallons per day. Friends of Perdido Bay asked for a public hearing on this permit which was held November 1, 1988. We discovered that this wastewater treatment plant was under a Consent Order to close in 1984. It was still open, however, because the local utility authority, Escambia County Utilities Authority (ECUA), was having trouble finding another suitable location to replace the Avondale location. Every time a new location for a treatment plant was proposed, local people would complain. In 1991, we were able to convince the EPA to put a more stringent phosphorus limitation on the new permit hoping that this would curb the nutrients going into Perdido Bay. Since 1988, we had begun to see blooms of drift algae at our beach during the winter.

Friends of Perdido Bay was also trying to get special protection for the Perdido River. The river had been designated a "Florida Outstanding Water" by the Florida environmental agency in 1979, but we were seeking additional protections. One federal program mentioned was the Federal "Wild and Scenic Rivers" Program. Our federal congressmen would have to get a bill passed in Congress to get monies to study the feasibility of giving the Perdido River a "Wild and Scenic River" designation. Members of Friends of Perdido Bay collected over 3,000 signatures of citizens who supported special designation and

70

contacted our federal congressmen who said they would help[1]. We also tried to contact the major landowners along the Perdido River - the paper companies. Champion owned much of the land on the Florida side and International Paper owned most of the land on the Alabama side. A bill was introduced in the Senate and a companion bill also had to be introduced in the House of Representatives. The bills were introduced but seemed to die for lack of support. There was a big silence from the major landowners along the Perdido River, whom I am sure didn't want restraints put on their use of lands. Later, however, much of the land along both the Florida and Alabama sides of the river was purchased by the states using the state land-buying monies. In 2002, Alabama Senator Richard Shelby got a $2 million-dollar federal grant for purchasing land along the Perdido River in Alabama.

Friends of Perdido Bay continued to work with the EPA on their "Interstate Project". We had been given a $50,000 grant to start a citizen monitoring program in 1988(described in the Studies chapter).

Our main concern was still the Champion permit and study they were doing and we continued to work with Champion. They would send us reports on the studies they were doing and we would offer suggestions. One Champion employee, Janet Price, would call weekly and we would have lengthy chats. For several years in 1988 through 1991, Champion and Friends of Perdido Bay would jointly sponsor a prize at the yearly science fair. We also continued to correspond with the local DER office and the EPA.

The guiding document for which Champion had to fulfil the requirements was the Consent Order issued in 1989. Paragraph 11 of the Consent Order stated: "This Consent Order shall constitute authorization required by Section 403.088(3), Florida Statutes, for the temporary operation of the facilities during the time periods covered by provisions of this Order."

71

Champion was required to: submit to the Department alternatives to increase the level of dissolved oxygen in their effluent; look at the factors affecting dissolved oxygen in Elevenmile Creek and Perdido Bay by modeling; evaluate alternative treatment technologies and implement them so as to address violations caused by Champion; analyze biological integrity as part of the study; look at technologies to reduce effluent transparency (color) to improve dissolved oxygen and biological quality of Perdido Bay; evaluate nitrogen sources and look at treatment for achieving compliance with un-ionized ammonia (NH_3) ; provide the Department with reports on dioxin studies; and *"...shall complete all corrective actions approved by the Department and shall be fully in compliance with all applicable standards and criteria and requirements of the Department prior to expiration of TOP .... unless otherwise agreed"*. The Temporary Operating Permit (TOP) and Consent Order issued in 1989 were set to expire December 1, 1994.

For the most part, Champion did meet most of the requirements of the 1989 Consent Order except for the installation of technologies which would bring them into compliance with Florida's Water Quality Standards. Champion studied alternative technologies. They looked at moving their point of discharge to lower Elevenmile Creek. They looked at wetland treatment and started a pilot wetland treatment project. They examined land application of their effluent. They increased the dissolved oxygen in their effluent by cleaning out some riffle ditches prior to discharge. They looked at coming into compliance with the un-ionized ammonia standard and said it wasn't going to be possible to meet. They did submit the 22 volume Livingston Study in July 1992.

In looking at some of the data we were given, I realized how complex the pulping and paper-making process was, and how many chemicals they use. It was a huge mill. In one list we were given (Nitrogen in process Additives Used During 1989), Champion used 99,000 pounds a day of Starch additives. They used hundreds of pounds a day of slimicides and biocides. They used 19,000 pounds a day of extended clays. Then there were all the chemicals coming from the trees used to make pulp. I thought that most of this stuff was sure to get into the bay. Champion concluded that most of the ammonia was being formed in the bottom of their treatment ponds. The amounts they were releasing were toxic but they couldn't do anything to solve the un-ionized ammonia problem. Several DER (P) people I spoke with thought Champion was using ammonia to tie-up the dioxin, thus forming chloramines. This helped make the dioxin in the effluent "non-detectable". The new effluent guidelines for the pulp and paper industry, published in December 17, 1993, also mentioned that EPA did not know all the chemicals contained in paper mill effluent. But it became apparent as time progressed that paper mill effluent contained chemicals, obviously toxic and even dangerous.

The federal (NPDES) permit was supposed to be issued in 1988. NPDES stands for "National Pollution Discharge Elimination System". The limits in the new NPDES permit were supposed to be based on the work the EPA had done on Perdido Bay in 1986 and 1987. EPA limits were also supposed to agree with DER limits; however no report was ever issued. EPA did do a modeling of upper Elevenmile Creek and found that the mill exceeded the assimilative capacity of the creek. An EPA scientist told me that the EPA could not issue a permit which the mill could not meet (or possibly desired to meet).

The State permit for Florida was issued in November, 1989. The next permit to be issued was the federal NPDES permit for Champion. The public hearing for the federal permit was held May 17, 1990, in the University of West Florida Field House. The draft NPDES permit which EPA proposed had some of the same limits and conditions as that of the state permit; however, the federal permit imposed more stringent conditions. Beginning on December 1, 1994, and extending to the end of the five-year permit (December 1995), the Biological

Oxygen Demand limits in the NPDES permit dropped about 1000 pounds per day. December 1, 1994, was when Champion was supposed to be in compliance with all Florida's laws according to the state permit. Nearly 150 people attended the hearing. People spoke against the permit; people spoke for Champion. Joe Trapp of the Perdido Bay Environmental Association spoke against the permit because he said chlorine was still being used for bleaching and dioxin was still being formed. The EPA representative, John Marlar, said that dioxin at the mill was currently not detectable. When a resident asked why EPA did not step in when they found out that Champion was not meeting water quality standards in the late 1980's, Marlar said that "EPA did not have a case"[2] . Alabama Assistant Attorney General Robert Tambling said the state of Alabama was opposed to the permit because the plant's discharge was contributing to the pollution of Perdido Bay. I was concerned because the NPDES permit did not mention a requirement to meet the species diversity rule. My husband, Jim, was concerned because there was no limit on nitrogen or phosphorus in the permit. I remember walking into the meeting with Vicki Tschinkel and Janet Price from Champion. Our relations were cordial enough. Joe Trapp said Perdido Bay Environmental Association was not going to accept the permit. Despite our comments, EPA issued the permit unchanged, effective August 7, 1990. Champion now had a Florida Temporary Operating Permit with a Consent Order and federal NPDES permit which would allow them to continue to operate.

On June 8, 1990, an article appeared in the Pensacola News Journal announcing that Escambia County was Number 2 in the state in toxic releases[3]. The two biggest contributors were Monsanto and Champion. The data came from 1988. A later study done in 2004 would find the same thing[4]. The war of words between Champion supporters and people on Perdido Bay continued weekly in the opinion section of the Pensacola News Journal for several years.

In September 1990, Alabama Attorney General Don Siegelman filed a request for an evidentiary hearing on Champion's federal NPDES permit. In the petition, Mr. Siegelman said Alabama was being subjected to Champion's pollution and the permit violated Alabama's pollution laws, in particular, turbidity and foam. Alabama requested that the Champion permit be reopened in December 1991 when Dr. Livingston's study was completed. Alabama also charged that the EPA did not take into consideration the paper mill's past record of noncompliance (*Pro Earth Times*, Oct 1990). Frank Westmark, Champion's spokesman, "...*said the company is in compliance with Florida's water quality standards, which are higher than Alabama's. We don't believe the company's permit is threatened as a result of this action*"[5].

Unfortunately, the federal government does not have the same administrative requirements as the state of Florida. People can ask for evidentiary hearings, but few hearings are granted. So Siegelman's request was ignored.

Despite Champion's promises in the early 1990's to comply, they were having trouble meeting limits in the state permit. Their wastewater treatment system continued to have "upsets". Maybe it was poorly designed and unable to handle the waste load coming from the mill. A series of upsets brought on by cold weather and heavy rains (according to Champion) caused the mill to exceed BOD limits in 1990 and 1991 (years for which we have data)[6]. We saw lots of foam and scum. We were beginning to see algae in the winter in 1988[7]. The bay continued to look worse. Some unusual encrusting sponge began growing on the cement groins at our beach. The EPA, Florida DER and NRDC assessed penalties against Champion of nearly $148,000 in 1990 and part of 1991. The year 1991 looked just as bad with 6 months of major problems. Unusually heavy rains caused the Total Suspended Solids (TSS) values to soar. On March 2, 1991, a heavy rainfall (5.6") swept 27,553 pounds of TSS into Elevenmile Creek and then into the bay. The maximum, daily limit in the permit is 27,000 pounds per day. The paper companies have long known about the problems with rainfall and exposed ponds. The old owners of the mill, St. Regis, were ordered to correct this problem in the 1970's. Champion should not have been surprised, nor should have the regulators. But the regulators who were there in the 1970's had long since gone. We learned that state and federal regulators have no memory of past history. Problems which are not quickly solved are forgotten. Regulatory personnel change jobs and the reports are forgotten. In the future these problems will arise again, and if not corrected will be forgotten again. For the paper mill, it is easier just to pay the fines and hope for a more lenient government administration, rather than fix an expensive problem.

The permitting situation continued to be fluid. Every day I had to read the legal notices in the newspaper to see if anything was being announced. On September 12, 1991, a legal notice appeared in the Pensacola News Journal announcing that Champion was being required to do a "Level II Water Quality Study", as part of the (1989) *Consent Order, Temporary Operating Permit and Variances*. Champion had been issued four variances from water quality criteria for iron, transparency, zinc and specific conductance. Perhaps it was the "new" Democratic administration in Tallahassee flexing their muscles. The Governor was now Lawton Chiles and Carol Browner was Secretary of DER. The 1989 Temporary Operating Permit and Consent Order had been drawn up under the Republican Administration of Governor Martinez.

The 1991 level II Water Quality Study was to establish *"Water Quality Based Effluent Limits in Perdido Bay and Elevenmile Creek"* considering all dischargers and tributaries in the entire bay including Alabama. This required a computer model of Perdido Bay. The EPA had been perfecting these types of models and most were fairly accurate. Tom Gallagher of the New Jersey firm Hydroqual was hired to take the data that Dr. Livingston had acquired and add water direction and flow to simulate continuous movement and flux. We assumed the deadline for this model was going to be December 1, 1994, or the expiration of the Temporary Operating Permit. On September 10, 1991, I received a letter from David Arceneaux, the Director of Environment, Health and Safety at Champion, announcing and outlining this "new" study. The Livingston study was part of this new study initiative. Among the study plan were recent dioxin values and other chemicals in the effluent for 1990. All dioxins and furans were "non-detect", but the detection limits seemed high (from 1.5 parts per quadrillion to 5.4 parts per quadrillion). Chlorinated phenols, benzenes, and other chemicals known to be present in paper mill effluent were also not detectable. From the data supplied by Champion, a couple of heavy metals were present but the concentration did not exceed state standards except for iron. Most of these chemicals are associated with the Total Suspended Solids coming from the mill and are diluted to "not detectable" levels in the whole mill effluent.

I was becoming more and more alarmed by the "Livingston Study" and Champion's plan to establish Water Quality Based Effluent Limitations for the Perdido Bay Drainage System. The Hydroqual model had not yet been done. A lot of work was being done, but the main problem, the Total Suspended Solids and their oxygen-consuming capacity, was being ignored or obscured by Livingston. I wrote several letters to Carol Browner, Secretary of DER under Lawton Childes; Champion; and other DER personnel. I pointed out that production at the mill had been allowed to increase. While perhaps some improvements in treatment had been made, it was not adequate to prevent more degradation. I also sent Carol Browner a video of the foam and algae at our beach. Champion answered my criticism in a letter to Carol Browner dated October 1, 1991. The essence of Champion's letter was that they had spent a $50 million at the mill for "pollution prevention" technologies, the centerpiece being the oxygen delignification bleaching technology; discharge limits were less than one-third of the technology-based discharge limits recommended by EPA for mills of this size; they had funded a study of Perdido Bay; had spent more than $10 million evaluating pollution prevention and treatment technologies. The letter said that the results of Dr. Livingston's study "will guide Champion's action to comply with the provisions of its Consent Order/Temporary Operation Permit." "Pollution prevention" was a popular environmental concept at that time. Champion's letter did not say that they were going to be in compliance with all state standards by the expiration of their 1989 Temporary Operating Permit and Consent Order.

One of the pollution prevention technologies on which Champion spent a lot of effort and money was recycling of their bleach plant effluent - called "BFR" "Bleach Filtrate Recycle". This process entailed removing chloride ions and then sending part of the bleach effluent to the recovery furnace. In Champion's report on BFR dated March 24, 1993, they listed reasons why some form of mill closure in the U.S. seemed inevitable. In the report, Champion engineers mentioned that mills in Europe which had gone to Totally Chlorine Free Mills (TCF) would be difficult to close. Champion hoped that this technology being developed at the Pensacola mill could be patented and then sold to other companies. BFR was the recommended process for closure of Champion's Kraft Bleach Plant and for meeting requirements in the Consent Order (or at least some of them). The projected environmental benefits were a 50% reduction in BOD, a 50% reduction in effluent ammonia, and a 70% reduction in effluent color. The saltiness of the effluent would increase slightly. One of the disadvantages of the project listed in the report was that the risk was higher than the traditional risks taken by the industry. It is interesting to note that two of the paper companies which had been working on mill closure, Union Camp and Louisiana Pacific, were sold to other companies. Both these mills are now closed. Another option which Champion mentioned to bring them into compliance was a direct pipeline to Perdido Bay.

The Pensacola News Journal ran a big article on BFR on January 7, 1996. In the article, Champion called BFR a "breakthrough technology" in helping to close the loop (go to zero discharge) at paper mills. *"BFR is expected to save energy, reduce chemical usage, cut down on water discharge and would be the first step in a closed-loop system for pulp mill bleaching plants - long a dream of the industry"*. (My opinion was that not all members of the pulp and paper industry would agree with this statement.) The article said that DEP expected to issue a draft permit January, 1996, which would allow Champion to continue to operate while working on further improvements. I was singled out in the article as being a harsh critic of Champion's "improvements". No permit was ever issued in 1996. This BFR technology was never installed at the Pensacola Mill. One bleach line at Canton NC mill installed BFR.

The environmental agencies continued to fine Champion for violations. An inspection of the mill by a DER inspector found several violations, especially in the manner the laboratory was run. Samples which were split between Champion and DER personnel found discrepancies. The settling ponds at the mill required cleaning to help retain more Total Suspended Solids (TSS), especially during rainstorms. Although Carol Browner had issued a Memorandum on July 30, 1991, clarifying use of *Temporary Operating Permits (TOP) and Consent Orders (CO)*, Champion continued to operate. The Memorandum said that: *"...No facility should be allowed to operate under a TOP or series of TOPs for more than 5 years. If a facility fails to come into compliance within 5 years of operating under a TOP or series of TOPs, the facility should be either required to cease operation or obtain a variance."* Temporary operation of a facility which is not in compliance may be authorized in a Consent Order. So according to Carol Browner, a temporary operating permit could only be issued once. The mill continued to operate on an expired permit.

Changes were occurring at the local DER office as well. Bob Kriegel was replaced by Bobbie Cooley as District Director of DER at the beginning of 1992. Bob Kriegel had been investigated by the state for bribery and favoritism allegations. Supposedly he withheld permits from his friend's enemies. Perhaps this was the way things operated here. With Bobby Cooley, we had hopes that he would be more forceful in enforcing environmental rules against Champion. I continued to write letters to DER. In one letter dated March 24, 1992, I complained about the drift algae blooming at our beach in the winter. I pointed out that this had been occurring for the past five winters or since 1987. The algae blooms lasted about four or five months. I ask the DER to investigate the source of the nutrients. DER said that the Livingston study which was supposed to be finished in August, 1992, and paid for by Champion, would address this issue. My worries about the Livingston studies continued. I wrote to the President of the Ecological Society of America about the unscientific methods being used to get "polluters off the hook. I did not receive any answer.

By the time the Livingston study came out, we knew it was going to be a "whitewash". Dr. Livingston concluded that Champion's wastewater discharge was the principal factor affecting dissolved oxygen in Elevenmile Creek. He also found that discharges of nutrients into the Creek affected the immediate receiving portions of Perdido Bay. He somehow also concluded that Champion's wastewater was having little effect on the low-dissolved oxygen in the bay when compared to other sources of nutrients and organic matter. Dr. Livingston determined that the source of oxygen depleting pollution was coming from the lower Bay. The salt water entering Perdido Bay from the Gulf was causing stratification, according to Dr. Livingston, and was causing the oxygen depletion, not pollution from the paper mill.

Dr. Livingston's study set off a fire storm of controversy. Shortly after the Livingston Report came out, DER biologists went out and determined that the source of oxygen-consuming material was coming from the upper bay and not the Gulf of Mexico. Four researchers from the Ecological Support Branch of the EPA disputed Livingston's results in unpublished reports. One researcher lamented that Perdido Bay should be a nursery area for fish, but was only a treatment pond for the paper mill [8]. The DER hired a reviewer, Dr. Jack Taylor, who also pointed out the fallacies in the Livingston conclusion. However, Vicki Tschinkel who was still working as a Champion consultant and who had been instrumental in hiring Dr. Livingston, got the reviews of two noted scientists praising the thoroughness of Livingston's work, although both admitted they also were too busy to do a thorough evaluation. Livingston's conclusion further was reinforced by a Wasteload Allocation Model which Hydroqual's Tom Gallagher was doing. I had received a copy of the Wasteload Allocation report, but several pages of the report were missing. (I did finally receive the entire report many years later.) The model did not account for Champion's Total Suspended Solids which were settling to the bottom of the bay, especially in the lower bay. In the model, these solids disappeared. So according to the model, the water would enter the bay from the Gulf, pass over the oxygen consuming bottom solids, and become depleted of oxygen. Just where these solids came from was unknown according to the Tom Gallagher model. By using models, it is easy to deceive.

Although the conclusions in the report were highly controversial, the Secretary of DER, Virginia Wetherell, sided with Champion and agreed with the Livingston Report; however, she conceded further study was needed since many questions remained unanswered.

Carol Browner, who had been the former secretary, had moved to head EPA. Of course, the media picked this up immediately: "DER agrees with Champion study". On June 16, 1993, the Pensacola News Journal (PNJ) wrote: "The Department (DER) concurs that the problem in the Bay is not the mill". However, not all editors at PNJ were so fooled. J. Earl Bowden, Senior Editor and Vice President wrote in the July 19, 1993 edition: *"Yes... Champion contributes to the problem in the Bay. Officials with the state Department of Environmental Protection are clear on that point"* and *"Champion - and DEP - can't expect people to forget that it took grassroots involvement by concerned citizens to get the state and Champion to get serious about cleaning up the mill's effluent."* In case Pensacola citizens did not get the news, Champion ran a big ad on July 4, 1993, in the Pensacola News Journal: *"Leading Scientists and DEP agree on Perdido Bay problems. Champion effect on the bay is minimal and limited to area near mouth of Elevenmile Creek"* read the headlines. The ad concluded *"Champion is working hard to solve the environmental concerns attributable to the company. We think it's time for others to put aside worn-out old disputes and work together."* I often wondered if the local newspaper, sided with Champion because they were buying full page ads. Champion's newsletter, *Champion News*, also touted the results of the Livingston study - *"DEP Agrees With Perdido Bay Study"*. Champion's newsletters were showcasing all the goodwill it was spreading around Pensacola. From sponsoring summer evening concert series in the park, to the fireworks display on the Fourth of July, Champion was working on winning community support. They were the good guys, and Friends of Perdido Bay and the other environmentalists from Perdido Bay Environmental Association were the "mean, trouble-makers" who were unreasonable. Janet Price, a Champion employee who was leading compliance with the 1989 Consent Order, had told me in conversations that "the truth was what the public perceived it to be". Champion's public relations efforts worked hard on molding public opinion into its version of the truth.

While we had been concentrating on making sure our side of the story was heard in the Livingston study debate, Champion was preparing to enact their "improvements". Champion had not told my husband and me anything about those improvements. On Saturday evening, March 13, 1993, as I was looking through the legal notices of the Pensacola News Journal, I saw the notice from the Department of Environmental Protection (DEP) (Note: DER merged with another state Department and became DEP): "NOTICE OF INTENT TO ISSUE PERMIT Champion International Corporation". My husband and I had just been down to DEP and no one had said anything about a permit. The following week we went down to the DEP office in Pensacola and got a complete copy of what Champion was intending to do. This 1993 air permit was for "improvements to their wastewater treatment system". This was their plan for compliance? Champion was doing their improvements through an air permit. The Champion proposal was to convert the bleaching process to 100% chlorine dioxide; add a bigger power boiler to support the generation of chlorine dioxide from chlorate; add more evaporators to reduce the contaminated water going to the wastewater treatment system; add a bigger lime-kiln mud drier; and go to extended cooking of the wood chips These improvements were consistent with the "pollution prevention" philosophy the government was pushing. The only problem was that these improvements were going to increase emissions of hazardous air pollutants. Champion determined that chloroform, chlorine and chlorine dioxide were going to significantly increase in the air. As of that date 1993, there were no chloroform standards for the air because they had been blocked by the Florida Paper and Pulp Industry.

Much of the residuals captured in the air scrubbers were dumped into the wastewater treatment system. Any improvement in the air usually meant increases in the water pollution. Any increases in production also meant increases in air and water pollutants[9] and Champion had plenty of air emissions. In a 2000 Fish and Wildlife Report, its facility consisted of: a tall oil plant, nine boilers, a lime kiln-mud dryer, two dissolving tanks, a coal crusher, a coal conveyor system, a paper machine including clay silo, a lime slaker, chlorine dioxide storage and generation, a bleach plant/scrubber system, a wood yard that included chipping and screening, plus numerous tanks for various liquid storage. All of these emitted pollutants into the air. The wet scrubbers which were used to control air emissions on tall oil plant, power boilers burning bark and coal, bleach plant and lime kilns all discharged collected material into the wastewater treatment system.

DEP hadn't followed its own permitting rules when it allowed Champion to "improve" air quality by modernizing the precipitators on its recovery furnaces. There was no public notice of this $2.1 million modernization. According to *Champion News* (Issue one, 1993), the first precipitator was completed November 1992 and the second precipitator was scheduled for completion the first quarter of 1993. According to a Champion spokesman, *"...With the completion of this modernization project, our recovery boiler precipitators will be on the cutting edge of today's technology."* Champion did not announce how much the air quality was being "improved." Champion had begun their "improvements" before DEP had issued the 1993 "Intent to Issue" air permit.

Several members of Perdido Bay Environmental Association (PBEA) and I decided to challenge the air permit and filed for an administrative hearing. Why? Mainly because we had hoped that Champion would go to totally chlorine-free bleaching.

At that time, several other paper mills were going to totally chlorine-free bleaching. The Union Camp mill in Franklin, Virginia was installing a bleaching process using a propriety ozone method. Louisiana-Pacific mill in Samoa, California, also was going totally-chlorine free. (The EPA had yet to publish its new air and water standards for the pulp and paper industry. They would appear later in December 1993.) Champion immediately made a Motion to Dismiss our petitions in the Administrative Court, calling them frivolous [10]. We were allowed to amend our original petitions. The administrative law judge allowed us to amend our petitions three times in response to Champion's Motions to Dismiss. Champion's last motion claimed that we did not have standing because we were not substantially affected by the "improvements". On January 27, 1994, nearly a year after we had filed our petitions, the administrative law judge agreed with Champion and dismissed our petitions because he said we did not have standing.

The whole time that our challenges to the air permit went on, Champion was running ads in the Pensacola News Journal questioning why we would hold up their progress. On Sunday June 27, 1993, a debate about Champion's new processes appeared in the Opinion section of the Pensacola News Journal. Frank Westmark, the public relations manager for the Champion mill, took Champion's side; Fred Garth presented our side. Westmark used the Livingston study to point the finger away from Champion. If Champion wasn't causing the oxygen depletion problems in Perdido Bay, then the $35 million "pollution prevention" project that Champion was planning would be perfect. Fred Garth from the Perdido Bay Environmental Association countered: *"Champion calls it a $35 million pollution prevention program...Once again, they think the people of Escambia and Baldwin counties are idiots. Here is a company that for the past 10 years has fought to increase its production capacity and thus its pollution output. In the 1980's, they spent over $200 million to convert the plant, which dramatically increased its pollution. Now, suddenly, they have a conscience?"*[11]

A Viewpoint article in the Pensacola News Journal by Nelson Bethune (8/29/93), a board member of Perdido Bay Environmental Association, was also very good because it contained some of the past history of citizens' efforts to clean up their Bay. *"Why don't we trust Champion? Read on. Consider this history;*
1942 - Mill starts operation, dumping untreated waste into Eleven Mile Creek and hence into Perdido Bay.

1965 - A mill engineer responding to a compliant from a Perdido Bay resident says about the crud in the water: It's the mill's fault, but he can't get the management to do anything about it.

1970- Government study concludes that effluent from the mill is "overwhelmingly" the major cause of the pollution problems in Perdido Bay. The report sets target for pollution reduction by the mill to be achieved by Jan. 1, 1973.

1970 - The mill hires its own consultant to study the effect of the mill on the bay.

1971 - The mill refuses to release their consultant's report, stating that it is not relevant since some changes have been made at the mill.

1973 - The mill owner, St. Regis Corp., announces in a full-page ad in the Wall Street Journal, a new process that will reduce pollution by settling out much of the bad stuff in their effluent.

1975 - The new process is quietly shelved, because the disposal of the material that settled out was a big problem - go back to just flushing it down the creek.

1985 - Champion acquires mill. Tells environmentalists: Give us a little time; we'll do the right thing for the environment.

1987 - Citizens file for an administrative hearing on the proposed DER water pollution permit for the mill.

1989 - The administrative hearing is pursued by the Perdido Bay Environmental Association and me; the hearing officer concludes that Champion needs some time to study and correct their problems.

1992 - Champion cancels a verbal agreement with the U.S. Fish and Wildlife Service to allow them to study uptake of dioxin by catfish in their effluent.

1992 - Champion embarks on a public relations blitz to influence public perception of the company.

1993 - Champion's public relations campaign is expanded to target school children by "adopting" schools and encouraging employees to participate in this program.

1993 - Champion's behind-the-scenes negotiations with DER concentrate on exploiting weak points in pollution regulations. The major projects being considered are: 1) Piping the effluent straight to Perdido Bay, or: 2) Continue dumping in the creek but dilute the effluent with water piped from the Perdido or Escambia River.

1993 - The mill has not yet achieved targets for pollution reduction set by the Federal Water Pollution Control Administration in 1970.

1993 - Citizens file for an administrative hearing on the proposed DEP Air Permit for Champion which requires a decrease in some air emissions but will allow others to increase.

We respect Mr. Tim's efforts. We ask that he and others understand why we hear a hollow ring in the mill's current theme:

"We're good neighbors. Don't ask questions. Trust us."

Besides running ads, Champion was also mailing out quarterly newsletters. The first quarter 1994 *Champion News* announced that "Mill's Major Environmental Project Clears Legal Hurdle". The newsletter said that the Champion mill would begin the construction of their $50 million project in May 1994. The project went from $35 million to $50 million. In this newsletter, Champion announced that the grass beds in upper Perdido Bay were flourishing and that they were holding a conference for local educators and said that they were supporting the EPA's proposal for bleached pulp and paper production. Champion was really spreading the money around the community trying to pass themselves off as "good community citizens". To get themselves ingrained in the community, Champion hired John Fogg, an ex-Blue Angel pilot and future mayor of Pensacola. I often wondered how much the military participated in this pollution fight. Was the industrial- military complex flexing its muscle?

We knew in 1993 that Champion was not going to meet the Water Quality Standards in the creek. In a May 14, 1993

87

Memorandum to Virginia Wetherell, Secretary of DER, Bobbie Cooley, District Director of DER, summarized the work being done by Champion. In the "Memorandum", he writes:

"...Our draft response to Champion contains our conclusions and recommendations on the various studies. We do not believe the proposed process modifications alone are capable of meeting water quality standards. However, rather than proceed with the pipeline alternative, we feel Champion should concentrate its efforts on further improving the quality of its discharge to Elevenmile Creek. We have also recommended that Champion investigate the use of flow augmentation, whereby additional fresh water from another water body, such as the Perdido River would be pumped into Elevenmile Creek to provide further dilution of the mill's discharge." Both proposals Champion was considering would be the death knell for Perdido Bay. Cooley's proposals would perhaps allow Champion to meet the water standards in Elevenmile Creek, but certainly not Perdido Bay. My husband and I were shocked and disappointed by these revelations. Champion had told us that they were going to do the "right thing," that they were going to do more than the letter of the law, but the "spirit of the law" as well. We found out that the "spirit of the law" meant that they could discharge "a little bit". A permit limit of 27,000 pounds a day of Total Suspended Solids was more than a "little bit". The Pensacola domestic wastewater treatment plant which treated wastes from 165,000 people was only permitted to discharge 844 pounds per day – an amount far less than allowed.

The color issue in the paper mill effluent was curious. Champion claimed they were spending $15,000 a day on a special chemical called polyamine to remove color from their effluent. Why was Champion spending so much money when engineers we knew told my husband that the simple chemical alum (aluminum sulfate) could remove the color. Earlier in 1992, Friends of Perdido Bay had been contacted by a chemist from Louisiana, Ray Doescher, who said he could remove the color using kitchen chemicals. He came to a meeting of Friends of Perdido Bay in June 1992 and demonstrated his "proprietary method". It worked fine. Mr. Doescher told us that he had demonstrated his technique at Champion in a bench test several weeks earlier. It had worked but Champion wasn't interested. Polyamine was removing something else from the effluent. Dioxin? Heavy metals? It remained unclear. Champion had also gone to using hardwoods as part of their pulping process. At one point, they were using 65% hardwoods and 35% pine. Use of hardwoods produced less color. And as we found out later, hardwoods do not degrade as much when chlorine dioxide is used for bleaching.

In April 1994, DEP announced that they were going to give Champion an extension on their Consent Order and Temporary Operating Permit which had been issued in 1989. Champion claimed that our administrative challenge to the air permit in 1993 had held up their improvements. To DEP's credit, no permit for a pipeline to Perdido Bay had been issued, but we were holding our breaths. Many of us knew that it was going to be difficult because of the pressure from the industry. We knew, as did all biologists that studied Perdido Bay, a direct pipeline to Perdido Bay would be much worse than the present situation. Champion's effluent would kill more life in the bay. To make matters worse, the DEP biologists were no longer sampling Perdido Bay. If we wanted to prove that Perdido Bay was "dead," we would have to provide the data ourselves. Dr. Livingston was still doing studies, but he was not to be trusted since he seemed to be in the pocket of Champion.

Champion applied for a permit renewal (not a temporary operating permit) on September 30, 1994. This was considered a "timely" permit application. In a letter from DEP's Bobbie Cooley to Doug Owenby, Champion's mill manager, dated November 22, 1994, Mr. Cooley said: *"Since you have timely applied for a renewal, your current permit will remain in full force and effect until such time as the Department takes final agency action on this new permit application"*. The ball was now in the DEP's court. It was the Department's authority to approve or deny the plan and they could take as much time as they wanted. The DEP continued to claim that they required more information from Champion about their "improvements". Until the DEP deemed Champion's permit application "complete", the DEP would continue extending the deadline, or as DEP termed "administratively continue" the old permit.

By the beginning of 1995, it was difficult to know what permit was in effect at the time. According to the 1990 NPDES permit, more stringent limits were supposed to go into effect December 1994. I wrote to EPA on January 13, 1995 about the fact that Champion was not meeting the new effluent limits. In March 28, 1995, I received a letter from EPA. Their response was a shock. It states:

*"Champion was issued a new NPDES permit in August 1990. Upon issuance of the permit, the Environmental Protection Agency (EPA) received evidentiary hearing requests from the State of Alabama Attorney General, Champion International Corporation and Friends of Perdido Bay. To date, none of the evidentiary hearing requests have been resolved. The NPDES which was issued to Champion in August 1990 has been stayed in its **entirety** (EPA's emphasis) pending a resolution of the requests for evidentiary hearing. Until such time as a decision is made to grant or deny the evidentiary hearings, the entire 1990 permit is stayed and the preceding 1983 permit is effective. The effluent violations that you refer to in your letter are violations of provisions and limitations required by the 1990 permit. As stated above, these limits are not in effect at this time due to unresolved evidentiary hearing requests."* This letter was sent certified mail. I began to wonder if the whole thing was a sham. EPA had contacted us once, about resolving our issues with the 1990 NPDES permit, but then we heard nothing more from them. To make matters even more confusing, DER personnel sent me a letter which had been written October 2, 1995 to DER by EPA. In the letter, the Champion federal NPDES permit which had expired on August

31, 1995 (original 1990 permit) was being transferred to the state. But EPA told me that the 1983 permit was supposedly in force. It had expired in 1988. There definitely was something wrong.

On May 1, 1995, Florida had been granted the authority to issue federal NPDES permits. That meant that dischargers seeking a permit would only have to get one permit - from the state. In the Florida law authorizing the state DER to issue federal permits, the more stringent permit was supposed to be the prevailing one. This meant that the state 1989 permit should have been the controlling document until 1994 when the more stringent EPA limits went into effect. But by 1995, the state permit had expired. The DEP issued an order to Champion transferring the NPDES permit to the state; however, the order expired on the expiration date of the state permit which was December 1, 1994. Because the Order was issued on November 15, 1995 the Order had already expired. The district director of DEP issued a supplement to the November 15, 1995 Order on April 22, 1996. The supplemental order stated that the effective NPDES permit for Section I was the 1983 permit which had more lax limits. This violated Florida's rule for combining permits, but we were unaware of all this chicanery until several years later. When I complained to Champion's attorney several years later that we had not been notified as required by law, he said "You have just been notified" - too late, of course.

Champion also must have been confused by the fluid nature of the changing permits. On January 30, 1996, Champion asked for a Florida administrative hearing on the issue of which permit was in effect. DEP's April 22, 1996 letter to Champion stated that the entire 1990 permit was "rendered ineffective" by evidentiary hearing requests. The enforceable permit was the January 3, 1983 permit. Once DEP clarified which permit was in effect and enforceable, Champion withdrew its request for an administrative hearing. No surprise there.

Champion submitted a "Modified Compliance Plan" one year later in September 1995. In the "Modified Compliance Plan, Champion said that: *"Consent Order paragraph 14 specifically directs Champion to develop a compliance plan to be submitted to the FDEP for review and approval"*. The plan was now DEP's authority to approve or deny. In the "Modified Compliance Plan", Champion said that they would complete Phase I (issued through an air modification permit) by December 1, 1995 and then Phase II by December 1999. The Company said it would not begin Phase II until the new combined federal and state NPDES permit, which they applied for in 1994, had been issued. Champion claimed that they had spent $20 million in research and development looking at new technologies.

"At the conclusion of Phase one, the Pensacola Mill will have installed the state-of-the-art-technology which forms the basis of U.S. EPA's proposed effluent standards for the pulp and paper industry. Phase Two (not yet specified) will take the mill even further" [13]. In Phase II, Champion talked about installing Bleach Filtrate Recycle which was being tested at the Canton, North Carolina mill. The 1995 permit application was accompanied by an Application for Variances. A variance from state standards was requested for Dissolved Oxygen and Un-Ionized Ammonia/ Biological Integrity. Champion claimed that the toxicity of un-ionized ammonia was causing lowered diversity of animals and fish in Elevenmile Creek. This was Dr. Livingston's conclusion. He did not address all the toxic chemicals which were being released. I noticed that several other water quality standards which Champion was violating were missing from the variance list. Among those were: specific conductance, pH, and turbidity (color). The "Modified Compliance Plan" contained a lengthy section on engineering plans for a pipeline to either dispose upland at the McMillian Tract or create a lower disposal at Elevenmile Creek Outfall. The Modified Compliance Plan also said Champion would meet all state standards by expiration of the permit in December 1, 1999. Despite Champion's promises to meet state standards, they had never been able to meet standards since 1970's.

In *Champion News* (Issue Four 1995), the company touted its new technology installed in Phase I, to reclaim and recycle lime, a byproduct of its chemical recycling process. *"The Pensacola mill is one of the first in the United States to employ this new technology, which will enable the mill to re-use the majority of the lime required in the manufacturing process."* The *Champion News* also announced that the mill had completely converted to 100% chlorine dioxide and that it would be in full compliance with all federal and state water quality standards by the end of December 1999. Many citizens on Perdido Bay were urging Champion to go to a land application and get out of the bay, including myself. It was apparent that Champion was not going to clean up sufficiently to meet water quality standards in the creek and bay. The bay continued to look unhealthy.

On March 12, 1995, a full-page ad appeared in the Pensacola News Journal announcing "Champion's Environmental Projects Scheduled for Completion in December". The ad said: *"The overall program is designed to meet all applicable state and federal water quality standards in Eleven Mile Creek."* I wondered if the people at the mill were delusional. From the modeling studies on BOD, Champion knew very well that they were not going to meet standards in the creek, unless they had high hopes that their chlorine dioxide bleaching would do more than it did or they could reduce their BOD by eightfold. *"Our goal is to meet all water quality standards and make the Pensacola mill one of the most environmentally friendly pulp and paper mills in the world. This goal is within reach, and working together, we will achieve it."*

The DEP did not issue any new agency action through the late 1990's.; they only extended the old permit while the regulators mulled over Champion's proposed fixes. No variances were issued. Champion continued to violate the law without the variances. By not taking any action and only extending the permit, Consent Order and variances, DEP prevented the public from intervening in any decisions being made. Florida does have a provision in their state rules which gives citizens authority to make the DEP enforce their rules. You must go to Circuit Court to make that happen. If one loses a court case (a possibility), one must pay the legal fees of the other side. Environmentalists would have to wait.

Friends of Perdido Bay kept busy with its grassroots efforts to preserve the bay area. We were working with another environmental group, Friends of the Prairie, to get the state to purchase the Tarkiln peninsula as a pitcher plant prairie on land adjoining the middle part of the Bay. The county held a referendum on buying the property and it almost passed. The state then bought the land. The Escambia County Utilities Authority decided to buy 1000 + acres of land surrounding the Avondale Plant and apply their effluent to wetlands. At the time, ECUA was permitted for 4 million gallons a day. Friends of Perdido Bay thought it was a good solution at the time. The effluent would still run into the bay, but much of plant nutrients would be removed. There was a small hurricane, Opal, in the Fall of 1995. A catfish kill occurred in the Spring of 1996 in the lower and mid-bay. Only adult, hardhead catfish appeared to be affected. One symptom was red lips and fins. No cause was ever reported. However, in the Fall 1996, red tide caused by a bloom of toxic algae, was detected in the lower bay. Since the state had abandoned their water quality sampling in the bay, I had begun doing quarterly sampling at about nine stations in the bay. There was still severe oxygen depletion in the deeper parts of the bay and on the bottom even though Champion supposedly was still working on various methods of meeting the dissolved oxygen standard in Elevenmile Creek, which spilled into the bay. They tried dilution with 4 million gallons pumped from the ground. They tried getting alternative criteria saying low dissolved oxygen is natural in the summer in many streams. The DEP biologists, who were always very helpful to us, countered that argument by producing average dissolved oxygen values for streams similar in flow to Elevenmile Creek.

94

You could begin to see the attitude of the state regulatory agencies change. Alabama always had a lax regulatory system, with their rules being less stringent than Florida's, but Florida also became friendlier toward polluters. In 1997, Virginia Wetherell, Secretary of Florida DEP, began promoting "a kinder, gentler" environmental agency. In the Spring of 1998, she told employees that they "could either get on the train or get run over". The buzz word was "sustainable". Not only had Florida biologists stopped sampling stations in Perdido Bay which they had sampled for 20 years previously, but the state's data storage program, STORET, selectively recorded data. I found out that DEP was only entering oxygen and salinity readings from the surface, something I was already doing at stations in Perdido Bay. They were ignoring oxygen readings from the deeper waters. There was no problem in the surface waters of Perdido Bay, especially if you tested them during daylight hours. It appeared, on the surface, that Perdido Bay had no problems. But we could see that it did. Dr. Livingston continued to work for Champion and do biological sampling in Perdido Bay, yet we knew his views were biased. The local Pensacola News Journal ads made it seem like Champion had cleaned up. Champion continued to run ads like that in Nov. 1994 - *"Champion Continues to Improve Water Quality"*. *"Huge environmental program includes new technology to meet state and federal standards; estimated cost near $100 million"*. Champion also continued to give money to the community. Champion's PR program was working at giving Champion a clean image. However, the clean-up was not enough, and DEP would not issue a new permit.

My husband and I had a meeting with Frank Westmark, Champion's spokesman, and Willie Tims, Champion Environmental Director in May 1997. They told us that they were considering going into the neighboring Escambia River and Bay. Champion came to a Friends of Perdido Bay meeting on May 28, 1997, to announce that they were looking at discharging to Escambia Bay. This was one scenario. The other was treating the effluent in a constructed wetland and piping it to lower Elevenmile Creek. Of course, the residents on Perdido Bay were very happy about Champion going to Escambia Bay, but those on Escambia Bay were not. It was a larger bay, but I was unclear about whether or not it could handle Champion's effluent. Escambia Bay already received effluent from several large chemical companies, a power company, and another paper mill in Brewton, Alabama. I was never sure, but I supposed those dischargers did not want anyone upsetting their site. The dischargers on Escambia Bay had gotten Escambia Bay to the point where it seemed O.K., but it wasn't really. The sediments were heavily contaminated, as were those in Perdido Bay's[13].

Champion's 1997 announcement set off a "Battle of the Bays." To test public opinion about going to Escambia Bay, Champion held a meeting at Pace High School in Santa Rosa County on July 16, 1997. It wasn't a pretty scene. About 300 people showed up and jeered Champion's environmental manager when he tried to explain Champion's plan. *"How can we allow an industry that employs 1,200 people to affect the lives of almost 300,000 people?"* asked Sandy Doll, the owner of Bay Realty. The meeting was boisterous. I got up and tried to tell the audience that Escambia River was a better place for Champion's effluent than Elevenmile Creek. The audience told me to sit down and shut up. Several Champion employees got up and spoke. One man said the effluent from Champion was as clear as a glass of water. Susan Ham of Pensacola said Champion would get what it wants. *"You are talking about big business vs. the little man. Who is going to win? Champion doesn't care for anything except what's filtered into their pockets"* [14]. After the meeting, I met up with Champion's PR person, Susan Shackley. She didn't seem too upset about the outcome of the meeting, nor did the employees she had with her. I have since wondered if that meeting was staged so that Champion could stay in Perdido Bay.

96

In October 1997, I read an article in the Pensacola News Journal about the decline in Champion's profits. In the second quarter of 1997, Champion reported a loss of $0.12 per share. They were putting certain mills up for sale and selling off 325,000 acres of timberlands. Champion still owned approximately 10 million acres of timberland. They were also cutting some of the workforce at other mills. Champion's local public affairs director, Susan Shackley, said local layoffs were possible. *"The company has not said when an announcement on layoffs will be made or whether there'll even be an impact here.... The good news for the Pensacola mill is that we continue to be an integral part of Champion's long-term strategy."* [15] I wondered if this threat to jobs spurred some of the supporters of labor to jump into the fight.

In the ongoing battle, to move its effluent to another bay, Champion had to do another water quality study, this time of Escambia Bay. Dr. Livingston was doing the study and it was supposed to be finished by June 1998. In May 27, 1998, Champion sent out a Press Release announcing
"...completion of the most comprehensive scientific study ever conducted on the Escambia and Perdido estuary systems. The study, led by a team of independent scientists from the state of Florida, was undertaken as part of an effort by Champion to determine the best location for the company to discharge its treated wastewater....The study indicates that after completing ongoing improvements to the mill's wastewater treatment system, the mill will be able to discharge into the Escambia River, which is larger, more open system and meets Class III water quality standards, with no variances or special considerations." But I knew our bay was not their priority and I was just holding my breath.

In the summer of 1998, a local attorney, Mike Papantonio, began running TV ads against Champion going into Escambia Bay. He said that he was spending $60,000 of his own money because people on Escambia Bay did not want

"...millions of gallons of toxic waste dumped into their bay...."
His T.V. commercials countered the commercial Champion was
running. It did not make us on Perdido Bay feel any better.
Champion began running ads complaining that the ads by Mike
Papantonio were playing politics with jobs at the mill. One
rumor that was circulating was that "powerful interests" wanted
to shut the mill down so that their forest lands could be opened
up to development. The mill's spokeswoman, Susan Shackley,
put a stop to the jobs issue when she said *"The Company has
never made a connection between going to the Escambia River
and long-term state of the mill."* Baldwin County Alabama
Commissioners voted to support the Champion proposal to move
their effluent to Escambia Bay.

In January 1999, more high profile help came to give
support to the Escambia Bay people. Bobby Kennedy, the
NRDC's main lawyer, came and spoke to a local civic group. I
went to the meeting. He did not directly say that Champion
should not go to Escambia Bay, but that it was important to
protect your backyard. It was O.K. to be a "NIMBY". The next
day, Champion's unions ran a full-page ad in the Pensacola
News Journal inviting Bobbie Kennedy to tour the mill. The ad
said they had one of the most technologically advanced paper
mills in the world. Linda Young of the *Pro Earth Times*
encouraged Champion to go to a "closed loop system" and stay
in Perdido Bay. The Clean Water network, which Linda Young
ran, encouraged people to attend a meeting in Tallahassee to
speak to the EPA against Champion changing bays. At the EPA
meeting in Tallahassee, EPA experts said that the closed loop
technology did not exist for paper mills making the type of paper
Champion made. EPA was going to assess the Champion mill in
the near future. The Pensacola News Journal had three or four
editorials against Champion going to Escambia Bay. We
Perdido Bay people were very hopeful and waiting for the new
NPDES permit to come out for a discharge to Escambia Bay.

In 1998, Curtis Golden, the State Attorney of Northwest Florida, empaneled a special Grand Jury to investigate the air and water pollution of Escambia County, Florida, and to assess the effectiveness of the regulators in protecting the air and water. Curtis Golden was from Santa Rosa County, the next county over bordering Escambia Bay. They heard testimony from many people and reviewed documents. The findings of the Grand Jury were no surprise to us. *"For reasons more fully set forth below, we find that although efforts to improve the degraded conditions of the surface waters have succeeded somewhat, surface water quality, in general, is degraded and will likely remain so. The causes are various, but degradation is the result primarily of discharges by industry (especially the pulp and paper mill and chemical factories), sewage treatment plants, and storm water runoff...."* (p 1)[16]. The report went on to name Champion as the largest single source of water pollution in Escambia County. The Grand Jury report said that Champion could not meet, and could never meet, the state water quality standards in Elevenmile Creek. The report faulted the local office of the DEP with failure to enforce pollution laws. According to the report, laws of Florida would be violated if Champion switched bays.[17]

We concurred with all the findings in the Grand Jury Report. I was told that Champion's plan to go to Escambia Bay precipitated the report. I was also told by Mr. Edgar, the Assistant State Attorney, he would try to have Champion stay in Perdido Bay as it was already polluted with paper mill wastes. Champion could not go to Escambia Bay without killing the oysters in Escambia Bay and doing great harm to its ecosystem. Perdido Bay's oysters were already dead.

On February 3, 1999, the Pensacola News Journal announced in big headlines "Champion suspends plan to route wastewater to river," so Escambia Bay was spared the fate of Perdido Bay. In the PNJ article, findings were shared:
"The scientists concluded that the Escambia River, which feeds into Escambia Bay just east of U.S. 90, can handle

the mill's wastewater. The river is 45 times larger than Elevenmile Creek and can better dilute chemicals in the wastewater, they say. But Livingston also said more tests should be conducted before they can be sure that releasing the wastewater into the river and Escambia Bay will not have an adverse impact, particularly on the fragile bay." Livingston was being truthful for once. It was very disappointing to us, but not to the Escambia Bay supporters. Whether the Grand Jury Report, or the Pensacola News Journal's editorials against going to Escambia River, or the outcry from the public was sufficient influence to deter Champion from going to Escambia Bay, we will never know. Perhaps it was just a ruse by Champion to bide time or to gain allies from Escambia Bay supporters to help them in Perdido Bay. Champion was going to seek a permit to remain in Perdido Bay at the same discharge site; nevertheless, it wasn't going to be easy. Recent studies in 1999 by Florida biologists documented Champion's violations to water quality standards in Eleven Mile Creek. Only Champion's consultant, Dr. Skip Livingston, was studying Perdido Bay.

On Sunday June 27, 1999, the Pensacola News Journal ran a full-page article on Perdido Bay written by Dr. Livingston. He said an "ecosystem approach" was needed to save the bay. The ecosystem approach was the new buzzword in environmental circles; you had to consider the entire watershed, not just point-source (industrial) polluters. We had been attending meetings of the Perdido Bay Ecosystem Restoration Group. These ecosystem meetings had been revived since the early 1990's. Several meetings were held but it was difficult to make any decisions about what to do. In Livingston's article, he wrote:

"The current condition of the Perdido Bay system is the result of the complex interaction of natural processes and human activities. Recovery of the upper bay, after reductions of phosphorus loading by the Champion International Corp. paper mill, is a positive response to efforts to control discharges from an identified point-source."[18]. I didn't know how Livingston

100

could say the upper bay was recovering. The water looked terrible and we had seen massive amounts of drift algae at our beaches that spring. The grass beds were "flourishing" but they had a red tinge instead of green. Livingston went on:
"...a more complete characterization of the pollutant loading in these areas is needed." These areas were in the lower bay. Livingston said Perdido Bay was a small basin.
"The Perdido drainage system is dominated physically by the Perdido River, an alluvial system of swamps, marshes and creeks that drain into the main stem of the river, which then flows into Perdido Bay." I have always disagreed with Livingston that the Perdido River is an "alluvial system". There are some swamps, but for the most part the river carries a low sediment load. Livingston, again in deflecting the oxygen-consuming characteristics of paper mill solids (sludges) wrote:
"...Model results indicated that Champion's wastewater discharges lowered the dissolved oxygen in the bay by relatively small amounts when compared to the other sources of nutrients and organic matter...." This was in direct conflict with what the EPA study had shown back in 1986 and 1987. But maybe that was the point of Livingston's research - to counter the findings of the EPA study. In a smaller article on the same page, Livingston touted the need for "ecosystem research". Ecosystem research is great if you have a lot of money and a lot of time. Otherwise, simple wasteload allocations usually provide enough information to help control pollution.

In the same June 27, 1999 Sunday issue of the PNJ, Livingston blasted environmentalists in a Viewpoint article - "Time to face Perdido Bay's real problems". Local environmentalists were NIMBY's. He included our group, Friends of Perdido Bay, and me as NIMBYs. Second, he blasted the news media, *"...major parts of which have deteriorated into an arm of the entertainment industry. Gone are the great environmental writers of old."* His third complaint was the *"...increasing ignorance of and lack of interest in environmental problems by the public at large...."* He went on to lament that

101

his reports on nutrient imbalances in Perdido Bay had been ignored by the public. He didn't say what had caused the nutrient imbalances but he did not put the blame on Champion. Rather he said it was "storm water runoff". Storm water runoff has over the years been a "boilerplate" reason for just about all pollution. He praised Champion for providing funds for a long-term, comprehensive study which was available to the public. Too bad his conclusion couldn't have been a little more objective and even agreed with his article on ecosystem research! We might have believed him.

Between June 1999 and January 2000, several articles appeared in the Pensacola News Journal about Champion looking for solutions to their water quality problems: a pipeline to wetlands adjacent to Perdido Bay or variances for water quality standards being violated in the Creek. An article in the Pensacola News Journal on January 24, 2000, announced that "Champion might keep using creek". According to the article, Champion was building a case for using mixing zones and variances for continuing to discharge to Elevenmile Creek. In the same edition, an announcement of Ester's Lawsuit (See Ester lawsuit) was made[19]. Her attorney was going to seek stiffer penalties. Champion assured us that they would be "in compliance" by 2002. At this point they had had 14 years to solve their problem. An EPA scientist said Champion was in a difficult situation. Perdido Bay folks anxiously awaited the new permit to be issued.

Jeb Bush was now governor and his Secretary of DEP was David Struhs. It turned out David Struhs was the Brother-in-law of Andrew Card, George Bush's Chief of Staff. In 1999, there was a downturn in Champion's profits and it was not a good time to be expending money. We also heard that Champion was running out of a local supply of hardwood, over half of which was used in making pulp. Pine trees - a softwood - were the only trees grown locally. Champion had asked the city of Pensacola if they could build a chips-handling facility along the waterfront in downtown Pensacola to import eucalyptus chips, from Brazil. The city of Pensacola turned them down. Friends of Perdido Bay got citizens on Perdido Bay to write letters to our politicians. We started attending legislative meetings. But we were just too small of a bay with too few people to have much impact. The Alabama politicians were no help. Alabama would like to have had clean water but not at the expense of their industries. Paper companies owned over half the land in Baldwin County, the Alabama county bordering Perdido Bay. We started looking for help from other local and national environmental groups. Escambia Bay had a chapter of Riverkeepers, a group founded by Bobby Kennedy. We tried to get Mike Papantonio, the lawyer who had run ads to keep Champion out of Escambia Bay, to help us on Perdido Bay. But no group or persons seem to be too interested in helping us save Perdido Bay from Champion's continued pollution.

I have always been interested in knowing who the major stockholders of these corporations are. Many times, stockholders have direct impact on management of a company. The old environmental supervisor at Champion, David Arceneaux, had told me that he had gone and made a presentation to the Champion's Board of Directors about going to a wetland treatment and they had turned him down. Some internet research produced the following: in 1989, Berkshire Hathaway bought $300,000 of new, preferred stock for $300 million. According to the New York Times article[20], this stock was purchased to avert a hostile takeover of Champion by Georgia-Pacific. In 1995, Berkshire sold this stock back to Champion for $387 million. The Loews Corporation owned by the Tisch Family of New York, bought a 7.92 % stake in Champion International in 1990. Loews Corporation owned insurance, CBS, a cigarette company, the New York Giants football team, and hotels. In 1994, Lowes sold all but 6.5 % of Champion's stock. Mr. Tisch was a member of the Champion's Board of directors in 1993.

103

After Champion announced that they were going to stay in Perdido Bay, Friends of Perdido Bay knew we were going to have a fight and we were ready! We had over $100,000 in the Perdido Bay Foundation from the settlement of the class action lawsuit in 1995. Friends of Perdido Bay kept watching for issuance of the new permit to Champion.

In spring 1999, drift algae and grass beds were blooming profusely. The grass beds, although lush, were not green. They were red! Some chemical was interfering with the chlorophyll. The snails I had been studying in the early 1990's were just about gone. The water quality in the bay was also bad. We saw lots of foam and scum. As we found out the next year, Champion was having problems with the sludges accumulating in their ponds. The bleaching agent, chlorine dioxide, was hard on pine chips and caused more loss of fiber to the wastewater treatment system. In addition, Champion was trying to use less nitrogen and phosphate in their treatment as Livingston had recommended. They didn't know if this was causing increased sludge production or not. Champion had to dredge out their ponds, which was disruptive to the wastewater treatment system. Champion reported various exceedances of their permit limits for BOD and Total Suspended Solids. Warning letters were going back and forth between DEP and Champion. Champion attributed the problem they were having with their sludges to higher than usual amounts of rainfall. The level of nutrients, nitrogen and phosphate, were also going up. Graphs of nutrients from 1999 showed higher levels of both. I am sure that is why we were seeing lush blooms of algae. The regulators continued to ignore our letters and complaints of red grass beds, blooms of drift algae, and allowed Champion to continue to operate. It was hard to see how Champion was going to come into compliance by 2002 as they kept promising.

CHAPTER 7 ~ Dioxin Days

During the time we were waiting to find out how the environmental agencies would handle Champion's expired 1989 permit, a very important national issue arose – dioxin.
In the mid-1980's, the Swedish Environmental Protection Board project documented biological effects of pulp and paper mill wastes on several species of aquatic life in the Baltic Sea.

"In 1983, the EPA issued a Dioxin Strategy to establish a framework for addressing dioxin contamination. An unexpected finding of the National Dioxin Study was that the dioxin isomer 2,3,7,8 TCDD was present in fish downstream from 57 percent of the pulp and paper sites samples...The data revealed that, within the paper industry, bleached Kraft pulp mills contained the highest levels of dioxin"[1]. Bleach Kraft pulp was the type of pulp Champion started making in1986; that same year EPA made plans to obtain detailed sampling data from one bleached Kraft mill. Then the study was expanded from one to five mills. After reviewing the results from the Five-Mill study, the EPA made the determination to look at all chlorine-bleaching facilities. This was called the 104-Mill Study[2]. (2, 3, 7, 8 TCDD is the most dangerous form of dioxin.) This study provided the EPA with analytical results of dioxins and furans in effluents, sludges and pulps along with details about processes in the mill and how the treatment systems operated. Fish downstream from bleached paper mills were also examined. Champion mill was part of the 104-Mill study.

Although my husband and I were not given the data, we found out from an article in the Oct. 13, 1989 *Perdido Pelican* that a sludge sample from the mill had 14.0 parts per trillion (ppt) of TCDD (the dangerous form of dioxin) and 21 ppt of TCDF, one form of a furan which was dangerous. The mill effluent sample showed TCDD present at 11 ppq (parts per quadrillion) and TCDF present at 38 ppq. It was difficult for us to know what these values meant although it was obvious from the article that dioxin was present in Champion's effluent and that it was associated with the sludges. As I look back, the late

1980's were the years my family used the bay extensively. We were in it constantly during the summer. I don't remember being particularly worried in the late 1980's about dioxin. Was I naive? Yes. As I learned more about how deadly and dangerous dioxin can be, my apprehension about my children's exposure grew into anger.

To try to give Friends of Perdido Bay some perspective on the emerging issue, I wrote an article for the Friends of Perdido Bay June, 1988, Newsletter *Tidings* about dioxin[3]. I summarized what EPA had found in the 1987 National Dioxin Study. Dioxin was very toxic to certain animals, even in very small concentrations. It was soluble in fat and stored in the fatty tissues of the body. The EPA had determined (in these early studies) that dioxin was a probable cancer-causing agent and it had been found in effluents from paper mills making bleached paper. It was also a contaminant of Agent Orange, the defoliant sprayed on Vietnam. According to the FDA, fish with dioxin concentrations over 25 ppt (parts per trillion) dioxin should not be eaten. A whole carp caught in Elevenmile Creek had a dioxin concentration of 25.5 ppt. Besides possibly causing cancer in humans, dioxin can cause skin boils called chloracne and flu-like symptoms.

Just after this article appeared in the *Tidings* newsletter, Vicki Tschinkel, the ex-DER Secretary who had gone to work as a Champion consultant, told me that EPA had caught a mullet in Perdido Bay near Soldier's Creek (middle bay) which had a dioxin level of 28 PPT in the whole fish. It was an ominous sign that dioxin was not going to be lower in the middle part of Perdido Bay, and it probably was not going away anytime soon. The following spring (March 4, 1989), I wrote a "Letter to the Editor" of the Pensacola News Journal. In the opinion letter, I asked the question "Was it safe to swim in Perdido Bay and eat the fish out of Perdido Bay because of the finding of dioxin?" On March 28, 1989, Mr. Kriegel, Deputy Assistant Secretary of DER replied to my opinion letter with a personal letter[4].

Mr. Kriegel's letter said we should not be discussing such an important issue in public and suggested a private meeting. He said DER had addressed the dioxin issue in the 1989 permit and how testing for dioxin in fish should begin in June 1989. I replied to Mr. Kriegel by letter dated April 5, 1989. I told him how my family and another family swam and water-skied in Perdido Bay on October 4, 1986, the day the clams died. I told him how I had gotten an infected finger and acne from swimming in Perdido Bay that fall. No one had warned us that the bay might have been dangerous. I told him that at the time we did not know what had killed the clams, but six months later as I was going through the DER files, I found the letter detailing how Champion had pulled the weirs on their ponds. I reminded him that Perdido Bay was used for recreation and to have just pulled the weirs on ponds without warning was very irresponsible. I can find no evidence that he replied to my letter. But my apprehension about dioxin was growing.

For the next several years, Friends of Perdido Bay were kept very busy reviewing the studies on Perdido Bay. Champion did share with us their dioxin data (at least some of it), showing that between February 5-9, 1990, dioxin was present in most fish caught in Elevenmile Creek. A composite sample of white cat fish from the lower creek had the most dioxin - 8 to 11 ppt (parts per trillion). The fish from Perdido Bay had non-detectable levels or just a trace amount (a composite sample of hardhead cat fish had 0.55 ppt). In the fall of 1990, a health advisory was issued for dioxin in Elevenmile Creek. No signs were posted, however, along the creek to warn the public that fish may be dangerous to eat. The EPA had issued a consumption warning for all fish over 7 ppt and, as noted earlier, fish from Elevenmile Creek already exceeded 7 ppt. The newspaper article (PNJ 9/22/90) announcing the ban said that "...*fish caught in Elevenmile Creek two years ago had dioxin levels ranging from 8.1 to 25.7 parts per trillion, more than four times the EPA limit of 7 parts per trillion....*" This was some dioxin data we had not seen[5] and was the first dioxin warning issued for fish in Florida. An advisory was also issued for the Fenholloway River downstream from Proctor & Gamble Cellulose in Perry, Florida. *"Spokesman for Champion and Proctor & Gamble said the EPA limit is unrealistic because a person would have to eat 6.5 grams of fish every day for 70 years to have any chance of getting ill."*[6]

Champion began running full page ads in the Pensacola News Journal in 1990 trying to make it seem like they had "cleaned up" and dioxin was no longer present. "We Want You To Know" was the headline in the May 6, 1990 ad. *"...Since 1986, we have upgraded our Pensacola mill to enable us to attain a leadership position in the pulp and paper industry with particular emphasis on environment...."* Among four or five improvements, dioxin was the first issue addressed in the ad. *"...Dioxin non-detectable...Scientific tests show that dioxin is non-detectable in the Pensacola mill's wastewater and the waters of Elevenmile Creek and Perdido Bay"*. Just what the detection limit was at that time, I do not know. Furthermore, while dioxin may have been non-detectable in the water, fish in Elevenmile Creek continued to accumulate it. Dioxin was still present, even if it wasn't being detected. At the end of the ad, Champion reminds readers that they had created 250 new jobs to bring the total workforce employed at the mill to 1,200 people. In addition, Champion claimed that they contributed $200 million annually to the area economy. "Champion Spirit - Community Pride". Of course, these ads enraged many in the community of Perdido Bay. At least once a week, letters to the editor would appear denouncing the paper mill and it's disguising the amount of pollution with ads. Supporters of the mill would also contribute letters praising the mill's efforts.

In May 1990, Greenpeace showed up. Greenpeace was on an eight-state tour to tout its "Chlorine Free by 93" campaign. There was a peaceful protest planned for Saturday May 12, 1990. Perdido Bay Environmental Association and its president, Joe Trapp, were the local coordinators for the Greenpeace movement. Joe was an eloquent speaker who reminded me of a peace activist from the 1970's. Greenpeace was urging the paper mills to go to totally chlorine free bleaching, using hydrogen peroxide instead of chlorine of any type. A motorcade from Lillian, Alabama to the Champion paper mill in Cantonment, Florida, was planned on that day. The event started the previous day with a town meeting at the Lillian Community Center. I went to those Greenpeace meetings and was impressed by the organizers and their methods. They used demonstrations to get publicity for their causes. We needed as much publicity as we could get. Seventy people showed up to protest the use of chlorine. The demonstrators chanted "Hey, hey, ho, ho, chlorine bleach has to go" and "Champion stop lying, Perdido Bay is dying". Several demonstrators also wore gas masks as they marched one mile from the Cantonment post office to the paper mill on U.S. 29.

The protest was on Saturday; on Sunday May 13, 1990, Champion bought another full-page ad in the local newspaper, the Pensacola News Journal. *"Ask Champion...When it comes to questions about the environment, sometimes it's hard to know just who to ask and what to believe...."* read the headlines. In the ad, Champion again said they were totally committed to meet federal and state water quality standards in Elevenmile Creek by December 1, 1994, the date the new permit was supposed to be issued, and that dioxin was undetectable in their wastewater. This statement about dioxin being undetectable in the wastewater may be true, but doesn't mean that dioxin was not present. Dioxin is associated with the paper mill sludges and not with the water portion. If the sample was not mixed thoroughly or just the aqueous portion of the sample was tested, even if there, dioxin would not be detectable. Later sampling showed that dioxin certainly was present in the sludges.

At the same time as the dioxin issue was getting a lot of publicity, dolphins (porpoise) were dying at an alarming rate in the Gulf of Mexico. Some people, including Joe Trapp, became

109

very concerned that dioxin might be killing them, so he started a fund to try and find the reason for the deaths. The previous winter of 1989/1990 had been an extremely cold. Autopsies and tissue samples from dead dolphins did not show dioxin, but mercury was elevated. Later, scientists concluded a virus was the culprit in the dolphin deaths, but that still doesn't rule out dioxin contributing to a lowered immune response.

In response to fish with dioxin, dolphin deaths, and other negative press, beside the ads in the Pensacola News Journal, Champion also sent a letter to its workers and 500 community leaders. The letter (which I did not see but gleaned its intent from a letter to the editor written by Jim Trapp, Joe's brother) attempted to paint Greenpeace in a bad light. *"Greenpeace comments will be misleading, exaggerated, and offensive."* *"Deprive Greenpeace the opportunity to confront or antagonize Pensacola Champions as they come and go."*[7]. The attempt by Champion to get their employees to take sides against Greenpeace was not well received by many local environmentalists. What most environmentalists found offensive were these big companies making money at the expense of the environment and then covering it up. Most environmentalists have no fight with the workers, even though worker's jobs depend on the polluting company.

While so many were discussing water quality, what no one was mentioning in the dioxin fight were the chlorinated chemicals Champion was spewing into the air. One Champion employee told me that dioxin and other chlorinated chemicals such as benzene and chloroform were higher in the air than in the water. *"...EPA has long known that pulp and paper mills emit chlorine and chloroform to the air. In the 1980's, the Agency attempted to get chloroform listed as a hazardous air pollutant, due to its carcinogenicity...After the 1990 Amendments to the CAA, the pulp and paper industry was listed as a category of major sources of hazardous air pollutants because of the known presence of chlorine, chloroform, and other metallic HAP's*

110

(Hazardous Air Pollutants) in pulp mill emissions...."[8]. Before converting the mill to chlorine dioxide, Champion estimated that 60 % of the chloroform was in the air and 40 % was in the water. During Earth Day (1988), a Champion employee stopped by our booth and poured out his ailments to me. He said that several workers at the mill had developed strange tumors and that he had a lawyer who was going to file a lawsuit. I watched for that lawsuit to emerge, and though Court is online, I never saw any lawsuits claiming dioxin had caused injury. We were given the data for 1991 air and water emissions from Champion. No dioxin data was mentioned; however, chloroform in the air was very high. 86,000 ppy (pounds per year) were emitted in the air versus 700 pounds in the water. Also, 110,000 pounds of acetone, a known carcinogen, was released in the air and 1900 pounds in the water. The data of toxic emissions releases can be found online on EPA's Toxic Release inventory. Years later, I sought the air dioxin data from the EPA through a Freedom of Information Act request. The EPA could not find any data on dioxin in air or water from Champion. Missing!

Friends of Perdido Bay was still working with Champion and trying to encourage a constructed wetland treatment. However, as I look back, I am not sure that a constructed wetland would have removed the dioxin. It would have captured the dioxin-laden sludges, but then they would have had to have been removed. "Totally chlorine-free bleaching" would have been best. But the American Pulp and Paper Industry decided not to go totally chlorine-free as they had in Europe. The American paper industry stuck with a chlorine compound for bleaching, and the EPA caved in to the paper and chemical groups, not enforcing the closed loop system that had been recommended decades before and was still ignored.

Interestingly, the paper industry began to push for a dioxin standard for permits in the water. Industry likes the certainty of permit limits, especially if they can set them. They can always say, "Well, we meet the limits." If they do not agree with the limits or do not get some sort of relief from the limit, then the industry or industries can go to court and block the issuance of the limit for years. New limits for toxic air pollutants which had been mandated in 1990 were still being challenged by industry groups. The Pulp and Paper industry had initiated their own dioxin studies and were pushing the states to adopt their suggested dioxin limits. The EPA had recommended a standard of 0.014 ppq (parts per quadrillion) in the water. The Florida Pulp and Paper Industry advocated a dioxin limit of 1.2 ppq, nearly 100 times more lenient. And the state of Florida DER was proposing a dioxin limit of 0.58 ppq. If the states did not adopt their own numeric limit for dioxin, then the EPA limit would apply. Florida DER got a directive from Lt. Governor Buddy McKay to use the 0.58 ppq standard. This standard had been recommended by a toxicologist working for Florida HRS using the pulp and paper data. Environmentalists also thought the fish consumption value estimated by the pulp and paper companies was too low. A later study by the University of Florida would confirm people ate more fish than had been considered in Florida's early risk assessment study of dioxin. But the pulp and paper industry would continue their campaign for weaker standards.

The Florida Pulp and Paper Industry met with DER officials several times in 1991 about dioxin limits. At that time the Secretary was Carol Browner who would later become Head of EPA under Bill Clinton. She was being pressured by the Pulp and Paper Industry to approve the 0.58 ppq limit for water. She also indicated that she wanted to wait for the results of the EPA reassessment before setting a rule. Georgia had adopted the number recommended by the pulp and paper industry, and the EPA approved this limit (1.2 ppq). On January 9, 1992, Browner sent a letter to Governor Lawton Chiles which said,

"...Lt. Governor MacKay and I met with representatives from all the Florida pulp and paper companies on December 18, 1991. The imminent threat of EPA promulgation of water

112

quality standards for toxic pollutants (including dioxin) has
resulted in the following actions: ... The Department agreed to
bring its original proposal for dioxin back to the ERC
(Environmental Regulatory Commission) ...0.58 ppq. We have
no evidence upon which to change our recommendation at this
time...." According to an article in the April 1992 *Pro Earth*
Times, however, Secretary Browner ignored the new evidence on
dioxin which the EPA had gathered

Perdido Bay Environmental Association members and
Joe Trapp also wanted to meet with Secretary Browner about
dioxin. She refused to meet with them.

In Florida, all new rules or changes to environmental
rules must be approved by an Environmental Regulatory
Commission (ERC) before they can become law. It so happened
at this time (early 1990's), that the Environmental Regulatory
Commission in Florida had people who were concerned about
the environment (this does not seem to be so today). In 1991,
the Florida ERC had held hearings on a proposed dioxin limit
and decided to wait until a new EPA reassessment of dioxin
came out. But the Pulp and Paper industry kept pressuring the
governor and Secretary Browner. At the January 17, 1992,
hearing of the ERC, the DER and the Pulp and Paper Industry
were hoping that a dioxin limit of 0.58 ppq would be passed.
The pressure was on the state to pass a limit. If Florida did not
adopt its own standard, then the EPA limit of 0.014 would be
used in permits. Leading the fight on the side of the
environment was the Legal Environmental Assistance
Foundation (LEAF) and their attorney David Ludder. Audubon
Society, Sierra Club members and the Florida Environmental
Alliance were also proposing caution at that first meeting. On
the other side were the Pulp and Paper Industry, all their friends
from other business groups, the Chambers of Commerce, and a
host of others. The hearing room was packed and very warm.
The ERC declined to adopt the standard of 0.58 ppt which DER
was trying to set.

The issue of the dioxin limit came before the ERC again on March 27, 1992. It was a marathon session which lasted from 9:00 AM to 11:00 PM. The evidence from different researchers was discussed. DER's recommendation of 0.58 ppq, which was 40 times less protective than the EPA limit of 0.014 ppq, was based on a recommendation from Florida HRS toxicologists Joseph Sekerke, Ph.D. Dr. Sekerke had based his recommendation on the comments of Dr. Vernon Houk who had worked for the Centers for Disease Control in Atlanta. In late 1989, Dr. Houk had announced that current research suggested that dioxin was only a "weak carcinogen". Dr. Houk had made his determination based on studies from the pulp and paper industry. Dr. Houk's determination was denounced by several prominent scientists[9]. Testimony given in a civil court trial in Mississippi by Admiral Elmo Zumwalt demonstrated how the American Paper Institute had influenced the Bush White House to make EPA re-examine the dangers of dioxin. Admiral Zumwalt had lost a son to cancer from the spraying of Agent Orange in Vietnam. In the end, the ERC committee voted 3 to 2 not to adopt DER's standard. The EPA limit would be imposed. Chairman Dick Batchelor told the citizens at the meeting, *"...our communities have hosted these paper companies for decades and I think they have an ethical obligation to be good neighbors and use the best technology available to them"*.[10]

Not only was the pulp and paper industry working on getting a more lenient dioxin standard as part of the state rules, but also trying to increase the standards for other known pulp and paper toxic water releases. At the time (1992), Florida's surface water standard for phenol was 300 micrograms per liter. Pulp and paper was trying to get the standard changed to 4,600,000 micrograms per liter in surface waters. As pointed out by district regulators, this level of phenol would cause objectionable odors and would taint the flesh of fish and shellfish. In 2015, the phenol limit in Florida's Water Quality

Standards is <400 micrograms per liter with a note that this is protective of human health and not aquatic life.

Champion was also sharing with me some of the literature which the pulp and paper industry was putting out. An article in the Pulp and Paper Journal, April 1991, entitled "Chlorinated Organics in Perspective: from Drinking Water to Mill Effluent" points out that chlorinated organics are produced naturally. Oceans produce vast tonnages of methyl chlorides and related compounds every year. This is natural. Wood-rotting fungus produces methyl chloride and peat bogs emit organochlorine compounds. The author, Bruce Fleming, describes how nature breaks down these chlorinated compounds, and by chlorinating our drinking water, how we consume lots of chlorinated organics. In the Conclusion of his 1991 journal article, Fleming says that the paper was an *"...attempt to challenge those who state that all chlorinated materials are man-made poisons. Chlorinated organics are everywhere in the environment. They are produced and destroyed naturally. Not all are poisonous, and, oddly enough, some chlorinated organics can even be found in the bloodstream...."* (p 117). Industry people always seem to take the other side; create doubt. It was sometimes difficult to find out what the truth really was.

The ban on eating fish in Elevenmile Creek did not last long which I am sure was due to the pulp and paper industry's prodding. On September 1, 1992, Florida lifted its ban on eating fish out of Elevenmile Creek, based on a composite of white catfish sampled in 1991. The level of dioxin had not been mentioned in the Pensacola News Journal Article. The limit of detection was 1 ppt. Linda Young, editor of the environmental newspaper, *Pro Earth Times*, criticized lifting of the ban. She indicated dioxin is toxic and dangerous at any level. In her newspaper, *Pro Earth Times*, she continued to follow the dioxin debate. In an October, 1992 issue, Linda Young writes

"...Dioxin, the infamous chlorine-based poison, poses a threat to public health at least twice as great as formerly

115

*thought, a draft report released last week by scientists at the U.S. Environmental Protection Agency (EPA) suggests....*Further in the article, *"...cancer may not be the most sensitive effect. Reproduction, development, and the immune system appear to be even more vulnerable to small dioxin doses...."* She went on to mention that the U.S. - Canadian International Joint Commission on the Great Lakes recommended phasing out chlorine entirely.

Despite the pulp and paper industry's pressure, the EPA came out with another study of dangers of dioxin. In 1994, EPA came out with its last dioxin analysis. *"...Exposure to even minute traces of dioxin, much of it through the food chain, poses wider health risks than had been suspected and may harm the human immune system and fetal development.... Cancer may not be the most troubling health concern posed by dioxin...."*[11]. The Chemical Manufacturers Association characterized the EPA study as flawed. *"EPA has relied on very inconclusive data from animal studies."* [11]. Whoever was right, dioxin was a very nasty chemical and it looked like my family had been exposed to it for years. I could only pray that my children would be O.K.

The dispute over dioxin led to a class-action lawsuit being filed by citizens of Perdido Bay, on November 9, 1992, in circuit court in Baldwin County, Alabama, (the Alabama County adjoining Perdido Bay). My husband and I were becoming frustrated with the slow progress Champion was making. More serious were my doubts about Champion's study of Perdido Bay. Champion's hired researcher, Dr. Livingston, just seemed to be missing the mark despite our "helpful" criticisms. And the environmental agencies appeared to be letting it happen. Friends of Perdido Bay's three-year agreement to not pursue legal action against Champion had finally expired. We had been talking to several attorneys for several weeks before the lawsuit was filed. I thought the date of the filing was interesting. This date was just after Clinton's election with Gore having been elected President/Vice-President. One of the local attorneys on the suit was Mary Murchison. She lived on the bay and had been a

Board Member of Friends of Perdido Bay. The lead attorneys who took the case on a contingency basis were a law firm from Birmingham, Alabama, Burr and Forman. Richard Freeze and Pete Grammas were Burr and Forman's lead attorneys. My husband, Eugenia Elebash and I were the representatives for the plaintiffs (citizens). Mrs. Elebash was Mary's aunt and had been involved with an earlier legal action against the paper mill in the 1970's. Skadden, Arps, Slate, Meagher & Flom, from New York, and Baker, Worthington, Crossley, Stansberry & Woolf from Knoxville, Tennessee, were the attorneys for Champion. The suit charged that Champion and the American Paper Institute knew of the hazardous nature of dioxin in mid-1980. Champion had failed to warn the public about the dangers of dioxin and concealed them. The suit was asking for damages in excess of $500 million. The suit also sought a temporary and permanent injunction (cessation) for dioxin releases by the mill. Besides Champion, the other plaintiff in the suit was the mill manager, Doug Owenby.

At the time, suing paper mills for dioxin had become popular. One of the attorneys in our lawsuit, Richard Freese, had filed a lawsuit against Kimberly Clark for a mill in Alabama. Citizens on Perdido Bay had also been in contact with a group of people who had filed a lawsuit against Champion Paper Company in Canton, North Carolina. In 1991, 2,600 residents along Pigeon River and Douglas Lake had filed a class-action lawsuit against Champion in U.S. District Court in Greenville, Tennessee. It was heartbreaking to hear of all the cancer and cancer deaths of the people who lived and fished in the Pigeon River Watershed. The Pigeon River was a beautiful clear mountain stream in North Carolina and Tennessee until it was grossly polluted in the early 1900's by Champion, the major employer in Canton. The hearing on the Pigeon River lawsuit resulted in a hung jury. According to a Google search, the Canton, N.C. mill is called Blue Ridge Paper Products today. It is owned by employees and Packaging Holding Inc., a New Zealand Company.

Like all lawsuits, a lot of paper is generated. The first thing that Champion did was move the lawsuit to federal court in Mobile, Alabama. Our attorneys made motions to move the suit back to Circuit Court in Baldwin County where they thought we had a better chance. The federal judge agreed. Then Champion made a motion to dismiss their mill manager as a defendant. The Baldwin County Court Judge Partin, agreed. The mill manager could not be held personally responsible. Our attorneys filed a second complaint on August 25, 1993. This complaint was filed to remove Mrs. Elebash and replace her with another Alabama resident, Bob Donnenwirth. The first big hearing in the lawsuit was scheduled for May 31, 1994, in Baldwin County Circuit Court in Bay Minette, Alabama. The Judge was hearing arguments on whether to certify Plaintiffs as a "class". To have a "class" everyone had to have common complaints and be injured in the same manner. If the class was not certified, then everyone would have to file a separate lawsuit. From the lawyer's perspective, it is a lot more work for a lot less money.

On the hearing date, May 31, 1994, more than seventy-five Perdido Bay supporters showed up for the hearing. The hearing had to be moved to a larger court room to accommodate all the people. We had a caravan of supporters drive from Lillian, Alabama to the site of the hearing. The distance is about 51 miles and takes about an hour. Many other people attended as well. The hearing room was packed. The hearing extended over into the next day, June 1. There were many witnesses, and testimony. As I wrote in the July, 1994, Newsletter, *Tidings,* "Perhaps 50 years of horrible pollution will finally end." Judge Partin did rule in our favor. The property owners on Perdido Bay were certified as a "class" and the boundaries defined as 1,741 parcels of property in Alabama and 948 parcels in Florida. Champion's liability was limited to property damages, not bodily harm. We were asking for $150 million in damages. Injunctive relief somehow had disappeared from the lawsuit and the lawsuit now seemed to now be focused more on nuisance issues like

118

foam etc., rather than dioxin. The "discovery" part of the lawsuit continued. Our attorneys asked people to send pictures of foam and scum. Depositions were taken of Champion employees. One of the pieces of information which we learned from the depositions was that Champion was working on a technology to recycle the bleach plant effluent and not release it to the wastewater treatment system. They called this technology "Bleach Filtrate Recycle" (BFR). According to several people, Champion was trying to get the other paper companies to buy this patented technology from them. Our attorneys told us that they were not going to install this technology at the Cantonment mill, but maybe at the Canton, N.C. mill. I never heard any more about this technology.

Our attorneys obtained privileged documents from Champion as part of discovery. Although the class representatives never saw any of these documents, one of the reporters following the class action requested documents which were not deemed confidential by Champion. He reported on the some of these non-confidential documents in an article for the *Foley Onlooker*, a local newspaper on March 1, 1995. A "Communications Plan for Pensacola Mill Consent Order" presented to an executive steering committee on December 12, 1991, stated its purpose was "...*to develop a course of action that will create an environment to enable the Pensacola mill to successfully secure an operating permit after 1994, and build a base of public support that neutralizes the mill's detractors....*'" This information was not what Champion was telling us. Champion had told us they were going to do the right thing and "clean up". This was Champion's other side. Another one of the "Communications Plans" strategies was to find "...*an advocate (recognized scientists) and/or organized group in the community who will publicly challenge and discredit critics, enabling the company to take the high road....*" This information was chilling. Fortunately, no one appeared to take the side of Champion although a few engineers did defend them from time to time.

After the class was certified, Champion made a motion to dismiss our Class Action lawsuit claiming that there was no evidence to support our claim that they were damaging our property. Our attorneys countered with pictures of foam and scum from many class members. DER biologists gave affidavits that Champion was harming Perdido Bay and our waterfront property. My husband and I and Bob Donnenwirth testified that we had lost our use and enjoyment of our waterfront because of Champion's pollution. Mr. Woolf, the attorney for Champion, said that we could not prove damages because we did not have "before Champion" and "after Champion" values for our property. Mr. Bethune, who was an Alabama Realtor and a property Appraiser, looked at property values on Perdido Bay versus values on Pensacola Bay and found the value of lots on Perdido Bay were $200 per linear foot less than Pensacola Bay. The hearing on Champion's Motion to Dismiss was held July 18, 1995. We waited for Judge Partin's ruling. After nearly six months of waiting for the Judge to make a ruling, our attorneys became nervous. They thought the judge was signaling that he wanted the parties to begin "settling" the lawsuit. So, in April 1996, we announced that our attorneys had begun settlement discussions with Champion. On May 3, 1996, Judge Partin approved a settlement between class members on Perdido Bay and Champion Paper Co. Champion gave $5,000,000 to the class members in exchange for immunity from past damages. Champion could still be sued for future damages, but you had to find lawyers willing to take the case. After payment of fees and expenses to the five legal firms which handled the lawsuit, about $3,000,000 was left over. That meant each property owner was getting $1,500. Property owners who lived closer to the mill got a little more, but the actual compensation was pitiful.

Personally, I was very disappointed in the results of the lawsuit, and not just because of the money. Our goal was not to get money as the Champion attorney, Lewis Wolff, stated, but to try and get the mill to clean up. The $5 million seemed like a drop in the bucket and Champion just seemed to go right on polluting, now with no redress by Perdido Bay property owners. Maybe the lawsuit was a money-maker for the attorneys, but not for the people on Perdido Bay. It seemed like once attorneys took a case on a contingency basis, they became the bosses. The three class representatives had very little say. Perhaps Champion installed some pollution control equipment, but it was not enough to make any difference in what we saw in the bay. As far as dioxin was concerned, Champion no longer had to test for it in their effluent or in fish because they said they were "non-detect". We had to rely on the EPA to determine if Perdido Bay was free from dioxin. I was not the only one disappointed. Ester Johnson and her husband, Welton, who had been members of Perdido Bay Environmental Association, opposed the settlement along with about 30 other property owners. I didn't blame them. Ester had worked for years to clean up Perdido Bay. One opponent to the settlement, Patrick Langan, said the settlement *"...is a slap in the face to all those who look out on the bay and see slime and brown sludge...."* I figured some of those people will probably never trust us again.

After the settlement of the 1996 class action lawsuit, the three main Class Representatives, Bob Donnenwirth, Jim Lane and I, decided to ask all the members of the class to donate their proceeds from the settlement back to a Foundation we were going to establish. Many people donated proceeds from their settlement checks back to the Foundation. We collected $120,000 from the donations and set up a not-for-profit foundation, called Perdido Bay Foundation. The Perdido Bay Foundation had five trustees: the three original class suit members, along with Mary Murchison and Thornton Garth. We usually met every other month. The Perdido Bay Foundation did some good things such as funding testing of the bay and eventually paying for attorneys to challenge a permit in an administrative hearing. After 2009, the Perdido Bay Foundation had spent all the money and ceased to exist, but Friends of Perdido Bay lives on.

While the class action lawsuit was progressing, we continued to push for totally chlorine-free bleaching, i.e., using hydrogen peroxide instead of a chlorine product for bleaching. Several Perdido Bay residents, including myself, had unsuccessfully challenged an air permit in 1993 allowing Champion to continue using chlorine-based products. Greenpeace also continued pushing for Totally Chlorine Free (TCF). We could never seem to get this issue to be part of the lawsuit even though the evidence was mounting against dioxin in other parts of the world. In Europe, researchers found evidence of a reduced sperm count in men which they hypothesized was linked to prevalence of chlorinated compounds in the environment. In February, 1994, the EPA considered amending the clean water act to completely phase out chlorine. The loud outcry from politicians supported by the chemical industry helped kill a bill in Congress which called for a complete phase out of chlorine in paper making. The paper industry and the chemical industry, like the tobacco industry, denied producing dioxin in their effluent. The paper industry said that they were "eliminating elemental chlorine" and going to ECF (Elemental Chlorine Free). "Eliminating elemental chlorine" was not eliminating chlorine, only changing the form of chlorine.

The Paper Industry and Chemical Industry lobbying must have worked. In December 1993, the EPA issued its new, proposed technical guidelines for the Pulp and Paper industry. These were going to be the new standards which EPA was going to enforce. Unlike past EPA guidelines, rules for air and water were combined into one rule. When I read these guidelines, my heart sank. The allowable limits for conventional pollutants like BOD and Total Suspended Solids were no better than before. Maybe they were worse. EPA was taking chemicals out of the air and putting them in the water. The new standards were horrible. Carol Browner was head of EPA and Bill Clinton and Al Gore were President and Vice President. Why hadn't they pushed for more stringent standards? Behind-the-scene deals? I

122

could only speculate on why the Clinton Administration had not gone with hydrogen peroxide or ozone instead of chlorine. It may have had something to do with the chlor-alkalai industry. To break down wood to get the fibers, Kraft paper makers use sodium. Sodium is manufactured from the splitting of the simple molecule, sodium chloride (NaCl), salt. Chemical companies which manufacture sodium also have chloride to sell. A Champion employee told me the reason the paper mill in Cantonment, FL, had always done a little bleaching was because they got a break on the price of sodium by buying chlorine. So, if the paper makers had eliminated chlorine, there would have been an imbalance in sodium/chlorine demand.

Prior to December, 1993, the last time the standards for paper mills had been revised was in 1986. EPA established guidelines for both air and water pollutants in the different methods of producing paper pulp from trees. EPA did a survey of all the paper mills in the U.S., both by survey and by visitation. From the answers received, EPA compiled a list of various technologies for the different ways of making pulp from wood. The technologies fell into various categories - Best Practical Control Technology (BPT), Best Conventional Pollution Control Technology (BCT), and Best Available Technology Economically Achievable (BAT) for what was termed "conventional pollutants". Conventional pollutants included "Biological Oxygen Demand (BOD), Total Suspended Solids (TSS), fecal coliform, pH, and any additional pollutants defined by the Administrator as conventional...BPT guidelines are based on the average of the best existing performances by plants in a category or subcategory...." (Federal Register/Vol 58, No. 241/ Friday December 17, 1993/ Proposed Rules). New mills had to follow more stringent standards. Existing mills, like the Champion mill, seemed to have the same water standards as before. The guidelines are developed by looking at the best existing technology and do not consider the water into which the effluent is discharged. For a little bay like Perdido Bay, it was disaster. Using this method for developing guidelines is not

123

going to encourage any innovation in treating wastes, since no industry is going to spend extra money developing a "new" technology which would force all the rest of the industry to "clean up".

The Clean Air Act also had to be considered. *"Title III of the 1990 Clean Air Act Amendments was enacted to reduce the amount of nationwide air toxic emissions...."* There were 189 chemicals deemed by Congress to be hazardous air pollutants (HAPs). These toxic air pollutants had to be regulated by national emission standards for hazardous air pollutants (NESHAP). All paper mills were considered "stationary sources". The Administrator (of EPA) was to develop emission standards for each category of HAP. The limits were based on maximum achievable control technology (MACT). These were the limits which the Florida Pulp and Paper Industry Group were challenging in Florida. Guidelines for paper mill sludges were also going to be adopted after the mills had converted to the newer form of bleaching using chlorine dioxide. These limits were going to be proposed under the Toxic Substances Control Act. The December, 1993, Federal Register lists a dioxin sludge limit of 10 ppt as the maximum allowable, but also deems it toxic. As the Federal Register conceded, there was no silver bullet.

In 1990, Congress passed the Pollution Prevention Act. "...Congress declared pollution prevention the national policy of the United States...Pollution should be prevented or reduced whenever feasible..." [13] All guidelines for both air and water had to be consistent with each different act which Congress had passed. The EPA used an integrated approach for developing guidelines for both air and water. According to the Federal Register, December 1993, *"The Administrator developed these proposed regulations jointly to provide greater protection of human health and the environment, reduce the cost of complying with both sets of rules, promote and facilitate coordinated compliance planning by industry, promote and facilitate pollution prevention, and emphasize the multimedia nature of pollution control...*" (pp 66093). Using this integrated approach, the EPA found that "*...there is no single control technology currently available that reduces pollutant discharges to the water and air to the levels required by the respective statutes....*" (pp 66094). What this meant for us on Perdido Bay was the chemicals scrubbed from the air using sodium hydroxide air scrubbers were going to be dumped into the wastewater treatment system. According to the EPA analysis,

"*...air controls did not significantly affect effluent loading of toxic and priority pollutants. Combustion destroys most compounds emitted from process vents, thus reducing the amount of pollutants that could enter surface waters due to deposition. Chlorinated HAPs remaining after the process changes react with the caustic in the scrubber, neutralizing the caustic effluent. Non-chlorinated HAPs that absorb into the caustic are biodegradable, and are not estimated to significantly increase the pollutant load to the wastewater treatment system....*" (pp 99094).   In short, the EPA technical guidelines took the pollutants out of the air and put them in the water. This was a blow for clean water in Perdido Bay, but the air around the mill would be better.

After accepting comments on the new "proposed" guidelines for air and water pollution in the pulp and paper industry, these rules, known as "cluster rules" went into effect April 15, 1998. It had taken nearly five years to finally get the rules adopted. The new guidelines contained incentives programs to encourage the paper industry to develop and install "closed loop" technology. The EPA guidelines estimated that "closed loop" technology could be achieved by 2015. "Closed loop" technology was also advocated by the regulators reviewing the data from paper mill treatment in 1970. It is possible to achieve, but resistance to developing this technology is obvious, especially since for over 30 years the "closed loop" has been discussed with no action ever taken.

The "cluster rules" did require the paper mills to look for chlorinated organic material at different phases of the pulp-making cycle. I heard a lot of grumbling from the paper personnel about the intrusion of government into the internal operating of the paper-making process. We did not know at the time if the new bleaching technology, chlorine dioxide, which Champion installed in 1996, reduced the formation of dioxin or not. We hoped it had. Several reports came out in the early 1990's which showed Perdido Bay's sediments were very contaminated with heavy metals and organic contaminates. Perdido Bay ranked number one in contaminated sediments in EPA's Region 4. These results came from the EPA's EMAP program. Remember, dioxin is associated with paper mill sludges more than with the water. Mike Brim's 1993 "Toxics Characterization Report for Perdido Bay, Alabama and Florida" report seemed to indicate that dioxin had been a problem in Perdido Bay at least since 1989, but supposedly was no longer. We found out later the danger was not over.

To understand the different interpretations of dioxin data you had to look at the different forms (isomers) of dioxin present. Dioxin is a very hazardous and toxic substance and even in very low quantities can cause cancer. It comes in various forms, called isomers - some more hazardous than others. The most hazardous form is 2,3,7,8 TCDD. The amounts of all the different forms of dioxin are found and then converted to a number which is the equivalent of 2,3,7,8 TCDD using toxic equivalents for each form of dioxin. The state of Florida had set a level of 7 ppt as the target clean-up value for sediments in domestic situations.

Most of the data showed very low or non-detectable levels of the most dangerous form of dioxin 2,3,7,8 TCDD in the sediments. However other forms of dioxin and furans were more prevalent. In the report, "Survey of Dioxin and Furan Compounds in Sediments of Florida Panhandle Bay Systems" published in 2002, Fish and Wildlife researchers found Perdido

126

Bay sediments contained the highest levels of dioxin in the Florida Panhandle. Dioxin had not gone away. Most of the samples came from Elevenmile Creek where the paper mill discharged. The one sampling spot in Perdido Bay was located on the Florida side in the lower bay. This is an area known for settling of sludges from the paper mill. The sample taken July 21, 1995, (before Champion installed chlorine dioxide) showed the OCDD form of dioxin to be high. If the toxicity equivalents are applied, this sample showed toxicity equivalent to 2,3,7,8 TCDD of 14.74 ppt. The OCDD form of dioxin is known to come from combustion. Burning of coal in the power boilers of the paper mill and other pollutants stripped from the air were the most likely source.

The big Champion/Livingston study on Perdido Bay during the years 1988 to 2007 did not measure dioxin directly. They claimed it was too expensive. The study did find chlorinated chemicals in shrimp. Very little was made of this finding and no health advisories were posted by the EPA.

Friends of Perdido Bay and the Perdido Bay Foundation also did dioxin and PCB analyses of sediments in Perdido Bay. The tests for dioxin must be sensitive enough to detect the very low concentrations. Sampling is done with special equipment and with care so as not to contaminate the samples. There were few laboratories which had the equipment necessary to run these tests and the tests were expensive - over $1,000 per sample. We couldn't afford many. We also wanted to make sure that there was no question about the validity of these tests. We chose our lab carefully. In 1999, I sampled the sediments in three areas of the bay - upper bay, mid-bay and lower bay. All samples had toxic equivalent dioxin values less than 1 ppt. At all sites, the most dangerous isomer of dioxin, 2,3,7,8 TCDD was non-detectable.

In February 2003, I sampled the sediments from the upper bay. Champion had sold the mill to International Paper in

2000. Bleached paper using chlorine dioxide was still being produced. The most toxic form of dioxin 2,3,7,8 TCDD was present (3.45 ppt). Other forms of dioxins and furans were present as well. Notably high was the OCDD form which was present at 4,660 ppt. Using the toxicity equivalent from all the different forms of dioxin produced a value of 33 ppt. The laboratory also analyzed for PCBs which also contribute slightly to dioxin equivalents. Several PCBs were notably high PCB-118, PCB-105, and PCB-156. We didn't know exactly what to make of these profiles.

We tested the sediments of Perdido Bay again, after Hurricane Ivan washed muck from the bay onto our properties. We took six samples. The toxic dioxin equivalents ranged from 9 to 31 ppt. Some samples had detectable levels of 2,3,7,8, TCDD, but most of the dioxin was in the form of OCDD. The same PCBs were high as in the sample taken in February 2003. People were shoveling this dioxin-laden muck out of their driveways, letting it dry and sweeping it out of their houses. This could not have been good for them.

Dioxin levels were also measured on crab meat collected July 3, 2005, and on a composite sample from ten clams collected August 20, 2007. The crab meat had barely detectable levels of dioxin with the OCDD form being the highest. But the PCBs were measurable, especially the same three which had been detected previously in the sediments. PCB-118 measured 97 ppt. This resulted in a dioxin equivalent of 0.058. The lipid adjusted value was 30.5 ppt. The clam tissue had slightly higher dioxin values than the crab. Again, OCDD dioxin was the highest. The same three PCBs were high with PCB-118 measuring 118 ppt. The dioxin + PCB equivalent for clam was 0.561 ppt. This data indicated that the dioxin and PCBs present in the sediments were contaminating the life on the bottom.

The last dioxin sampling was done November 9, 2014 on sediments from Tee Lake, a tidal lake in the northern part of

Perdido Bay through which International Paper's effluent now flows. There was a trace amount of 2,3,7,8 TCDD, the most dangerous isomer. Again, as with the previous samples, OCDD was the highest dioxin isomer with a concentration of 1470 ppt. Other forms of dioxin were also present. The total dioxin equivalent was 7.1 ppt. The same three PCBs were also high with PCB-118 measuring 105 ppt.

The similarity of PCB profiles throughout the 10 years of sediment testing was interesting. I asked several experts but no one could help. Then I ran across a paper published in 2012 in the *Journal Environmental Forensics* which gave the PCB values for Escambia Bay, a neighboring bay. Even though the values in Escambia Bay were ten times higher than the values in Perdido Bay the same three PCBs had the same profile. The researchers attribute the PCBs to an old spill; however, I concluded that the PCBs were coming from the material washed off the smoke stacks of industries in Escambia Bay. The PCBs which were showing up in both Perdido and Escambia Bays probably come from coal which is the main fuel used for power at industries in both bays.

The dioxins which were still present in the sediments of Perdido Bay in 2014 are probably coming from the burning of chlorinated compounds. These compounds are then disposed of in the wastewater treatment system as mandated by the EPA's "Cluster Rules". While EPA's rules may have reduced the chlorinated compounds in the air, they are being disposed of in the water. I believe this poses a risk to human health in Perdido Bay. We have sent our data to environmental agencies but no one seems interested. Dioxin is no longer part of the national dialogue. I am not even sure that by converting to chlorine dioxide instead of using chlorine, dioxin was lessened in the sediments of Perdido Bay. How different would it have been if the paper industry had eliminated chlorine, used some other form of bleaching, or stopped using coal mixed with wood products for fuel? I wonder how different everything would be if the paper mill simply had adapted the closed loop system recommended some thirty years ago? Meanwhile, as recently as 2015 in the state of Texas, at least, where dioxin lawsuits raged for several years, a Bill was signed into law making it tougher to sue big polluters like the paper mills.

CLOSE-UP OF FOAM GENERATED BY PAPER MILL

CHAPTER 8 ~ Management Plans

As the dioxin crisis unfolded, the EPA addressed their problem by changing to a different bleaching chemical and establishing new guidelines for the paper industry. The EPA and state environmental agencies were also changing the focus of their environmental programs from compliance monitoring of "point" sources or known dischargers to ecosystem problems - looking at the problems in the entire watershed. The new environmental focus was less confrontational toward big business and fit in with the world economy. Perdido Bay was a good model for the ecosystem approach because it was small with a lot of information. The water quality in the tributaries and bay was monitored quarterly at fixed stations. Biological sampling was also done at these stations. Generally, Alabama looked at the lower bay and Florida biologists looked at the upper bay. After 1986, biological sampling of the bay stopped in Florida and Alabama curtailed its sampling. Except for Livingston's studies which ended in 2007 and an occasional special sampling, no entity is monitoring the biological health of the bay.

Florida's earliest attempts to manage water bodies using an integrated approach came in 1987 when the Florida legislature passed the Surface Water Improvement Act.[1] The SWIM program was delegated to different water management districts around the state and the funding to run the water management districts came from local property taxes. While water management districts did not issue permits for "point" sources such as industries, the Water Management District's job was to restore and protect surface waters in their districts by land acquisition, by water monitoring, by permitting storm water and wetlands, and by use of Capital Improvement Funds for erosion projects. The water management districts regulate ground water through issuing consumptive use permits for wells. The Water Management Districts write management plans (called SWIM plans) for the water bodies in their districts. These plans are usually written by Water Management District staff. Because Perdido Bay is an interstate body of water, the local water management district did not write plans for the Perdido Bay until 2012. The "draft" 2012 SWIM (Surface Water Improvement and Management) plan for Perdido Bay does mention that the paper mill remained the largest discharger into Perdido Bay and inferred that the plan to relocate its discharge was going to bring it into compliance with state rules. Unfortunately, as of the date of this book, 2016, the paper mill plan did not work and it is not meeting state rules and is operating on an expired permit.

Citizen-based management plans were supposed to begin with EPA's 1988 Cooperative Management grant for Perdido Bay which was to culminate in a management plan. The whole ecosystem and its problems had to be addressed, not just individual dischargers. In June 1989, the states of Florida and Alabama announced that money had been appropriated in the state budgets for a "new" joint Florida and Alabama Water Resource Council. This Council was different from the committees the 1988 Cooperative Management Grant had established. The article announcing this council prominently displayed the names of the two Republican governors of the states, Guy Hunt of Alabama and Bob Martinez of Florida, who supported this initiative. My husband, Jim, was selected as one of the members of the Council. In the letter to Jim dated August 31, 1990, Secretary of DER, Dale Twachtmann, wrote: "The Florida and Alabama state legislatures have jointly established a committee to submit recommendations concerning the protection and restoration of the Perdido River and Bay System. This committee will review and advise both states on necessary environmental programs and activities for the river." The first meeting was held Nov 8, 1990. There were 10 members on the council, composed of two citizens from Perdido Bay, my husband, Jim, and Thornton Garth; academic members; several local people from both states; and co-chairs John Carlton, District Director of Alabama Department of Environmental Management's Mobile Office and Bob Kriegel, District Director of Florida Department of Environmental Regulation in Pensacola. The co-chairmen had gotten together and outlined a long-term agenda. The Water Resource Council (officially named the Florida/Alabama Water Resources Coordinating Council or FAWRCC) meetings were held monthly or bi monthly with the locations alternating between Florida and Alabama. For each meeting, there was an agenda of speakers on various ecosystem topics, such as regulatory structure in each state, ongoing studies, forestry, land-use issues, septic tank permitting, storm water permitting, wetland permitting. Occasionally, special topics were assigned to the council members to research. After the presentations, the floor was open to the public. Jo Ann Allen and Ester Johnson from Perdido Bay Environmental Association usually made remarks about conditions in the bay. At the November 29, 1990, meeting, topics for management strategies were handed out. At the May 15, 1991, meeting, an informal priority list of most important issues was voted on. Champion's impact on Perdido Bay was number one, non-point impacts (those sources not requiring a permit) came in second. There were always problems, however, defining the role of the Council. It was only an advisory group and held no regulatory authority. At the December 12, 1990, meeting, Jo Ann Allen handed out a written comment.

"In my hand I hold a January 26, 1967, letter sent to me by the Alabama Water Improvement Commission, a predecessor of ADEM, which states that my written statement filed with the Commission concerning the degraded water quality of streams and waters of the Perdido River Basin, would be included in the record of the public hearing on water quality standards for the Perdido River Basin which had been held in Bay Minette on January 18th (1967). Council, this was 23 years ago!"

Jo Ann went on to point out that the same problems which existed now, existed 20 years ago. Public monies had been wasted on studies, management meetings and reports and nothing positive had been accomplished. She didn't see much hope in the current management initiative. In the letter, her frustration with the situation was obvious. I also began to use the Council as an outlet to vent my displeasure with the Livingston Report. My letter to Bob Kriegel about the deficiencies in the Livingston Report dated February 15, 1991, was passed out to the group.

The FAWRCC did not issue a formal, written management plan for Perdido Bay until June 1995. The group had stopped meeting, but was called on to review draft proposals written by a staff person at DER and pass a final management plan. The findings of the June 1995 management plan are as follows: "1. The Perdido Basin and Bay have been negatively impacted by human activities. 2. The most significant problem is the increase in available nutrients, particularly nitrogen. 3. Non-point and Champion Paper discharges are the greatest contributors to the increase in nutrients. 4. Toxic pollution is not presently a severe problem in the basin.
5. There are other less severe environmental problems throughout the basin. 6. There is the potential for increased environmental degradation resulting from various land use practices."

I thought that these findings were very interesting because it showed how government agencies would downplay the impact of Champion and change the focus from organic matter which paper mills put into the environment, to nutrients which paper mills must add to help degrade their wastes. Originally the council voted Champion to be the number one problem in Perdido Bay but by 1995 the Champion problem had slipped to third behind non-point source problems.

134

In addition to writing management plans which ignored the damage by local industries, Florida had formally decided to lessen "compliance monitoring" and go to "common sense regulation" by combining two state departments into one. In 1993, the Florida Legislature merged the Department of Environmental Regulation (DER) with the Department of Natural Resources (DNR) to create the Department of Environmental Protection (DEP). The DNR had a history of being aligned with the large landowners in Florida and with "corruption and favoritism"[2]. The new agency was charged with "...developing a strategy to protect the functions of entire ecological systems.... A fundamental goal of ecosystem management initiative is to promote good stewardship". The Ecosystem approach stressed "common sense regulation." "It recognizes that traditional regulatory programs perform a vital function and must not be abandoned, but at the same time there is a need for workable alternatives that provide incentives for the regulated public to voluntarily go beyond compliance to stewardship." [3] Who could argue with these lofty goals, especially since the U.S. was going into a world economy where regulatory programs of other countries were missing? Despite the lofty goals, the ecosystem management approach was never well-funded. The Secretary of DER, Carole Browner, had gone to Washington to work in Bill Clinton's EPA. Governor Lawton Chiles appointed Virginia Wetherell who had been Secretary at DNR to head the new, super-agency, DEP. With her appointment to DEP Secretary, key DER personnel were replaced with DNR managers who had never done "regulation" and "enforcement". The whole focus of the Florida environmental agency had changed.[4]

Using the EPA's new "Clean Water Action Policy" as the initiator, another management plan for Perdido Bay came out in 1998. It was prepared by the Perdido Ecosystem Restoration Group (PERG) with monetary support from NOAA and Florida Department of Community Affairs. The group was composed mainly of members from governmental agencies with only two citizens being represented, me and one other member of Friends of the Prairie. Friends of the Prairie had advocated for purchase of land along Perdido Bay on Tarkiln Peninsula as a wetland prairie, and were successful. The PERG group met several times, usually during the day. Government employees don't like to have to work at night. The problem is that many citizens work and cannot attend day meetings. In the Executive Summary, the background and purpose of the 1998 Management Plan is given. "The Florida-Alabama Water Resources Coordinating Council (FAWRCC, the previous council) authorized the creation of this document as the final unifying element of the Perdido Bay Cooperative Management Project in 1995. This current 1998 version is the result of revisions suggested by the Perdido Ecosystem Restoration Group which was formed in cooperation with the FAWRCC in January 1997."[5] I don't know who on the FAWRCC group was contacted to make or authorize the new revisions. My husband, a faithful attendee of the 1993 FAWRCC group, didn't know about the revisions or the report.

The report had many different types of data and was a good reference. Much of the water quality data had been taken from USGS (United States Geological Survey) sampling. Of the 157 pages (plus additional pages in appendices), one sentence addressed the pollution from the paper mill. "The most voluminous and concentrated pollution source is from Champion Paper Company which discharges into Elevenmile Creek" (Page 157). This one sentence was buried in the report. The report outlines many, many other possible sources of pollution but did not give any sort of ranking as to the importance of that source. Under the "Point Source Pollution Control Strategies", the recommendation was "…to build on the existing regulatory foundation…." (p 76).

In the Introduction to the 1998 report, the federal initiatives which were being developed at that time are summarized. One in particular - EPA's "Clean Water Action Policy, Restoring and Protecting Americas Waters," was singled out as the impetus for the 1998 report. *"In his 1998 State of the Union Address, President Clinton announced a major new Clean Water Initiative to speed the restoration of the nation's precious waterways. This new initiative aims to achieve clean water by strengthening public health protections, targeting community-based watershed protection efforts at high priority areas, and providing communities with new resources to control polluted runoff."* It sounded good, and some things may have been made better. Escambia County Florida did get a federal grant to construct storm water ponds. Wetland protections seemed to be enhanced, but degradation of Perdido Bay continued.

The last management plan for Perdido Bay, of which I am aware, was written by the Nature Conservancy of Florida, and the plan was called *"Perdido Bay Community Based Watershed Plan,"* published December 2014. This management plan was written to help identify projects which might receive some money from the fines of the BP oil spill in the Gulf of Mexico in 2010. Four or five meetings were held, again during the day, where attendees tried by consensus, to define the problems on Perdido Bay and find solutions. Nearly all the attendees were people from government agencies, county, state or federal. As far as I could see, there were very few interested citizens present, as these meetings were not announced publicly. *"The community-based watershed planning provides a process for making thoughtful science-based decisions that help to both assess already proposed projects and identify new projects that help solve recognized and documented problems in the watershed."*[6] Nowhere, unfortunately, in this management plan was the industrial pollution from the paper mill identified as a "root cause". Of course, even if it had been, money for a project would not have helped the problem. One project which was proposed for funding was dredging the solids from the bottom of Perdido Bay.

Despite all the management plans, the degradation of Perdido Bay continues. Without any long-term monitoring, it is nearly impossible to develop management plans or to gauge if management plans are working. The requirement for "citizen input" is input by government employees working for environmental agencies. Either the government employees are unaware of the problems on Perdido Bay or they are afraid to say anything for fear of their jobs. Over the years, the type of government employee has changed. In 1995, the Secretary of DEP, Virginia Wetherell, asked the legislature to amend the Florida Statutes to remove Florida Career Service Protection for senior DEP employees. This meant that without this civil service protection, career employees could be fired without cause. Environmental employees were told "Either get on the train or get run over". When Jeb Bush took over as Governor, the protections of the Florida Civil Service were removed for even low level employees. Even low-level biologists could be fired for speaking out. The agencies hire different types of people, many of whom are not biologists. As an ex-DEP employee who is a biologist recently told me: he doubted there was anyone in the DEP who knew what the bays in North Florida were like. The same is true for the EPA. They push paper, and rubber-stamp reports, often erroneous reports, but have no idea what is happening in the environment. And while the heads of most environmental agencies change along with newly-elected governors or presidents, the bureaucrats who are second in command remain entrenched in their positions because of their moderate points of view, frequently in favor of big industry polluters. The low pay of environmental employees results in high turnover rates. With the recent election of a U.S. president who is focused on eliminating environmental rules and programs, which he claims are "job-killers", environmental protections will further be eroded. It is not an encouraging picture.

CHAPTER 9 ~ Nuisance Algae, Nutrients and Lies

The use of management plans to try and control pollution and restore bodies of water were in vogue during the 1990's, especially in big estuaries like the Chesapeake Bay.[1] The pollution most targeted for control was nutrient pollution like nitrogen and phosphorus - fertilizers for plants. In water, a little bit of fertilizer is O.K. as it can increase productivity of a body of water. Too much is not. It can cause algae blooms and turbidity, excessive growth of plants, and general decline. As recently as 2016, blooms of algae - some considered toxic - have occurred off Atlantic and Pacific coasts of the U.S., causing great economic damage. These plants die and settle to the bottom where they consume oxygen. Scientists call this process eutrophication, or enrichment. It is too much of a good thing. Florida, has especially, lost a lot of productive lakes and streams to over-fertilization of waterways. The Everglades is a good example of what happens with the presence of too many nutrients. Rivers and lakes are choked with water weeds and algae. The nutrients come from many different sources and controlling the release of nutrients into waterways is difficult. Nutrients are associated with storm water runoff from farms, septic tanks and people's yards. Domestic wastewater treatment plants discharge nutrients into waterways; some more than others.

The effluent from the paper industry is just the opposite of domestic wastewater: it is nutrient poor. There is so much carbonaceous material (material that consumes oxygen) present, that bacteria living on and degrading paper mill effluent quickly use all of them up. Bacteria need nitrogen and phosphorus to multiply. When bacteria use up the nitrogen (nitrogen is present in paper mill effluent, but not in a form useable by bacteria) and phosphorus, the breakdown of the carbonaceous material in paper mill effluent slows down. Paper companies must add nitrogen (usually in the form of ammonia) and phosphorus to their treatment ponds to grow sufficient numbers of bacteria to treat the carbonaceous (alcohols, wood fibers, and other organic materials) materials. They must also add oxygen by agitating the effluent. Without adding nutrients, paper (pulp) mills would not be able to meet limits which are in their permits. Treatment of paper mill effluent is directly proportional to the number of bacteria growing in the big ponds. When bacteria die (they only live a few days), the nutrients which were incorporated into their dead bodies, settle to the bottom of the paper mill ponds and become part of the paper mill sludge. Thus, the sludges from the paper mills contain the nutrients (usually organic nitrogen and phosphorus), as well as lots of organic material which uses up oxygen. Sludges also contain toxic materials like dioxin.

Back in 1993, Florida had a water quality standard which addressed excessive nutrients. The standard said that nutrients were prohibited to be released in quantities which caused nuisance algae blooms. It was a difficult rule to enforce, because one person's definition of nuisance may not match someone else's definition. But in the spring of 1993, I thought we had a case of nuisance algae, we would later learn was being caused by excessive nutrients from the paper mill. It was a green drift algae, the exact genus depending upon the salinity of the water, at our beach. Beginning in the winter and spring of 1988, these algae flourished in the upper and middle bays. In the spring of 1993 and again in 1999, the bloom was so excessive that it covered the entire beach, including our crab traps. The kids would ball it up and throw it at each other. Most occurred in the very shallow inshore waters. I think one summer I dried it and used it as a Halloween costume for the following fall. In the Friends of Perdido Bay Newsletter, *Tidings*, we asked for algae recipes as a joke. But this was serious. We had numerous times reported this issue to DEP. One of the Assistant Administrators from Tallahassee had been out to our house to look at the algae. We had sent pictures and videos of it to Carole Browner, Secretary of DER. The regulators were well aware of the problem. In 1993, I wrote a "Verified Complaint" to DEP about the nuisance algae to get them to do something. They responded and said the Livingston Study, which was being funded by Champion, would address the problem.

As far back as 1979, I had started doing research on the animals in the bay. The two most abundant animals were the clams which paved the bottom and the snails which lived on the groins and other hard surfaces. The snails grazed on the very small algae which grew there. Some people call it scum algae. I call it periphyton. As I watched the bay, I noticed that the snails had become more and more numerous over the years, since the algae had become more abundant. Four years later, in 1983, I measured 352 snails per square meter on the cement groins at our beach. We had not yet seen the massive amounts of drift algae which would come a few years later, but nutrient enrichment already was underway. (It wasn't until many years later (1996) when I saw the figures for paper production at the paper mill that I realized why we were seeing more algae. The mill was increasing its production of paper.) Productivity of certain parts of the bay was increasing. In 1983, I decided to measure the productivity of scum algae (periphyton) and the feeding of the snails. I would put wooden frames holding glass plates into the water. The periphyton would grow on the glass plates and then I would scrap it off, dry it and weigh it. I began measuring the feeding rates of the snails on the glass plates. I expanded my studies of the snail feeding, looking at concentration of periphyton, preference of snails for different types of periphyton, etc. [2]

Since my family and I were in the bay almost daily during warm weather, it was easy for me to notice any changes. In the summer of 1984, seagrasses began appearing at our beach.

This was exciting for me. Seagrasses add another dimension to the habitat. Different animals started appearing that live in seagrass beds. The seagrasses appeared to be proliferating. I even saw them flowering, something I had never seen before. Seagrasses are just like land plants - they flower, produce seeds, and lose their leaves in the fall. Not everyone likes the feeling of walking through seagrasses. My husband told me that his mother would tell her children to pull them up. But I loved them. I began to measure their growth. My husband, a civil engineer, devised a simple way of measuring the area of the seagrass beds. Their area expanded rapidly in the summer. In the winter, they would lose their fronds (leaves) and the area would shrink. But every spring from the late 1980's until 1999, the seagrasses came back. Our family would delight in pulling a seine (a length of net held at both ends) through the seagrass beds and see what animals could be found. Baby blue crabs, pipefish, sculpin fish and snails would fill the seine net. The clams were usually not very abundant in the sand at the base of the grass beds, but were found slightly further offshore where they did not grow.

The seagrass beds extended in patches up and down the neighbors' beaches. We knew of a very large bed across the bay in Alabama at Grassy Point, just outside the mouth of the Perdido River. We figured it was called Grassy Point because of the large grass bed having been there for as long as anyone could remember. The Fish and Wildlife study which was done on Perdido Bay in 1990[3] (See study section), found that the Grassy Point seagrass bed had actually expanded in size since 1941[4]. The Grassy Point bed is where Livingston found the greatest diversity of life in the upper bay. At our beach, they continued to come and go. The seagrasses totally disappeared, however, after the 1986 clam kill. In Spring 1992, they reappeared again. Again, my husband and I continued to follow their progress, but little did we know that the days of seeing seagrasses would be numbered.

In the Spring of 1994, there was again a lot of nuisance, drift algae at our beach. It seemed to be interfering with the grass beds. I noted that many small clams finally appearing after the 1986 clam kill also appeared to have died. I continued to work on the snail feeding studies. Hurricane Erin hit Pensacola on August 3, 1995. Hurricanes are tough on shallow grass beds as they stir up the sediment and either bury or uproot the grass beds. I continued to study the growth of periphyton on the glass slides. Although we were seeing lots of nuisance drift algae at our beach, the growth of periphyton on the glass slides was slowing down. I wondered if anything from the paper mill was interfering with the productivity of the periphyton, so I began experimenting to find out.

In May 1995, I tried growing periphyton on glass slides in paper mill effluent. Nothing would grow but I figured that my experimental setup might be flawed. The following summer (1996), I put my glass plates back into the bay in the frames. The glass plates were in the water from June 15 to September 30, 1996 and very little algae grew. Only a type of encrusting sponge was found on the plates. Something was wrong. I continued to try and grow periphyton on my glass slides in the bay without any luck. The population of snails also seemed to be declining. In the summer of 1997, I saw snails lying on their backs in shallow water. Was something toxic in the water affecting the snails? I had given up trying to grow periphyton on glass slides in the bay; it just wouldn't grow. This finding I reported to the Champion Consultant, Dr. Livingston, was ignored.

In the Spring of 1998, seagrasses had started growing again at our beach and were very luxurious. But something was wrong with the grass beds. The fronds appeared red. Seagrasses are normally green due to the chlorophyll in the chloroplasts. The red color was an accessory pigment showing through where normally it is masked by the chlorophyll. I looked at a seagrass frond under the microscope and saw that the chloroplasts were

143

crenulated (crinkled up). Something definitely was wrong. I went over to look at the large grass bed off Grassy Point in Alabama. That grass bed also looked red. I noted all these observations in a data book which I kept on the seagrass experiments, along with the area experiments my husband and I had run since 1984.   I reported this strange phenomenon to DEP and Dr. Livingston, who again seemed disinterested.

In the summer of 1999, there was yet another clam kill, but the sea grasses were still there. In the Spring of 1998 and 1999, excessive blooms of drift algae at our beach were reported to DEP. Nothing happened. By the early Spring of 2000, all life had disappeared from the bay. There was not a single clam, snail, grass bed or any algae of any type growing in the bay. The grass beds at Grassy Point had vanished. Even the shoreline vegetation had been affected by the disaster. The scrub trees which had been growing on the small island by the exposed pilings had disappeared. The white herons roosting in these trees at sunset and appear as giant white flowers, were gone. It was a disaster. We reported this to the environmental agencies who said it was caused by "salinity changes." International Paper had bought the paper mill and taken it over in early 2000 while Jeb Bush was Governor of Florida and Bill Clinton was President of the United States.

It was very difficult to try and figure out what had happened, especially given the disinterest of the environmental agencies. I checked on the EPA's website. They listed Perdido Bay's water quality as fair. The Florida DEP had been trying to take Perdido Bay off the list of water bodies not meeting state standards for "fishable, swimmable" (Class III). However certain parts of Perdido Bay were still listed as "impaired waters" for dissolved oxygen and excessive nutrients. But the answer to what had killed the bay was not found on any lists.

The problem appeared to begin toward the end of 1995, when periphyton would not grow on the glass slides I had been

144

using in my experiments. I began to look more closely at what the paper mill was doing. In late 1995, Champion had converted their bleaching process from elemental chlorine to 100% chlorine dioxide. Champion had also begun using their Lime Kiln Mud driers and washing the residue from the scrubbers into their treatment ponds. Between 1995 and 1999, we had seen a lot of foam on our beaches. It was as if Champion was having problems controlling some aspect of their process. I later found out that bleaching with chlorine dioxide caused more degradation of pine fibers than did chlorine. I began investigating chlorine dioxide. Chlorine dioxide is generated from sodium chlorate at the mill. It is an energy intensive process which required Champion to install a larger power boiler and use more fuel. It also produces a sodium salt.

In November 1995, I sampled Elevenmile Creek water twice for chlorate and chlorine dioxide, once on the 28th and 30th. Each day, I sampled two places - the upper creek and then the lower, tidal section of the creek. I sent the samples to a lab in Indiana having the capacity to analyze chlorate and chlorine dioxide amounts. The level of chlorine dioxide was the same on both sampling dates and in both the upper and lower parts of the creek. The level was 0.4 milligrams/liter. Chlorate was also present on both sampling dates, with reduced amounts in the lower creek. This probably reflected the dilution of the creek by other smaller tributaries, or by the breakdown of chlorate. The highest chlorate level was 8.7 milligrams/liter. Was this causing the decline in periphyton production? Since the EPA and Florida have no standards or limits for chlorate or chlorine dioxide, the amounts I found did not violate any standards. I wanted to sample the creek water again. When I contacted the lab, they said they could not run any more samples for me because the effluent, which was high in salts, had *damaged* their equipment. This was the last time I could check to determine if these chemicals were present in paper mill effluent.

145

From the literature (listed below), I knew that chlorate was a potent herbicide. It was used to control small plants in forests. Research in the literature was also appearing about the toxicity of chlorate to aquatic organisms. In one review paper (Wijk and Hutchinson, 1995), the researchers found that chlorate could have adverse long-term effects in concentrations at low as 0.015 milligrams/liter, especially to macro brown algae. This number was much lower than the concentration found in Elevenmile Creek. Another piece of research, *"Effects of treated and untreated softwood pulp mill effluents on Baltic Sea algae and invertebrates in model ecosystems"* (Rosemarin *et al.*, 1990) concluded, "The trend toward oxygen bleaching and replacement of chlorine by chlorine dioxide definitely reduces overall toxicity as long as the chlorate can be removed. Without chlorate removal, this effluent has a major destructive effect on Fucus-based ecosystems found in the Baltic Sea." Several other researchers also found pulp mill effluents to be toxic. This research was all done in Europe. The three papers which the American Paper Industry presented to the environmental agencies to show that chlorate and chlorine dioxide were not harmful, were done by the research arm of the pulp and paper industry: The National Council of the Paper Industry for Air and Stream Improvement. Other research put out by the National Council of the Paper Industry for Air and Stream Improvement had been accepted unchallenged by the EPA. While concentrations of chlorate I found in Elevenmile Creek are known to be toxic, the paper mill in Cantonment was not reporting any toxicity in their quarterly toxicity tests with the water flea as required by their permit.

In a report we later received in 2004 from a bleaching consultant, Dr. Norman Liebergott, he reported that chlorine dioxide can change back to chlorate during the bleaching process. He mentioned the literature which measured the toxic effects of chlorate but said that it could readily be removed by actions of anaerobic bacteria (these are bacteria that grow in environments without oxygen) or by treatment with sulfur

146

dioxide. But I had no idea if International Paper was removing this toxic bleaching agent or not. To me, it appeared that the effluent was herbicidal.

The presence of a constant level of chlorine dioxide in Elevenmile Creek was interesting. Chlorine dioxide will register as oxygen when measured with certain oxygen meters. I began to wonder if Champion was hoping to meet the dissolved oxygen level in Eleven Mile by using this deception. The company continually insisted they were going to meet all water quality standards in the creek. Perhaps chlorine dioxide was their plan. It didn't work, and it was after installing 100% chlorine dioxide that Champion began to look for alternatives to meeting dissolved oxygen water quality standards in the Creek. They were looking at diluting the effluent with clean water, trying to get lowered dissolved oxygen standards in the creek, or going to another bay. None of these alternatives appeared to look feasible to Champion.

In September, 1998, Dr. Livingston came out with a report on his studies in Perdido Bay. He had been studying the bay for ten years as a Champion consultant. His report underscored what we were seeing: the bay was getting worse, especially since 1994. He attributed lowered numbers of animals living in the sediment to sediment toxicity caused by a bloom of toxic algae. This was more or less consistent with earlier sediment studies which ranked Perdido Bay as highest in toxic sediments. He did not mention any toxicity in the water. What I was seeing was associated with the water and not so much with the sediment. But clearly, there was something causing a decline in the life of the bay. He did mention that Champion had increased their release of phosphate. He presented a graph which showed that Champion's increased release of phosphate in a nearly perfect bell-shaped curve, beginning in 1993. The peak of the curve occurred in 1995 and declined after that. A graph of the levels of total nitrogen and total phosphorus in Elevenmile Creek from 1990 to 2000 showed the excessive amounts of

147

nutrients which the mill was putting out. Both nitrogen and phosphorus were well over the guideline limits, but phosphorus spiked to very high levels in early 1996. I decided this must have been the reason we were seeing such excessive algae at our beach. It was also after Champion had converted to 100% chlorine dioxide and started dumping smoke stack pollutants in their wastewater treatment pond. I wondered if Champion was having trouble keeping the level of bacteria high enough in their treatment ponds to achieve compliance with the limits. Why would Champion be adding so many nutrients?

In his 1998 report, Livingston postulated that increasing levels of phosphate had stimulated phytoplankton blooms which may have been responsible for reduced levels of fauna in 1997 and 1998. In a much larger report put out in August 2000, *Eutrophication Processes in Coastal Systems: Origin and Succession of Plankton Blooms and Effects on Secondary Production,* Livingston further developed his argument that toxic phytoplankton blooms were killing life in the bay. In the Introduction of this report (Page 16), Livingston is candid.

"Perdido Bay in the NE Gulf of Mexico is somewhat unique in that it is a relatively small system with only one primary source of pollution in the upper bay, a pulp mill. Pulp mill effluents tend to have relatively high concentration of nutrients. Although there is some agricultural runoff into the Perdido River, such activity is concentrated principally to the west and south of the upper bay. Most of the land in the upper Perdido drainage basin is lightly populated. The highest agricultural and urban runoff is thus located in the lower bay. This combination of factors establishes upper Perdido Bay as an excellent place to carry out research concerning nutrient loading and eutrophication since the upper bay is small, and relatively free of pollutants other than a single point source of nutrients....Accordingly, there was an emphasis on the determination of the effects of nutrient loading and seasonal/interannual responses of water and sediment quality and associated biological interactions with a series of mill-

148

related changes in nutrient loading over an 11-year period of study. Field descriptive data were used in conjunction with field and laboratory experiments and modeling efforts to determine the response of the Perdido system to this single source of anthropogenous (human) nutrient loading.......By closely following nutrient loading from all sources (including the pulp mill) over a prolonged period, information was gathered concerning the origin, incidence and impacts of a series of plankton blooms that occurred from 1993 through 1999." After reading this, I began to wonder if this was a planned experiment, where the mill would introduce nutrients to the bay, and Livingston would follow the results. It could be a planned enrichment experiment. Why would such an experiment be carried out? Was it possibly to promote development of a better nutrient rule or to cover up the damage from the new bleaching system?

Livingston turned his 2000 report into a book with the same title, *Eutrophication Processes in Coastal Systems* (CRC Press, 2001). Much of the data in the book comes from his studies on Perdido Bay. He summarizes his conclusions.

"The primary plankton blooms in Perdido Bay started during the 1993-1994 drought at which time there was prolonged high orthophosphate loading by the mill to Elevenmile Creek....No blooms were noted during the early years of net and whole-water sampling. Bloom initiation occurred during a major drought at which time turnover rates in the bay were low; water temperature was higher than usual; water clarity was high; and salinity in the upper bay was relatively high. During this period, orthophosphate concentration gradients at the mouth of Elevenmile Creek were consistently high. These orthophosphate gradients generally coincided with the increased mill loading and were located in areas where most of the blooms originated........Thus, although the most intensive bloom activity occurred in the upper bay......some of these blooms extended throughout the bay.....There was no significant relationship

149

among chlorophyll a, b, and c concentrations and phytoplankton bloom numbers..." (P. 91)

His conclusion that blooms of toxic phytoplankton caused by increased nutrients killed life in the bay was not consistent with what we had seen. For the most part, blooms of toxic algae produce fish kills and destruction, but we had only one fish kill in Perdido Bay in 1996 where only catfish had died in the lower bay. A cause was never found. Second, blooms of algae can be measured by increases in chlorophyll. According to the Livingston data, there was no relationship between chlorophyll and the algal blooms. Again, maybe the new bleaching agent had detrimental effects on the chlorophyll in the phytoplankton, just as we had seen in the chlorophyll in the seagrasses.

Livingston continued to study Perdido Bay until September 2007 for the new owners of the mill, International Paper. He also testified for International Paper at several hearings. In December 2007, Livingston put out his last report. It was 340 pages plus appendices. He said the report culminated a 20-year study of Perdido Bay. As in past studies, he noted that several severe droughts occurred during the time frame 1999 to 2007. The droughts caused insufficient dilution of the paper mill effluent and nutrients became significantly higher in Perdido Bay, especially upper Perdido Bay. There were no plankton blooms however during these times of elevated nutrients. He indicated that the mill was putting out low levels of nitrogen plus phosphate in these later years. However, it was still putting out relatively high levels of carbon material (26,400 pounds per day). His conclusions were both honest and alarming. For fish species throughout the bay, he found that
"...the patterns tended to show high population numbers during the early years with precipitous decreases during the 2005-2006 period (the end of study)" (Page 144). "The overall trends of the combined species richness index were down in all parts of the bay with lows reached during the final 3 years of

sampling." (P. 155). "Infauna, invertebrate and fish numbers and species richness in various parts of the bay plummeted to levels never seen before in the 16-year sampling period. There was almost total collapse of numbers of trophic units (TU's) during 2002-2003. In some ways, the biological impacts were subtle; there were no fish kills or obvious signs of the plankton blooms. The bay simply slipped away without any observations by local residents or state and federal agencies." (P. 254). At times, Livingston was candidly honest and this was one of his most honest statements. But by late 2007, he had been fired by International Paper. He also noted that the Avondale sewage treatment plant (called Bayou Marcus) was now contributing nutrients to Perdido Bay. Bayou Marcus had gone to discharging their effluent to a wetland surrounding Perdido Bay, originally permitted for two million gallons of sewage a day; DEP had allowed them to expand their discharge to 8 million gallons a day. "Despite claims to the contrary, the Perdido River-Bay system has not been treated as an integrated ecological system by planning and regulatory agencies, and the neglect has led to the decimation of a potentially productive system."[7] This was pretty much what we had seen happening. It was tragic for those of us who cared about this bay and whose families had used it as a place for enjoyment as we raised our children.

As I look back at why Robert Livingston would have "changed his tune" about what was happening in Perdido Bay, I can only conclude that it was politics. Livingston was friends with Vicki Tschinkel who was working with Champion. She was trying to help them get a permit. The Clinton/Gore EPA worked with the Paper and Chemical Industries to find a solution to the dioxin problem. The solution they came up with was chlorine dioxide/ chlorate. The fact that chlorate was toxic was probably considered, but ignored. Paper mills located on bays and rivers with more flushing, probably never saw a problem. On Perdido Bay, it was obvious. Were they going to close down a major industry which provided jobs for people? Not likely, but

151

they should have come up with a better solution, especially since the closed loop system had been recommended since the 1970s.

It is my opinion that the experiment of adding nutrients to the bay to cause "eutrophication" was a joint "deal" between Champion and the environmental agencies. The Perdido Bay example of what excessive nutrients can do was used to promote stricter nutrient rules. Rather than just having a "narrative" nutrient rule which was difficult to enforce, the EPA and Florida were pushing for "numeric" nutrient limits; actual nitrogen and phosphorus numerical limits for water bodies. I believe that numeric nutrient limits could not have been established without the help of some "big players" and their politicians. This was the trade-off for allowing chlorine dioxide instead of going to chlorine free: help from the chemical industry in establishing numeric nutrient limits.

On January 14, 2009, the EPA exercised its explicit statutory authority to establish "numeric" nutrient criteria for Florida to meet the Clean Water Act. A series of Florida environmental groups sued EPA to try and get limits established. On August 25, 2009, the EPA and the Florida Wildlife parties entered a Consent Order that required the EPA to propose and adopt nutrient criteria for Florida Waters. The first phase was nutrient criteria for lakes and flowing water. The second phase was coastal and estuarine waters. The deadline for adopting these rules was January 14, 2011. If the state DEP adopted numeric rules first, the EPA would approve them. The state got busy proposing a rule to determine what the numeric criteria should be. Should all waterbodies have the same limits? Should different parts of the state have different limits? The EPA's approach was to use modeling for the different bays. DEP wanted to use an "historical" approach. Each bay would have a different numerical limit depending on past values. This approach was called a site-specific approach.

On July 26, 2012, DEP held a meeting in Pensacola to present its draft nutrient rule for local estuaries using the "historical" or site-specific approach. Dr. Livingston attended to make sure that the historical approach was used, and that the years 1988 to 1991 would be used to set the nutrient limits on Perdido Bay. I objected, citing the fact that we reported algae blooms at our beaches during those years. The years which Dr. Livingston chose were years when the bay was obviously enriched. The draft nutrient report for Perdido Bay was full of false assumptions; one of them being we never had any grass beds in the upper bay. It was a "whitewash." I was going to write a report detailing our past studies of grass beds at our beach to counter the false claims that there were never any grass beds in the upper bay. I usually keep all my data books in one place. I found all my past data, except for the data on the grass beds. The data book, along with the computer printouts of growing and shrinking grass beds over the years, however, was gone. Someone had come into our house and taken my data. There were never any signs of forced entry. It was chilling that someone or some organization might be so desperate as to enter my home and steal my data.

The argument that toxic algae blooms killed life in the bay just didn't make sense to me. It wasn't toxic algae blooms, it was paper mill chemicals. But where did the toxic algae originate? I asked Livingston this question while cross examining him in court. He said he didn't know. I believed he would not make up these toxic algae; he actually did find them. One was called *Heterosigma*. Whether or not it was toxic was never determined. However, regulators and politicians assumed that it was toxic and responsible for the decline of life in the bay. How did the algae get into Perdido Bay? Livingston did not know. We never again had blooms of *Heterosigma* after Livingston stopped studying the bay in 2007. In retrospect, I believe it is possible that someone or some entity could have planted these "toxic" algae in the bay. If they were desperate enough to enter my house, they certainly would be desperate

153

enough to "plant" toxic algae. I call them the "Make it happen gang." I have since become a believer in some conspiracies. Like Perdido Bay, blooms of toxic algae, *Pfiesteria*, were used as a reason for developing nutrient limits in Chesapeake Bay.[8]

Livingston did what he was paid to do - he got very high limits for Perdido Bay and accommodated the nutrients put out by the paper mill. Today, Upper Perdido Bay has the highest limits for Total Nitrogen (1.27 mg/L) and Chlorophyll (11.5 µg/L) in the state of Florida. The limit for phosphorus is almost the highest. This is amazing considering that the average Total Nitrogen in the river which feeds the upper Bay is 0.5 mg/L[9]. Livingston never addressed our problems about massive blooms of algae which occurred at our beaches in the 1990's. When I tried to challenge these levels of nutrients, established by the state in 2013, I was told that our challenges to International Papers' permit during the administrative hearings satisfied Florida's "due process" requirement. The state agency, the Department of Environmental Protection, did not want any more discussion of their limits for nutrients in Perdido Bay. Nuisance algae blooms do not occur anymore. We have no grass beds, and periphyton still will not grow at our beach. In my opinion, given the very high level of nutrients, there should be massive algae blooms. There are not. It appears to me that herbicides (maybe chlorate) are being used to prevent algae blooms. The bay is being "managed" much like a swimming pool. I wonder if the environmental agencies have addressed the nutrient problem by allowing a "managed" (herbicidal) solution to the nutrient problem. Environmental agencies are aware of the situation, and nothing is done. Beside a few mussels and snails, the bay is nearly dead.

CHAPTER 10 ~ The International Paper Years

As the year 2000 rolled in, the new century began with a dead Perdido Bay and a new owner for the paper mill sold by Champion to International Paper. In the dead winter of those early months of 2000, my husband and I had not yet comprehended that the grass beds and all animals were permanently gone until spring, 2000, when nothing returned to life in the bay. Friends of Perdido Bay reported this to Florida DEP who said it was abrupt salinity changes caused by heavy rainfall which had killed everything. The preceding summer in 1999 we had an especially bad bloom of drift algae. The grass beds were lush but discolored; red instead of green. 1999 was the last time we would see blooms of drift algae or grass beds at our beach (See Nuisance Algae).

Champion had not said anything to us about selling the mill. We knew that Champion wanted to bring in hardwood chips from its Brazilian eucalyptus plantation. In the late 1990's, they had sought to build a chips handling facility on Pensacola's downtown waterfront but had been turned down. The hardwoods produced less pollution because they do not degrade as much as pine using chlorine dioxide bleaching, and Champion was running out of local hardwoods. Pine chips were also very expensive at the time, so Champion had sought an alternative. Meanwhile, Jeb Bush had become Governor of Florida (1999-2007) and his Secretary of the Florida Department of Environmental Protection (DEP) was David Struhs. Despite a new year, new government, and a new paper mill owner, we were still left with the same old problems. Our beloved Perdido Bay was lifeless.

On Sunday, June 11, 2000, headlines in the Pensacola News Journal confirmed what we had been hearing for months, that Champion was being bought by International Paper (IP). We had heard that a Finnish Company, UPM Kymmene, was going to take over the mill in Cantonment. We had hoped UPM

Kymmene might install totally chlorine-free bleaching. Unfortunately, International Paper had outbid them by half a billion dollars. Two full pages in the Pensacola News Journal were devoted to this merger. International Paper was a much bigger company than Champion with sales of $24.6 billion versus $5.3billion for Champion. International Paper was the world's largest paper and forest products company. From other environmental groups, we had heard negative things about IP and their labor and environmental record. International Paper had eight mills in Alabama and none in Florida. The Pensacola News Journal's two-page article on the merger included an article about IP's good environmental record. IP was given an "A" on its environmental record by a non-profit group, Council on Economic Priorities. Champion's record by the same group had earned only a "C". We would see. The article said that there were still discharge issues with the mill in Cantonment.

"In the past 10 years, Champion has spent more than $100 million to try and meet state standards, said Jo Ann McKeithan, the mill's community relations manager. It has resolved to be in full compliance by the end of 2002......Areas still unresolved: excessive nutrients in the discharge water, salinity and biological integrity. Meeting the first two will ensure meeting the third, she said"[1]. When I read this statement, I knew it was not true. Dr. Livingston's research[2] ignored the huge amounts of particulate carbon which was released by the paper mill and only focused on the nutrients. His research also ignored the toxicity of the effluent which was becoming increasingly obvious since the bay had died. The various articles did highlight the importance of the paper mill to the local economy - more than 1,000 jobs and a payroll of $81 million. IP not only took over Champion's mill but their timberlands as well. IP's stock soared with the announcement of the Champion purchase.

In August 2000, the Pensacola News Journal ran several more articles that tried to cast IP in a good light. In one editorial IP's frank language and pledge to correct pollution problems won high marks. The News Journal considered this a good sign. According to the editorial, IP openly addressed the problems the mill was causing in the bay. Under IP's ownership, Dr. Livingston said that the paper mill *"had destroyed the upper bay with their nutrient loading. Let's make that clear."* The editorial went on to say that this new position was

"in stark contrast to the position taken for so long by Champion officials, who tried hard to spin Livingston's study as demonstrating that the mill had negligible impact on the bay. Champion only grudgingly moved toward acknowledging that some of the bay's problems indeed were connected to the mill."

According to the News Journal, Livingston had won credibility by recommending against piping the mill's effluent to the Escambia River. I thought that Livingston's recommendation had come only after stiff public opposition to the Escambia River Plan. In another article dated August 12, 2000, the headline read - "International Paper Vows to Help Bay." There must have been fears that IP would shut the mill down. Tom Jorling, IP's Vice President for the Environment dispelled those fears. Further Mr. Jorling promised IP would not consider piping their effluent to Escambia River, and would continue working with ECUA on the "plan". I did not know what "the plan" was. The article said that the Cantonment facility was the only one of IP's 250 American manufacturing plants that could not meet local water quality standards. He said, however, that it was still one of the top three or four environmentally sound bleach-using paper plants in the country.

Although the paper mill was under new ownership, we were not finished with Champion, the previous owner. In 1999, DEP had tried to issue a new Consent Order to Champion. (Consent Orders are legal agreements between the DEP and the regulated community to pay fines or fix problems.) We had been following the progress of this Consent Order. The Consent Order had fines for violations of BOD, TSS, and Dissolved Oxygen permit limits for years 1998 and 1999. A report on the

157

Champion's storm water problem had showed that Champion's ponds had filled up with sludge material and needed to be dredged or cleaned out. This was an expensive and laborious process. Because the ponds had filled up, the effluent was not being treated properly. The storm water report also showed how a 2.4" rainfall in 24 hours would increase the flow to over 40 million gallons a day. This had been a continuous problem with paper mill ponds. Rainfall in even small amounts would increase the flow through these large ponds and wash out the accumulated sludge. This usually caused violations in their Total Suspended Solids limit. From the mill's own records, it appeared that chlorine dioxide bleaching caused more plant fiber to be lost and hence the settling ponds filled up faster. Also, more nutrients had to be added to meet permit limits. Phosphorus was being removed with alum which was also filling up the ponds. The paper mill was going to have to dredge their ponds more often and do better maintenance.

Beside penalties, this proposed Consent Order also had permit limits. We had several attorneys review the Consent Order and all the documentation. One attorney who reviewed the Consent Order said that it definitely was acting like a permit. We did not want DEP to sneakily give IP a permit with the same old (or higher) limits which had been in the previous permit and which on its face, had expired. So, my husband and I challenged the issuance of this Consent Order in an administrative hearing (Division of Administrative Hearings Case (DOAH) #00-0628 and 00-0629) in February 2000. Steve Medina had also filed a petition for Ester Johnson.

Prior to filing our requests for administrative hearings, we had protested in July, 1999, against this Consent Order outside the DEP office in Pensacola. As an article in the Naples (FL) News pointed out, "…the proposed consent order also would set slightly higher caps on water quality criteria than under the mill's temporary operating permit."[3] …. When the reporter for Naples News asked Bill Schaal, DEP's program

158

administrator, why the state had not ordered the company to meet the state's requirements, Schaal said: "I don't have a ready answer for you"[4]. Susanne Shackley, Champion's spokeswoman said: "...the company which has spent millions of dollars to clean its effluent, wants to meet all water quality standards."

The administrative hearing went back and forth between IP's attorneys and us. We asked for entry on IP's property and their documents. They objected. Twice the judge dismissed our claims in telephonic hearings. Twice Secretary of DEP, David Struhs, returned our petitions to the Division of Administrative Hearings for more consideration. We amended our petitions five times. One of Mr. Medina's petitions filed by fax was "lost." In the end, DEP wrote a short form Consent Order for fines ($135,000) only, no permit limits, and the case was sent back to DEP. That ended the battle over the Consent Order Permit. The case was closed April 2, 2001. According to documents we later saw, this Consent Order settled all problems of past violations, including continuing violations in Elevenmile Creek and Perdido Bay.

Secretary of DEP, David Struhs, was also addressing the violations to water quality standards which IP was causing in Elevenmile Creek and Perdido Bay. By reinterpreting the old 1989 Consent Order to mean that IP *only* had to meet water quality standards at its point of discharge, violations to Florida standards in Elevenmile Creek and Perdido Bay magically disappeared. IP's point of discharge was a location back on the paper mill property which was inaccessible to anyone, except paper mill staff. This reinterpretation of what the old 1989 Consent Order meant, allowed millions in fines for IP to be negated. I considered this a completely erroneous interpretation of rules which were based on the Clean Water Act Rules. I asked for a clarification through a Declaratory Statement from David Struhs. He refused. This was a rather interesting move, especially since in June, 2000, a full-page article had appeared in the PNJ about how DEP and David Struhs were putting "teeth"

159

in enforcement. The article highlighted how fines had gone up under the current DEP regime. An example of an enforcement action was a $50,000 fine and 30 days in jail for a man illegally transporting oil. The article quoted David Struhs as saying: "What's the philosophy behind enforcement? It is to create a deterrent effect." The article also pointed out how Champion only had to pay $135,000 for recent water-quality violations in one of the most polluted streams in Florida. David Ludder, general counsel for the Legal Environmental Assistance Foundation, pointed out in the article that "It doesn't do any good to assess a penalty that does not recover the economic benefit from the violation and impose something additional as a deterrent"[5]. DEP was hard on little guys; the big ones got off the hook.

This lack of enforcement and misinterpretation of the rules was frustrating to many of us. I had been speaking with an attorney and decided to try to make the Courts make DEP fine Champion which had now become International Paper. I filed a Writ of Mandamus in Escambia County Circuit Court. I was trying to get the Court to order DEP to fine IP for *all* ($47 million) violations, not just a few at the point of discharge. The permit which had been issued in 1989 did not give IP permission to violate all standards in the creek and in the bay. This had also been the interpretation of several local DEP enforcement personnel. To allow these types of violations, variances are issued. For a Mandamus, you must show in the filed papers what the violations were and what fines should be collected. There should be no need for witnesses. The whole case is presented in the filing. I filed the document June 23, 2000. It was a large file. I finally was able to get a date in the Circuit Court on August 27, 2001 before Circuit Court Judge Bell. He dismissed the case because he said I should have filed the case in Tallahassee. It supposedly was the wrong venue. I disagreed but decided not to file another case in Tallahassee. It was all too much of a disappointment. Judge Bell later became a Florida Supreme Court judge.

160

The transfer of the old, expired permit to IP was another problematic area for DEP. DEP claimed the 1989 permit had not expired but had been administratively continued because Champion had made a "timely" permit application in 1994. When the Public Notice for transferring the expired NPDES permit to International Paper was published, I immediately asked for an administrative hearing. I claimed that the DEP was violating their own rules. The permit had expired and standards were still being violated. The hearing officer dismissed the case saying I did not have "standing". The paper company claimed it was simply a "name change" and I was not affected by a name change. The paper mill also claimed it would meet the standards by going with a direct pipeline to Perdido Bay, and they had the money to do this. The expired permit was transferred to IP on October 8, 2002 in spite of the fact that state standards were still being violated and no "clean-up" had occurred.

Friends of Perdido Bay and the Perdido Bay Foundation decided to start spending some money from the dioxin lawsuit which had been settled in 1995. I did some testing of the sediments in Perdido Bay and ran toxicity tests on the IP effluent. The sediment samples revealed very low levels of 2,3,7,8 TCDD dioxin. The metals in the sediments were high. Sediment mercury was twice as high as sediment mercury in Escambia Bay. Cadmium was also high, the highest values being in Elevenmile Creek's sediments. We sent water samples from IP's boil to a lab in Gainesville. They found that, while the effluent was not acutely toxic to a water flea and a fat-head minnow, it did significantly lower reproduction and growth. The effluent was having an effect, a chronic effect. Algal growth was another test we had run by the lab. The paper mill effluent did not inhibit the growth of algae. The same test which we had run two years before showed that paper mill effluent had previously inhibited algal growth.

We also started doing coliform testing in Perdido Bay. A 1999 study by DEP on coliform bacteria in Eleven Mile Creek

161

had found extremely high levels of coliform bacteria, especially after rainfall events. Not only were solids washing out of paper mill ponds but the bacteria which helped degrade paper mill wastes were also washing out with the sludges. Among these coliform bacteria was one known as *Klebsellia pneumoniae*. This bacterium was known to cause diseases and infections. *Vibrio cholera* was also found in the bay. Bacteria levels in Perdido Bay were known to be high. The Florida shellfish people had done sampling in the bay to determine if shellfish in Perdido Bay could be eaten. There was a ban on eating shellfish from the bay and Florida stopped sampling for shellfish harvesting. People got infections after swimming. Friends of Perdido Bay tried to get this information in the news by putting out press releases. But none of the local newspapers or T.V. stations would publish this news. It seemed like the media had gone silent on the issue of the paper mill. They would not even publish our letters to the editor.

In the spring of 2000, and again in the spring of 2001, we did not see any signs of drift algae or grass beds in Perdido Bay as we had in past years. I kept wondering what had happened to the algae blooms. Since International Paper had taken over the mill, we had seen no algae blooms or much life of any kind in the bay. Had the paper mill been better able to control their nutrients? How? It was sickening to think IP's effluent was killing life in the bay. In August, 2000, Robert Livingston had published another large report on Perdido Bay. He had continued to take samples every month in the bay since 1988. The report was titled *Eutrophication Processes in Coastal Systems*. The report summarized his research for the past 12 years on Perdido Bay. This report would be the precursor for a book he published in 2001 with the same title by the CRC Press. Livingston's research found that invertebrates in the bay had declined through 1999, the last year of sampling.

"There were progressive declines of infauna in the upper bay that continued to low levels in 1999. In the lower bay, the declines were even more extreme, with reductions to

162

negligible infauna biomass during the last 2-3 years of sampling" (P.92). "The fish primary carnivores tended to undergo major reductions at most stations during the last two-three years of the project, especially in mid-to lower bay areas". (P96). He did not blame this on paper mill chemicals but rather on enrichment processes of the paper mill nutrients. According to Livingston, the high levels of nitrogen and phosphates which the mill put out resulted in blooms of toxic phytoplankton. It was these blooms of toxic phytoplankton which presumably killed life in the bay; hence the name of the book, Enrichment (Eutrophication) Processes. Environmentalists disagreed. Blooms of toxic phytoplankton are obvious. You see lots of dying fish and other life in distress. We saw none of that in Perdido Bay. Nor did Livingston ever report all the blooms of drift algae and grass beds at our beaches. These signs of enrichment could not be correlated with disappearance of animals in Perdido Bay. It was the paper mill chemicals which were toxic, not blooms of toxic algae (see chapter on Nuisance Algae).

In 2000, the Bush/Struhs people began pushing a new plan. The plan involved the local utilities, Escambia County Utilities Authority or ECUA. ECUA was a local government authority which provided water and sewer to the local county in Florida. It had a paid, elected Board. The Board hired an administrator. We had been hearing a lot about public/private partnerships since the Bush people had taken over state government in Florida. A lot of behind the scenes negotiations were going on. The new plan called for ECUA to build a small wastewater treatment plant (2.5 million gallons per day) on IP mill property, and allow IP to re-use ECUA effluent as part of IP's process water. The IP/ECUA effluent would then be piped to a treatment wetland. We were not sure where. By getting ECUA involved, IP could tap into ECUA's ability to borrow money from the low-interest, state revolving loan fund. Using recycled domestic wastewater was also becoming popular. The paper mill pumped 27 million gallons a day from the groundwater for their processes. This large withdrawal of water had created a big "zone of depression" in the groundwater under the mill. We knew the mill wanted to increase production but any increased pumping of ground water by IP was being discouraged by local regulators.

In the early phases, this public/private partnership did not have many details, but it did have a considerable amount of unanswered questions. This was an interesting proposal. I knew the Executive Director of ECUA, Mr. Van Dever and the head engineer Bernie Dahl. Both had always been very helpful to us in the past. One Saturday afternoon, Mr. Van Dever called me. He told me that ECUA was being strong- armed into participating in this plan with IP. Since there were so many unanswered questions, he said that it was difficult for him to make any decisions. After I talked to Mr. Van Dever, he came under fire for some problems which I thought spurious and perhaps fabricated, and shortly thereafter both he and Mr. Dahl were replaced by the ECUA Board, which also was undergoing changes.

Friends of Perdido had been pleased with the results coming from ECUA's Bayou Marcus Plant's limited discharge to wetlands. They had gone to advanced wastewater treatment. In testing the water along the wetland beach, we saw no increase in nutrients coming off the wetlands. Matter of fact, it looked like the Bayou Marcus water was diluting the effluent coming from IP and Elevenmile Creek. But in late 1999, I flew over the Bayou Marcus wetlands. From the air, you could see a definite brown stain coming off of them. Water testing a couple days later revealed the color came from an increase in Total Organic Carbon. I wrote to DEP and sent them pictures of the brown color. It was coming from a breach in the beach berm on the wetlands. ECUA adjusted the flow through the wetlands and fixed the breach. Everything was O.K. for now, but wetlands were not trouble free. Later ECUA had to fix another breach in the berm which allowed wastewater to flow into a roadside drainage ditch, thereby bypassing the wetlands.

Pensacola's main domestic wastewater treatment plant also owned by ECUA, called the Main Street Plant, was in downtown on some prime downtown property. It had been built in 1937 and rebuilt several times. According to the engineering people, it probably had another 10 years of life. It was a modern looking building for a sewage treatment plant. Most of the Pensacola's domestic wastewater (approximately 15 million gallons per day) flowed down hill into the plant. The tertiary-treated effluent was discharged by an extended pipeline into Pensacola Bay. The one negative about the downtown plant was the odor. There always seemed to be a sewer smell hanging over downtown and was hampering any re-development plans by the city and the downtown board. People wanted to move the plant but the cost was going to be prohibitive. The plan to build a treatment plant at the IP mill was to take some of the sewage from the northern part of the distribution system and direct it to the new plant. It did not call for closing the downtown plant although many people were hoping that would happen. One local leader, Crawford Rainwater, had written to Governor Bush and the Secretary of DEP proposing to use the effluent from the downtown wastewater treatment plant as process water at IP. One ECUA Board Member, Larry Walker, also was particularly vocal about moving all the ECUA domestic wastewater to Perdido Bay. At the time, there was no state money for this costly project.

In June 2000, my husband and I were contacted by IP's Vice President for Environmental Affairs, Tom Jorling. IP had just taken over the mill and he wanted to meet with us and discuss the environmental issues at the mill, so we met with him there. We stressed the importance of increasing the treatment for BOD and TSS so there would not continue to be oxygen depletion problems on Perdido Bay. We put Tom Jorling on the

Friends of Perdido Bay newsletter's mailing list. The mill had stopped putting out the newsletters.

While DEP was stressing enforcement for some, IP seemed to be "cheating" on their self-reporting. The flow from the mill seemed to be higher than normal, even though IP was not reporting an increased flow. I had also been taking samples of the effluent just as it is released into Elevenmile Creek. This was called the "Boil". IP's official sampling site was back on their property at the "Flume". The public had no access to the "Flume" unless you trespassed onto IP property, which would not have been wise. I got close to IP's property line once, and immediately a company truck came along. Even DEP was required to give the company notice of several days before arriving for inspection. Comparing the samples we took at the Boil with what IP was reporting, showed their results were always lower. The laboratory at the DEP office ran the samples for us. An example; on August 29, 2000, we found a BOD of 25.6 mg/L and a TSS of 22 mg/L. IP reported a BOD of 7 mg/L and a TSS of 20 mg/L for the same day. This was quite a difference. DEP in previous years had done "surprise" inspections (with notice to the company). It seemed that the mill had always under reported their values. A reply from Bobby Cooley, the District Director of DEP, about the discrepancies, said they could have been "real" since I did a one-time grab, and the mill is required to do a 24-hour composite sampling.

I had also asked Bobby Cooley about the leachate from the IP landfill. IP's landfill was about 6 miles down the road from the mill and close to the Perdido River. They dumped the sludges from their treatment ponds into large clay-lined pits. The leachate and rainfall which would accumulate in the pits would be pumped out and taken back to the mill's wastewater treatment ponds in a tank truck for treatment. I saw this old tank truck and did not believe it could move. Also, I noticed that a gas pipeline had been installed which transversed the landfill and ran to the Perdido River and beyond. This was a very short distance. Koch Industries had built the pipeline. IP would never have gotten a permit to discharge into the Perdido River as it was an Outstanding Florida Water. But I was suspicious. DEP denied knowing anything about a pipeline. This is one thing we found out about big industry, sometimes it is just easier to "cheat" and risk a fine rather than build a costly project.

I also had begun looking at the ground water monitoring reports which the mill was required to submit to DEP as part of their permit. In the intermediate depth wells, many of the parameters that were being tested, like pH, saltiness, sulfates, arsenic, and chlorides, were above the levels in the background wells. This meant that paper mill effluent was getting into the ground water. The ground water under the mill was contaminated and might even be another "superfund" site. Nobody, however, was saying anything.

On August 16, 2000, another article appeared in the Pensacola News Journal. Dr. Livingston announced that he had come up with a plan to "restore the health of upper Perdido Bay in three to four years." He said his plan "aimed at controlling the state's top water pollution problem: nutrient overload caused by urban and agricultural runoff and industrial wastewater."

"Livingston is confident that International Paper Co. can help restore upper Perdido by reducing the nutrients in the wastewater of its Cantonment mill. The mill has been following Livingston's guidelines since September with success, he said." *"They destroyed the upper bay with their nutrient loading. Let's make that clear....This system will be fixed."*[6] The news article contained the most direct statement published yet that the mill had destroyed upper Perdido Bay. I just kept wondering how IP was controlling their nutrients and Champion couldn't. The herbicidal properties of the paper mill effluent appeared to be getting worse. Was Livingston's plan the same as the IP/ECUA project?

Friends of Perdido Bay followed the progress of the ECUA/IP plan to get out of Elevenmile Creek. At the end of 2000, according to IP the estimate for building a pipeline to a discharge site was $35 million. IP and ECUA obviously had an idea about where the pipeline was going, but they were not sharing that plan with Friends of Perdido Bay. The idea was to get public grants to pay for this project. But the local state representative, Jerry Maygarden, said that he doubted that the legislature could come up with that much money. There was also talk about moving the downtown wastewater treatment plant out of downtown. In a letter from Jeff Miller, our federal representative, he said no monies were available for that large a project.

We had received about 12 CD's of IP "confidential" papers as part of my participation (intervening) in a lawsuit against IP filed by Ester Johnson. Although I was never completely able to go through the entire set of discs which Jones Day law firm sent, I did review several discs. Many of the "confidential" reports on the discs pertained to decisions by IP corporate executives on whether or not to go along with the ECUA project. One report, written August 19, 2000, and titled "Technical Feasibility of Reusing Reclaimed Water at the Pensacola Mill" by Joel Bolduc, an environmental engineer at the Cantonment site, reviewed the options for IP corporate. Mr. Bolduc concluded that IP could use ECUA's water, but there may be an increase in the saltiness of IP effluent. I noticed that the report had been edited to take out any reference to using reclaimed water from the Main Street (downtown) plant. Also in the "Feasibility Report", some background information on the project was given. I thought it was interesting because the idea for an ECUA/IP partnership had been proposed by DEP as far back as Fall 1999. The "plan" which had been proposed by DEP was holistic in that it proposed removing both domestic and industrial wastes from direct discharge to local waters and included IP reusing some of ECUA's effluent in their processes.

Another confidential paper from this period was an e-mail dated November 14, 2000 from Mike Steltenkamp, the mill Vice-President for the Environment to Harvey Westervelt, an IP Corporate Vice President for Printing Papers. The e-mail discusses the need for more research by Skip Livingston on Perdido Bay:

"...Based on all the data to date, Skip has prescribed nutrient levels that if met, should reduce or avoid the frequency of blooms. Furthermore, he believes that the absence, or a reduced frequency, of blooms will allow for the Bay's recovery, again measured by the return of secondary production. The DEP is currently evaluating the data and is in the process of using this information to set water quality standards for our effluent discharge into 11-mile creek, and the Bay as it pertains to nitrogen and phosphorus. Currently, there are no standards. We hope that the state will set the same limits prescribed by Skip, but the state needs to be convinced that these levels are in fact adequate." According to this email, the corporate people apparently believed Dr. Livingston's hypothesis about nutrient discharges and the need to curtail these discharges. The reply from Mr. Westervelt in the same November 14, 2000, e-mail was also illuminating. *"I don't understand why we need to spend $270,000 on this. Let's discuss. How much is because we're worried about how he might re-act if we said "no"?"*

This last comment by Mr. Westervelt made me believe that maybe Dr. Livingston was holding IP hostage. If they didn't continue to fund his research, would Dr. Livingston finally tell the truth about this paper mill effluent? Also, after I read this e-mail I thought IP didn't seem to be concerned about their TSS and BOD permit limits - two of the parameters with which we were most concerned. Maybe IP planned on fixing the BOD and TSS problems in another way.

Among other information contained on the confidential CD's were lists of chemicals IP bought from Buckman Laboratories. The number of chemicals was massive - biocides for the cooling towers, deformers, polyamine, flocculants, phosphates for the mill water. Some of these chemicals were very likely to end up in Perdido Bay.

IP and ECUA continued to work on their "public/private" partnership. In December 2000, we heard that the IP paper mill in Mobile, Alabama was shutting down. We kept wondering where the combined IP/ECUA effluent was going. We heard that it was going to be sent to 5,000 to 6,000 acres of IP forests north of the mill. IP said they were getting out of Elevenmile Creek and Perdido Bay. DEP also expressed the same sentiment to Senator Richard Shelby of Alabama. We heard that Jeb Bush had removed money for the IP pipeline. DEP's budget was getting cut and the laboratory which was in the Pensacola office of DEP was going to close. In one of our many legal battles with IP, I was able to visit IP's treatment ponds in December 2000. I was struck by how little aeration IP had in their ponds. Aeration was very important to meet the permit requirements and they had definitely decreased the aeration from 1997 when I last visited the ponds. Running aerators cost money. I also obtained aerial photographs of the ponds. In 1997 the aeration appeared to be about three times greater than 2000. IP was saving money. But how were they meeting their permit limits? And why weren't they having the same problems with solids and BOD that Champion had?

Friends of Perdido Bay tried to be positive and support a project which we believed would improve water quality in Perdido Bay. The details about the IP/ECUA's public-private partnership were sketchy but we understood the effluent was going to be diverted away from Perdido Bay. My husband, who was president of Friends of Perdido Bay at the time, wrote a letter dated May 28, 2001, to George Watson, Board Chairman of Escambia County Utilities Authority, encouraging ECUA to approve the agreement with IP.

In fall, 2001, Friends of Perdido Bay invited IP to come and speak about their plans at our meeting in December. IP declined and told us that they were not going to build a "constructed or engineered wetland". There was no need. This was a blow. It began to appear more and more like IP was just going to use the wetland as an overland flow; something the EPA had frowned on several years before.

Friends of Perdido Bay had been told that this plan for a wetland disposal had been formulated several years before at an international conference on environmental reform held at Yale in the mid - 1990's. Tom Jorling was one of 15 high level environmental policy makers who were on the Advisory Board of "Environmental Reform: The Next Generation Project". Along with Mr. Jorling were Vicki Tschinkel, Champion's consultant, Frances Beinecke of the NRDC, and William Reilly, ex-EPA Director under George H.W. Bush, and more. According to the Yale Bulletin (Vol.26, Number 17)[7], the next generation project was a two-year environmental-reform effort sponsored by Yale and directed by Ms. Chertow, who was on the faculty of the Yale School of Forestry and Environmental Studies. The project brought together about 500 scientists, environmental activists and industrials for two international conferences as well as 14 regional workshops, each of which resulted in a book chapter. According to the Yale Bulletin (Vol. 26, Number 17), "While the first generation of environmental reform targeted big business, the next generation needs to include thousands of smaller companies and millions of consumers". According to the co-chair, Daniel Esty, director of the Yale Center for Environmental Law and Policy, "Significant reductions in pollution from big factory smokestacks and effluent pipes have been achieved. Our water and air are significantly cleaner." A book, "Thinking Ecologically - The next generation of environmental policy", published in 1997[8], outlined the "new" environmental policy. In the introduction, editors, Daniel Esty and Ms. Chertow, write:

171

"Thinking Ecologically argues for a next generation of policies that are not confrontational but cooperative, less fragmented and more comprehensive, not inflexible but rather capable of being tailored to fit varying circumstances. We see a need for a "systems" approach to policy built on rigorous analysis, an interdisciplinary focus, and an appreciation that context matters". Was this the "ecosystems approach" which Livingston and others were advocating? (See Chapter 6 Waiting and Chapter 8 Management Plans) From this new environmental policy, conventional pollutants like TSS and BOD were no longer relevant. According to the thinking, the old environmental policies had taken care of these problems. This new policy would fit nicely into the new global environment where our industries would be competing with industries in other countries where environmental control was less stringent. Unfortunately for Perdido Bay, the policies of the past had not succeeded, mainly because they had not been enforced. Perdido Bay was just too small to assimilate "big factory" pollution. Groups setting environmental policy in the U.S. have their own agendas. This policy group with roots in a School of Forestry was obviously trying to point the finger away from paper mills which have large pollution loads. Paper mills were the markets for the managed forests in the U.S., and the bodies of water to which paper mills discharged would suffer under this new policy.

In the fall of 2001, ECUA upgraded their downtown wastewater treatment plant. ECUA was having trouble controlling their solids. This resulted in a weekly article in the Pensacola News Journal about ECUA's solids violations. To me, these solids violations were hardly noticeable compared to IP's. We were not hearing any more about IP's solids or their violations. In the summer of 2001, DEP made the determination that IP's 1989 permit was still valid and had not expired. In 1994, Champion had submitted a timely application for a permit renewal, but DEP had not acted on the request. According to DEP, the permit had been "administratively continued." In July,

2002, DEP also made the decision not to fine IP for any violations in Elevenmile Creek. According to DEP, the "...1989 Consent Order had granted the paper mill a blanket exemption from meeting any standards in the creek...."

People on Perdido Bay were unanimously opposed to anymore wastewater entering Perdido Bay as several members of the ECUA Board were proposing. On March 7, 2002, eighty people came to a Friends of Perdido Bay meeting to oppose wastewater going to Perdido Bay. Someone arrogantly told me, "the Golden Rule applies; he who has the gold, rules." Our supporters were writing their politicians. One supporter wrote Senator Richard Shelby, who in turn forwarded the letter to the EPA. The reply of EPA on April 24, 2002, to Senator Shelby's letter was interesting because it sounded so rosy. The International Paper mill's discharge was going to be relocated to an "interior wetland". The Bayou Marcus domestic wastewater treatment plant was discharging to a receiving wetland with no direct discharge to the bay. Even though this discharge was not "direct," the effluent was still entering Perdido Bay. We didn't know where IP's "interior" discharge was. But the answer the EPA gave Senator Shelby was not exactly honest.

In May, 2002, I got a call from Tom Jorling, IP's Vice-President for the Environment, asking if I would like to tour the proposed IP wetland site with him and his new wetland consultant, Wade Nutter. My husband could not attend because he was teaching. Jo Ann McKeithan, IP's PR person, met me part way and then I accompanied her for the rest of the way. We all climbed into Dr. Nutter's Ford Bronco and took off over the few roads which existed on the 1500-acre property. The land had been partially cleared several times and had regrown. I remember having to get out and use the woods for a bathroom as the tour was taking a long time. One thing which really struck me was the slope of the property; it wasn't a flat wetland. Any effluent applied to this piece was really going to flow fast. Also, they kept stressing how large the property was. But according to

173

what I had read about "treatment" wetlands, the amount of effluent that IP planned to apply to land would require at least four times as much land to be effective. After the tour and before leaving, Tom Jorling asked me what I thought about the plan. I told him I wasn't sure, but that I had misgivings. He got angry and started shouting at me. At which point I also got angry and started shouting back. I remember Dr. Nutter staying quiet - that was how it ended. As I look back, I am glad I raised my voice. These big companies think people are just going to swallow anything they say. They use their money to get people elected and buy influence. Tom Jorling was nice, but he worked for what I considered "a bully." Stepping on average people like me, as well as affluent people, is how they make their money. Since International Paper had taken over the mill in 2000, the bay looked terrible; turbid and dark with little life. You could tell IP was not treating their effluent properly. Unfortunately, the DEP allowed IP anything it wanted to do.

On October 1, 2002, International Paper submitted their "Revised Discharge Permit Application." According to the covering letter, the original permit application had been timely, filed on September 29, 1994, eight years past. This was a revised permit application! IP gave us a copy complete with engineering drawings, results of wetland modeling, and all details. I was grateful that they had included us. To have had this massive application copied would have cost a lot. From the permit application, IP was planning on changing their treatment process to collect the solids better and then re-introduce these solids back into the main basin. This was similar to a process called activated sludge. In recycling sludge bacteria back, the treatment is much faster and it tends to remove more nutrients. Friends of Perdido Bay didn't know what the down side of activated sludge treatment was until much later (2011). Activated sludge produces a sludge which is very difficult to settle and is much finer. For this reason, (we didn't know it at the time) they removed most of their settling ponds since the sludge would not settle there anyhow. They were going to pipe

174

the treated effluent to a 1,500 (acreage was given in the permit) wetland between Elevenmile Creek and the Perdido River, known as the Rainwater Tract. Champion had purchased this property prior to being bought by IP. The pipe was going to be built by public bonds bought by ECUA. IP was going to give ECUA 20 acres of their property to build a wastewater treatment plant and then use some of the treated effluent in their processes. The capacity of the pipeline was going to be 37.5 Million Gallon a Day. IP and the DEP touted this as "…getting out of Perdido Bay." It wasn't at all. This was just an overland flow to Perdido Bay. They were getting out of the headwaters of Elevenmile Creek, but their effluent and now ECUA's would be dribbling (gushing in rains) to Perdido Bay. This was pending murder disguised as an accident.

Right away we saw a million things wrong with the project, both permit-wise and environmentally. For using wetlands to treat their effluent, IP used a Florida rule which had been written for applying domestic wastewater to wetlands, not industrial. The rule, called Experimental Use of Wetlands for Low Energy Water and Wastewater Recycling (Rule 62-6660.300 (1)) said that the wastewater which was allowed to be applied to the wetlands had to be tertiary-treated to the 5:5:3:1 standard. This meant a concentration of 5 mg/L TSS; 5 mg/L BOD; 3 mg/L total nitrogen; and 1 mg/L total phosphate. Maybe IP's effluent would achieve this total nitrogen and total phosphate concentrations, but certainly not the TSS and BOD concentrations. These concentrations were running about 20 mg/L, at best. IP tried to get DEP to define "exemption" to mean an exemption from water quality standards. According to DEP this was not what exemption meant. Class III (swimmable, fishable) water quality standards still had to apply in the wetlands. There had to be sufficient dissolved oxygen, etc. for animals to survive. In later modifications of this permit, IP would have to ask for variances for the water quality standards which they were not going to meet in the wetlands.

The design of the wetlands looked more or less reasonable. The effluent was going to sheet flow over land but be stopped by a series of berms. The berms would retain the water for a period of time, depending on the height of the berms, and prevent the flow of the effluent from eroding streams in the wetlands. At first, we were told that the effluent would remain in the wetland for an average of five days. (The longer the residence time, the greater the treatment.) The last design before the hearing, however, turned out to be that the effluent would flow through the wetland in 12-hours or less. The question of whether or not the property could even be classified as a wetland was another issue. Certainly, there were areas which were low and wet on the property. Several endangered species of pitcher plants were growing there. The remainder of the property was considered upland. The drop in elevation from where the effluent was released to the edge of the bay was sixty feet. The area over which the effluent was going to flow was supposed to be 1,500 acres. It turned out to be approximately 1,300 acres. From IP's engineering, 30 % of the effluent would enter lower Elevenmile Creek (the part which was tidal), and 70% would enter small Tee and Wicker marsh lakes in the northern end of Perdido Bay. IP wanted to close off these lakes to the public. Fortunately, the state did not allow this to happen. These were beautiful lakes full of marsh grasses and wildlife, and favorite spots to fish (or they used to be). The lakes did receive some paper mill effluent previously, from tidal action bringing Elevenmile Creek water into the lakes, but most of the water entering the lakes came from artesian springs on the property to the north. The average spring water welling up in the Rainwater Tract was estimated to be 13 million gallons a day. In the end, these beautiful lakes became nothing more than settling ponds for paper mill sludges. Any life would disappear with the toxic sludges.

A simulation of what treatment would occur to the effluent once released on the property was done using a mathematical model of nutrient uptake. Dr. Wayne Nutter and

176

his company from Athens, Georgia were hired to conduct the wetlands research. I was impressed by Dr. Nutter's science and honesty. However, he could only estimate what would happen to the effluent from the data which IP provided. He found that total nitrogen would be reduced by 13% and total phosphorous would be reduced by 9%. He said that BOD and TSS would be reduced to "background" concentrations or 99% would be removed. No definition of "background" concentrations was provided. I thought this was optimistic as paper mill sludges are known to take over 100 days to degrade. Dr. Nutter did not look at the "other material" which was contained in the complex paper mill effluent - chlorate, sulfur, dioxin, heavy metals, phenols, and all types of strange chemicals coming from pine trees, some of which caused female fish to become masculinized. He was probably not given this information, and he probably did not want to know it. The conclusion of the modeling report was that "no significant adverse impacts are expected" (P 77)[9]. Again, this conclusion was based on an effluent from a mill which was producing a 1600 air dried tons per day of bleached Kraft pulp and paper using 65% hardwoods in an aerated stabilization basin wastewater treatment method. We didn't know how long the simulation estimated the effluent remained in the wetlands, maybe 5 days. What would eventually end up going into the wetland was an entirely different effluent. The effluent would come from a pulping process of 70% unbleached and 30% bleached pulp using 100 % pine. The production would increase to 2300 air dried tons of pulp a day. So, the simulation that IP presented originally was practically worthless to predict the final outcome. The characteristics of the effluent would change. Perdido Bay would continue to be overloaded with toxic effluent.

Among the information that the revised permit application provided was "Significant Leaks or Spills." In 1999, 40,000 gallons of fuel oil and 100 gallons of diesel fuel were spilled. In 2001, another 400 gallons of fuel oil was spilled, and in 2002, 60,000 pounds of chlorate was spilled. According to the

177

report, "all releases were collected and were treated by the mill's wastewater treatment system...." I wondered if any of these spills had caused everything to die in the bay.

Champion was supposed to have done a water quality-based effluent limitation study (WQBEL) on Perdido Bay and Elevenmile Creek to establish permit limits, including BOD and TSS. This required another modeling exercise. However, the only WQBEL presented in the permit application was Livingston's conclusions from his 2000 report about nutrients, and how nutrients had caused toxic algae blooms. Livingston's recommendations for dissolved nitrogen (notice: not total) and dissolved phosphorus were included. Most of the nutrients in paper mill effluent are found in the sludges (TSS) as particulate or organic (not dissolved) nitrogen. These sludge nutrients were totally ignored by Livingston in his recommendations. The DEP didn't seem to care.

I could not see how IP was going to prove that they were not going to cause damage to the plants and animals in the wetlands. This was part of the state requirements that you had to
"...affirmatively provide the Department with reasonable assurances based on plans, test results, installation of pollution control equipment, or other information, that the construction, expansion, modification, operation, or activity of the installation will not discharge, emit, or cause pollution in contravention of Department standards or rules." (62-4.070 (1) Florida Administrative Code (FAC)). Another rule (62-4.030, F.A.C) states: "...The Department may issue a permit only after it receives reasonable assurance that the installation will not cause pollution in violation of any of the provisions of Chapter 403, F.S. or the rules promulgated thereunder." If the IP effluent was doing so much damage to animals and plants in Elevenmile Creek, the smaller streams in the effluent area would really suffer destruction. These were arguments that Jim and I would have to save for the hearing. The Departments (DEP) position seemed to be "Rules be damned".

178

At the same time that we received the revised permit application from IP (October 1, 2002), a headline in the Pensacola News Journal announced on October 1, 2002,

"Sewage Pipeline Gets Final O.K. $84 million plan by ECUA, International Paper aims to cut pollution. After more than two years of behind-the-scenes wrangling, International Paper Co. and the ECUA have agreed to embark on an $84 million plan to clean up Perdido Bay and offer sewer service to central Escambia County." [10] The article outlined the different steps involved in the project. In the first step, IP was going to significantly upgrade the wastewater treatment system at the mill. Cost $27 million. The second step was construction of the 10-mile pipeline. Cost $27.3 million. Step 3 was construction of a wetland disposal area. Cost $6.5 million. Step 4 was construction of a new wastewater treatment plant on 20 acres at the IP site. Cost $23 million. Total costs were $83.8 million. IP was going to pay 80% of the cost of pipeline construction and wetlands. Under the complicated 20-year financial deal, the Escambia County Tax collector would put a special assessment on IP's annual property tax bill to pay for IP's share. (Note: after 2005, Escambia County Commissioners granted IP a property tax break for 10-years.) According to the article, the work crews would begin breaking ground soon and the project should be finished by December 2005. The article put a positive spin on the project –

"When finished, the project should put an end to six decades of pollution in Elevenmile Creek and Perdido Bay caused by 25 million gallons of industrial wastewater the paper mill dumps every day." Tom Jorling, IP's vice president of environmental affairs was quoted as saying, *"I feel confident, having spent an entire career in wastewater treatment, that this project represents a partnership that will be emulated across the country."* Notice he did not say that IP would be in compliance with state rules. David Struhs, Secretary of DEP, who had been pushing the project, gave a prepared statement. *"This is a model that all states can follow. Any partnership that protects the environment and jobs at the same time is successful in*

179

everyone's eyes." The article[11] said that the mill will be able to meet water quality standards by upgrading its wastewater treatment system. There were critics of this plan, including myself. I was quoted as saying that there were not enough details to really know if water quality would improve and I did not think that the public should be involved in paying for a private company's cleanup. One of the ECUA board members who voted against the plan said he didn't believe that the utility needed a new wastewater treatment plant in the area, even a small one. But, of course a new domestic wastewater treatment plant was necessary for the partnership to occur; otherwise, there would be no need for an IP/ECUA pipeline.

The Mobile Press Register also ran an article[12] on the new plan. The headline announced
"Florida, IP Say $84 Million Plan Will Clean Perdido Bay." "...Supporters say new plant, pipeline will reduce pollution from mill; critics skeptical." The article said, *"...the state provided a $1 million grant last year and a $1.5 million grant this year to help cover the cost of building the pipeline and a distribution system that will spread the treated waste over the 2,000-acre wetlands. State loans will cover the remainder of the $34 million cost. The utility which will own and operate the pipeline and distribution system, will pay 20 percent of that loan and IP will pay 80 percent."* The Mobile Register had several quotes from Board members of Friends of Perdido Bay. "I would just hate to have the bay be experimented with again," said board member Barbara Lenn, who added that she had seen a marked decline during the 15 years she has lived in the area. "I certainly hope it will work." Bob DeGraaf, another board member of Friends of Perdido Bay, added: *"It's a plan. We haven't had anything before that was near adequate....Something's got to be done, or we're going to have a real mess to leave our children."* (Bob DeGraaf moved from Perdido Bay in 2012 and died July 2016.) Barbara Lenn's comment about the bay being an experiment came from a

paragraph in Livingston's 2000 Report *Eutrophication Processes*. On Page 16 of the report, Livingston wrote

"Perdido Bay in the NE Gulf is somewhat unique in that it is a relatively small system with only one primary source of pollution in the upper bay, a pulp mill. Pulp mill effluents tend to have relatively high concentrations of nutrients. Although there is some agricultural runoff into the Perdido River, such activity is concentrated principally to the west and south of the upper bay. Most of the land in the upper Perdido drainage basin is lightly populated. The highest agricultural and urban runoff is thus located in the lower bay. This combination of factors established upper Perdido Bay as an excellent place to carry out research concerning nutrient loading and eutrophication since the upper bay is small, and relatively free of pollutants other than a single point source of nutrients." From this paragraph, it sounded to many of us as though Livingston, perhaps in collaboration with Champion, used the upper bay as a research site for nutrients. Just why the environmental agencies would have allowed this "experimentation" was hard for me to understand.

As expected, the Pensacola News Journal endorsed the new plan (Oct 2002). The editorial showed some ambivalence[13] however.

"...DEP must be able to certify that this time, the plan works and the improvements are not just real and measurable but meet state standards. If not, IP has to continue to take the steps needed to meet water quality standards. All in all, the plan shows the difficulty - and the possibility - of crafting complex solutions to seemingly intractable pollution problems." We were not the only ones worrying about the impact of piping the effluent to a wetland. Residents of Hurst Hammock, a small community on the Perdido River, adjacent to and south of the wetlands, relied on wells for their drinking water. Because there was uncertainty about groundwater contamination, ECUA decided to install a potable water line to the residents of this area in May 2001.

181

Beginning in January 2003, a series of public meetings were held to introduce the public to the IP/ECUA project and get public comment. Most government projects require public comment, but from my experience, I don't know of any projects that have been changed due to public comment. Maybe slightly, but nothing major. However, as a member of the public one still feels compelled to comment. In light of this, my husband, members of Friends of Perdido Bay and I started to attend public meetings about the project and write public comments.

On January 13, 2003, the ECUA held a public information meeting to consider feasible alternatives for replacing the downtown Main Street Wastewater Treatment Plant. The ECUA was going to do a feasibility study of replacing the Main Street Plant and they wanted public comment. ECUA had representatives there to discuss this proposal. No replacement alternatives had been developed. According to the flier, "The public is encouraged to provide written comments for the benefit of the study effort."

On January 28, 2003, ECUA and IP presented an overview of the entire IP/ECUA plan. There were maps and diagrams and project representatives to speak with the public. The meeting was held at the ECUA building in mid-Escambia County. It was fairly well attended, especially by IP employees. Mr. VanDever was no longer Executive Director at ECUA. He had been replaced by Mr. Sorrell. Bernie Dahl was no longer chief engineer. He had been replaced by Bill Johnson, who had been an engineering student of my husband's. Both my husband and I attended the evening workshop, and wrote comments on the comment sheet. There were no oral comments accepted; only written. The fact sheet which was part of the information packet put a positive spin on the project. This project was going to enhance 2,000 acres of wetlands and restore it to a more natural and historic hardwood system, improve the quality of industrial and civic effluent, prevent adverse impacts to the environment by reducing current and future dependence on septic systems, had potential to reduce groundwater consumption by up to five mgd, and more. Who could argue with all these positive benefits? The fact sheet on IP's target effluent quality looked better, although still probably not sufficient to protect oxygen levels in Perdido Bay. The target TSS (Total Suspended Solids) daily maximum was the same as in their current 1989 permit (27,000 pounds per day). The improvements in the wastewater treatment system included installing a better way of handling sludges. At that time, a continuous dredging operation removed the sludges from the primary settling basin. Sludges were stirred up during this dredging operation. This new way of handling sludges, according to IP's modeling, was going to decrease the TSS released to the environment by nearly one-half. This looked pretty good, however there were no guarantees. Maybe DEP would incorporate these lowered projections in the new NPDES permit which was being contemplated.

For this ECUA wastewater treatment plant to get public funding and be built, Florida had to do a "Finding of No Significant Impact." The Bureau of Water Facilities Funding did the analysis and as we expected, found "no significant" impact. Have they ever found any "significant" impact? We wrote comments about the finding. In a letter dated April 4, 2003, I said there would be an impact. Uplands would be flooded, and small tidal lakes would be impacted directly with effluent. Additional wastewater would be entering Perdido Bay, and ECUA did not need, nor could afford, a new wastewater treatment plant. In response to our comments, Mr. Berryhill, Chief of the Bureau of Water Facilities Funding, wrote back: *"There is an environmental impact, but the positive impacts, far outweigh the negative impacts of this project."* Mr. Berryhill pointed out that IP was modifying their treatment system and the effluent would meet water quality based effluent limits for Perdido Bay. We had not seen what TSS and BOD water quality based effluent limits were because the WQBEL (Water Quality Based Effluent Limits) had never really been published. The letter pointed out that the wetlands were not considered

183

treatment wetlands but only a wetland effluent distribution which would "polish" the highly treated effluent. The NPDES operation permit and the permit to build the pipeline would have to be in place before the loan was issued.

It was becoming more and more obvious what the IP/ECUA plan was and where the effluent was going. In June 2003, Friends of Perdido Bay Board voted to oppose the IP/ECUA project. At the time, we opposed the plan, we were still being led to believe that the wetland site contained 2000 acres and once released from the pipe, the effluent would take six days to reach Perdido Bay. DEP issued the "Intent to Issue a Permit for Pipeline Construction" on May 20, 2003. While we were opposed to the pipeline, challenging the construction of the pipeline would be superfluous. Engineering plans showed that some wetlands would be impacted, but our main fight was to not allow effluent to be put into the pipe. The permit to build the pipeline was contingent on the operating permit for the wastewater treatment system being issued. Friends of Perdido Bay intended to fight the new NPDES operating permit.

Friends of Perdido Bay got busy and began rallying people to oppose the new NPDES permit. We ran radio ads in the summer of 2003. We figured our allies were Alabama politicians. We went to the Baldwin County commissioners who voted to oppose the plan. We held meetings and got petitions against the plan. People who lived on Perdido Bay overwhelmingly opposed the plan. In the end, we got signatures from 840 people who opposed the IP/ECUA plan. But unfortunately, as I look back now, I can see how late we were in opposing the plan. Our protests were too little and too late. The plan was being pushed by power and money. We were just too small to have much impact. (I was told 10 years later by environmental regulators, Perdido Bay was already degraded.) It was also during the summer of 2003, that Ester's lawsuit was being turned into a "Class Action" (See Ester's suit). An article appeared in the Pensacola News Journal on July 16, 2003 announcing the expansion of Ester Johnson lawsuit to include hundreds of waterfront owners in Florida and Alabama. "We are alleging the bay has been severely impacted by the discharges from the mill," said Steve Medina, a lawyer at Levin Papantonio. An ad appeared in the Pensacola News Journal advertising a meeting for Perdido Bay waterfront owners on Thursday July, 24, 2003. According to the ad, as an intervener, I (and any member of my family) was specifically excluded from the meeting.

DEP had not yet issued an "Intent to Issue" the permit to operate the wastewater treatment system. The processing of the permit would begin with a draft permit and a public meeting where comments would be taken. Based on the comments (comments rarely change anything unless they are from industry), the DEP would formally issue a permit and announce this issuance through an "Intent to Issue". At this point, anyone who is a "substantially affected party (public, government or regulated community) can challenge the permit through Florida's formal Administrative Hearing process. Before the draft permit was formally issued, a series of letters were going back and forth between the DEP and IP. DEP said the permit application was not yet complete. IP had to answer a series of "completeness questions". IP would send in answers to the questions which DEP had asked, often with a protest that these questions had been asked before.

In July 2003, a public notice appeared in the Pensacola News Journal announcing that a public meeting was going to be held before the Escambia County Commissioners to consider re-financing pollution control bonds for International Paper. These bonds would have a lower than the "going" interest rate. Public meetings are required any time public government proceeds to get loans. I didn't think there was any chance that the commissioners would turn down the request to refinance; however, I still had to write my letter protesting the use of public bonds to finance the pollution of Perdido Bay. Both the states of Florida and Alabama were buying land along the Perdido River from IP for preservation. This was a positive move.

In 2002, a review of Livingston's book, *Eutrophication Processes*, was published in the Journal, *Limnology and Oceanography*. The reviewer, a Swedish ecosystem researcher, did not give the book a good review. He said there was a lot of detail, but correlations were unclear. *"Effects on secondary production are clear during droughts, but it is not evident to me that an influence from toxic constituents in the mill discharge can be entirely ruled out" (P612).*

Livingston also published a draft report in July 2003 titled "Effects of Sewage Disposal (Bayou Marcus Creek Water Reclamation Facility), Agricultural Runoff and Urban Development on the Perdido Bay System." Notice, International Paper is not included in the title. IP was probably more pleased with the findings in this draft report. Number 12 in the Summary of Conclusions states:
"Even though there have been recent reductions of nutrient loading from Elevenmile Creek pulp mill in the upper bay (with associated reductions of bloom frequency), the combined effects of the Bayou Marcus Facility in the upper bay and agricultural and urban runoff in the lower bay have led to an overall deterioration of environmental conditions in the Perdido Bay system." He said the pulp mill has reduced their nutrient loading to the bay (2001-2003), but during October 2002, there had been a massive bloom of *Heterosigma akashiwo*, a toxic algae, which extended from the sampling station in front of the wastewater treatment plant all the way down the bay. We had not noticed any dying animals or dead fish, as would be expected with blooms of toxic algae. But the bay did appear "dead". Livingston blamed these blooms on nutrients from Bayou Marcus. Livingston also noted that during heavy rainfall from Hurricane Isidore in December 2002, his field crews had smelled "chlorine" in the vicinity of Bayou Marcus. Livingston also said that dozens of water and sediment samples contained

heavy concentrations of chlorine. *"...All of the data aim at a new source of pollution in the upper bay, and it's the Bayou Marcus plant." "There's no other place it could be coming from."*

The people at Bayou Marcus Creek Water Reclamation Facility denied that they had used chlorine[14]. Their method of disinfection was U.V. light and they hadn't stored chlorine at the Bayou Marcus site since 2000.

"I'm just astounded that someone can make comments like that about the Bayou Marcus plant, said ECUA Executive Director, Steve Sorrell. It's apparent to me that the necessary amount of scientific research was not conducted, since the conclusions are grossly in error." The News Journal article went on to speculate that *"Livingston's research, if correct, would indicate the Bayou Marcus plant, not International Paper's troubled Cantonment mill, is now the largest single source of pollution in Perdido Bay."* I wondered if IP hadn't gone back to using chlorine in their bleaching processes. They didn't seem to be having the same "problems" which Champion had, using chlorine dioxide, even though the bay looked worse. Or perhaps the spill of chlorate which IP reported in 2002 could have caused the "chlorine" smell. But the DEP never investigated this "chlorine" smell. The Escambia County Health Department did not come out to take samples for bacterial counts. The bay continued to be lifeless. One of the ECUA Board members defended ECUA in a Letter to the Editor in the local newspaper "Pelican"[15]. He said that Dr. Livingston chose money over honesty and that IP would do well to terminate their relationship with him.

This charge by Livingston that Bayou Marcus had released "chlorine" into the bay and was now the major discharger of nutrients had been preceded by a large article in the Pensacola News Journal on July 20, 2003, about how the Bayou Marcus plant was touted as "exemplary." That year, the National Association of Metropolitan Sewage Agencies honored the Bayou Marcus plant with its top award for having no

187

wastewater permit violations in 2002. *"Until proven otherwise, the facility is an example of how sewage treatment plants should work."* said Mary Jean Yon, director of DEP's Northwest District. *"We consider that plant to be top of the line in terms of a well-designed, well-run and well-maintained facility."*

In the fall of 2003, I found out that when EPA granted DEP the authority to issue the national (NPDES) permit in 1995, there was a Memorandum of Agreement between EPA and DEP. DEP was prohibited from changing Champion's 1989 permit. So, the EPA was ultimately the agency at fault for not stopping the pollution in Perdido Bay. Mike Brimm, from the Fish and Wildlife agency in Panama City, Florida, told us that sediments in Perdido Bay could be classified as "hazardous" and would make Perdido Bay a "superfund" site. Friends of Perdido Bay continued to have meetings and rallies against the upcoming permit. One meeting held on September 25, 2003, was attended by about 50 people in Lillian, Alabama. Joe Trapp, who had been active in fighting the paper mill since 1986, said *"This is a horrible plan. It's like putting lipstick on a pig...They could, but they don't want to spend the money for state-of-the-art treatment."*[16] Sally Cooey, a DEP spokeswoman, said the department believes *"...this particular project has environmental benefits over the current system."* Ms. Cooey was referring to the IP/ECUA project. I said "No permit for IP." We had bumper stickers made saying the same thing. We also held a demonstration on October 2, 2003, in front of the DER building in downtown Pensacola protesting the plan to empty into wetlands around Perdido Bay. We got T.V. coverage for our protest. Another local environmental group, Clean Water Network, joined with us in protesting the IP/ECUA plan. Linda Young, who runs the Clean Water Network and has ties to NRDC, understood that the plan was not going to reduce pollution to Perdido Bay. As she said in her flier, IP was proposing to increase production by 10% and increase BOD. Friends of Perdido Bay also began taking out monthly ads in a local newspaper, "The Lillian." We have been running monthly

188

ads ever since. For the remainder of 2003, IP and Friends of Perdido Bay were attending county commission meetings. IP was saying the plan would be environmentally superior to what was now happening. We said the plan would bring more pollution into Perdido Bay. IP had a meeting for the public in December 2003 where they presented their plan. They handed out a slick brochure which explained the project. As they pointed out in the brochure, Class III standards still had to be met in the wetlands. IP was proposing to get "exceptions" for the water quality standards they would not be meeting. IP's projected benefits were not overly rosy.

A Pensacola News Journal article on October3, 2003, announced *"Wastewater Project Draft Nearly Done." "Plan would ease International Paper's pollution problem."* Jo Ann McKeithan, International Paper spokeswoman, said the wastewater from the treatment plant *"...will meet water-quality standards before it enters the pipe to the wetlands. However, the company is seeking exemptions to water quality standards for salinity and pH."*[17] They would later have to ask for variances for dissolved oxygen, turbidity, and color as well. Another article in the News Journal on October 11, 2003 announced that *"Cantonment mill to cut 21 jobs."* These job cuts were part of the company strategy to increase profits by $1.5 billion by 2005. Tom Jorling said this mill's position in the company was strong. *"The mill was also experimenting with eucalyptus pulp and chips."* [18]

The engineering report for the replacement of the ECUA's Main Street (downtown) wastewater treatment plant came out in December 2003. The report was a professional analysis of alternative sites and the cost. A site had been chosen in the northeastern part of the county to build a new wastewater treatment plant and pump the effluent from downtown to this site. In two of the alternatives, the small wastewater treatment plant to be built at IP was still included in the estimates. In one alternative, there was no ECUA plant at IP. To move the Main

Street plant was going to cost $164,745,000. To allow the Main Street Plant to remain where it was with effluent pumped into Pensacola Bay was $30,000,000. This option was obviously the cheapest. Funding sources were identified, but the cost, per ECUA Board members, was too high.

In December 2003, Friends of Perdido Bay collected another 700 signatures of people who opposed the IP/ECUA pipeline. IP had presented their plan to the Baldwin County, Alabama, Commissioners. The Commissioners for the most part agreed it was a good plan. They said if any harm came to Perdido Bay, IP would be fined. This was not very reassuring to us because we knew how wishy-washy the Commissioners could be. Alabama did not even measure the oxygen concentration in the bay below six feet and were cutting all the funding for their different environmental agencies.

We knew the DEP was drafting the permit for ECUA and IP to discharge to wetlands and Friends of Perdido Bay wanted to have a say. But according to a December 6, 2003[19] article in the Pensacola News Journal, Linda Young said environmentalists keep getting shoved aside and blown off by the Department and International Paper. Friends of Perdido Bay had not known about this meeting between DEP and other environmentalists in Tallahassee and were not invited. Linda Young and the Coastkeepers wanted their own experts to review the finer points of the permit. IP was willing to meet with the environmentalist's experts. Jerry Brooks from DEP said all that was happening was posturing on both sides. Increased discharge of organic matter was being allowed in the proposed NPDES permit. Jo Ann McKeithan, IP's spokesperson, said this was *"...O.K. because the company will no longer be discharging to a small water body."*[20] When I read this in the paper, I wondered what planet IP was on. The small streams in the wetlands were far more susceptible to oxygen depletion than the larger Elevenmile Creek.

In January 2004, the news that the Secretary of DEP, David Struhs had left Florida's DEP to become Vice-President for Environmental Affairs at International Paper was almost unbelievable. In an editorial from the St. Pete Times[21], Governor Jeb Bush said he didn't see how it was a conflict of interest! The people David Struhs had left behind at DEP were all pro-IP/ECUA plan. They would do whatever it took to make this plan work. David Struhs had called me and asked me to support the plan a year or two before. I told him I would see. Many of the original people who worked at DEP in the 1970's and 1980's had left or retired. Governor Bush had lowered the protections of the Florida Civil Service System so that even lower level people could be fired if they took the wrong position on an issue. Most of the people who were hired in the later years were either not biologists or many were scientists from industry. I sent a reply to the St. Pete Times editorial. In my letter, sent February 6, 2004, I said that David Struhs was not the first Secretary to be hired by the paper mill. Champion Paper, the previous mill owners, had hired Vicki Tschinkel, who had been Governor Bob Graham's DEP Secretary. The move had paid off. The paper mill had been allowed to continue to operate on "expired" permits and violated all the same rules. David Struhs remained IP's Vice President until the IP/ECUA plan was approved by the State of Florida in 2010.

The Pensacola News Journal was covering progress in the IP/ECUA plan. It was a big news story for them. On Sunday, February 1, 2004, the News Journal ran a full-page article about the IP/ECUA plan. I considered the author of these environmental articles, Elizabeth Bluemink, an excellent reporter who tried to get both sides' points-of-view. Bluemink's article began with the headline *"Paper Mill's Pipeline Under Microscope."* She reported the EPA was reviewing the plan, quoting James Giattina, director of the Atlanta-based region's Water Management division: *"…We need to make sure all important questions are carefully evaluated."* Interestingly, while old-time EPA people were well aware of Perdido Bay's problems, most were no longer at EPA. Mary Jean Yon, director of DEP's Northwest District said the IP/ECUA project was *"...still about getting the company into compliance."* Notice, she did not say it was about protecting Perdido Bay. Bluemink's article said the effluent would flow through the wetlands for three to four days before entering Perdido Bay. Bluemink reported the EPA *"needs assurance that the wastewater is of sufficient quality not to impact Perdido Bay."* Ms. Bluemink included some history in her long article.

"The Perdido Bay watershed once supported a thriving estuary, but pollution ran off its commercial shrimp and fisheries harvests decades ago. Numerous scientific studies show the bay's problems are chronic - it suffers from too little oxygen and too many nutrients. Both choke aquatic life." Dr. George Crozier, an expert on Gulf Coast estuaries, was quoted by Bluemink: *"...the bay also suffers from toxins that were dumped for decades, including chemicals that disrupt hormones in aquatic creatures. The bay is a poor choice for any pollution discharge because it cannot flush itself adequately."*

Dr. Crozier had decided to stay out of the fight between "environmentalists" and industry. He ran the laboratory on Dauphin Island, Alabama and probably didn't want his funding cut by Alabama politicians who were heavily supported by "timber interests". Bluemink's February 1, 2004, Pensacola News Journal article included comments by Dr. Wade Nutter, IP's wetland consultant. I always thought Dr. Nutter was a good choice as he seemed honest. An editorial in the same Pensacola News Journal issue said: *"...There is no point in spending millions of dollars to treat wastewater in new ways if the water that emerges isn't clean enough."* They were right. However, it did allow IP to operate for the next 12 plus years and pollute Perdido Bay.

People in downtown Pensacola were still pushing to get the downtown Main Street plant out of Pensacola, per another article by Ms. Bluemink in the February 1, 2004, News Journal.

192

Downtown people were trying to use the money which had been allocated for the wastewater treatment plant at the IP site to build a new, larger wastewater treatment plant in the northeastern part of the county. The cost for the new plant would be $165 million. But changing the plan for a new wastewater treatment plant might possibly hold up the IP/ECUA project. Linda Young said in the article that IP's permit had expired in 1994, adding: *"…The mill is violating the law every single day. They don't have several years to come up with another harebrained scheme."*

Linda Young of the Clean Water Network continued fighting the permit which DEP was getting ready to issue. She pointed out in her editorial dated March 9, 2004, that the ECUA board had voted in December, 2003, to not build a wastewater treatment plant on the IP site, but on a site further to the east, and pipe five MGD (million gallons a Day) of the effluent to IP (thus still the need for a combined pipeline). Ms. Young pointed out that the wetlands were not treatment wetlands. Wetland experts hired by IP had recommended 4,875 acres for the disposal area. The total amount of land actually inundated by the effluent would be only 220 acres with a depth of one foot. However, during rainfall, the depth could increase to 6 feet. The draft NPDES permit which was circulating would allow more pollution of BOD, not less, and IP was going to request more variances for their pollution. She pointed out that IP was a big company which could afford to install the technology to clean-up their effluent, but had in fact chosen the political route. Under David Struhs' command, rules had been changed, especially those concerning heavy metals, in order to protect the paper industry. In the end of her article, Young said *"…The citizens of Escambia and Baldwin counties must speak out now, if this further assault on Perdido Bay is to be prevented."* We did speak out, but our voices were too few.

The Fish and Wildlife Service office in Panama City, Florida, a part of the U.S. Department of the Interior, was asked to review and comment on the IP/ECUA plan. One review letter was sent on February 5, 2003, one on February 25, 2004, and one on June 4, 2004.

Gail Carmody, who was Field Office Supervisor of the Fish and Wildlife Service Office in Panama City, signed all three. The February 5, 2003, letter commented on this project for the State Revolving Fund consideration. She said that the site for disposal of effluent contained wetlands, and the impact on these wetlands and mitigation should be considered. She also said that for general treatment of wetlands, 110 acres for every 1 million gallons of effluent is required. Therefore, of the 40 MGD proposed, 4,400 acres would be required. She also added some monitoring requirement should be included. In the final review letter, Ms. Carmody basically panned the sampling program for the wetlands which had been proposed at the time. She said it was insufficient. In the end, Fish and Wildlife recommended the permit, as proposed, be denied. Copies of the letter were sent to EPA Atlanta, DEP in Tallahassee, and to Dr. Nutter, IP's wetland consultant. Apparently, Fish and Wildlife's opinion didn't carry much weight either. When we tried to have these letters entered at the administrative hearings as evidence for the short falls in the project, we could not get them entered. We also tried to use Ms. Carmody or other wetland experts from the Fish and Wildlife Service as experts, but the U.S. Solicitor General's Office did not permit it.

Friends of Perdido Bay continued to voice concerns about the proposed NPDES permit. We were collecting contributions for the upcoming administrative hearing. We had gotten the Perdido Bay Foundation to pledge $50,000 toward our expenses at a hearing. At one meeting, which we held on May 20, 2005, the law firm of McKenzie, Taylor and Zarzaur came and passed out questionnaires. We had scheduled the meeting in a room at the Southwest Branch of the library. There was an overflow crowd in attendance.

The summer of 2004 was one to remember. Beginning at the end of July, Hurricanes began to hit Florida. We were told a strange type of el Niño was occurring. That summer, there were 15 storms, six of which were major hurricanes. The draft permit for the IP/ECUA plan had been circulating for about a month; however my husband and I had yet to see a copy. On September 3, 2004, DEP gave Notice of the Public Hearing and Meeting for the IP's NPDES in the legal notices in the Pensacola News Journal. The public hearing was scheduled for October 13, 2004, at Pensacola High School between 6 to 9PM. There was also to be an informational session preceding the public meeting. The IP/ECUA draft permit was complex and had several parts. There was a draft permit accompanied by a draft Consent Order that included corrective actions and a schedule for completing the corrective actions. There was an authorization to implement an experimental wetland project which would allow IP *"...the opportunity to develop information necessary to amend the water quality standards."* Not mentioned in the Notice were the Variances which IP had to obtain to discharge their effluent to the Class III wetlands. The length of the entire permit was 200 + pages. The Pensacola News Journal also carried an article on the Notice of a Public Hearing on IP's NPDES permit on October 13th. Publishing of the draft permit formally opened a public review and comment process. According to Jerry Brooks, deputy director of DEP's Water Resource Management division as mentioned in the news article, *"...This is a solid plan. It's clearly the best solution, given the circumstances."* My husband, who was president of Friends of Perdido Bay, said he had not seen the draft permit and was quoted as saying the following: *"...What they are getting is a permit to pollute the bay. We expect to put up a fight like DEP has never seen before."*[22] I noticed, the News Journal article said the mill employed 850 people. This was down from 1,000 people the last time I was aware of the employee count.

Before the public hearing on IP's proposed NPDES permit scheduled for October 13, 2004, Hurricane Ivan hit the

Gulf Coast on September 16th. It was a slow, huge storm which filled the entire Gulf of Mexico at one point. The storm's eye went over the beaches of the Gulf of Mexico between Gulf Shores, Alabama, and the Florida line. It came ashore as a Category 3 with winds of 120 mph. 4,600 homes were destroyed locally with 54 fatalities and $18.8 billion in damages. It drove a tidal surge into Perdido Bay of over 18 feet and was a devastating storm from which the community took a long time to recover.

My husband and I had evacuated with our dog and cat before the storm hit. We stayed with our children who were attending the University of Florida in Gainesville. We watched the T.V. news in Gainesville showing the I-10 Bridge over Escambia Bay being destroyed by the huge tidal surge. We wondered about our home. One of our sons who lived on Perdido Key had also evacuated inland from Pensacola. After the second day, we were able to contact him and find out that he was safe. He was able to travel to our house and let us know it had survived with minimal damage. He said, however, that it was impossible to get back into our house with a car. "Bring a chain saw." We waited several days before returning to Pensacola; we knew there was unlikely to be power or gasoline for cars or chain saws. When we did return, the last thing we thought about was a public hearing on IP's NPDES permit. It took us several days of cutting trees before we could drive through to our house. Once the roads were cleared, we started driving around the community looking at the devastation along with everyone else. People who lived on the beaches couldn't get back to their homes for nearly a month. The infrastructure had to be rebuilt. Whole areas in one section, Big Lagoon, had been completely wiped out. All homes were gone because of the tidal surge. Some of the homes had been washed back into Big Lagoon State Park. I figured we had been lucky.

The water had washed into our carport, but not our house. So many other people we knew did not fare as well. Homes flooded, trees fallen on roofs, windows blown in. It was horrible.   We also noted that the storm had washed a black muck into our properties and beaches. We thought this black muck had come from the bottom of the bay which had been stirred up by the hurricane. Downtown Pensacola had been inundated by a 15-foot tidal surge.

As my husband used to say, "It's an ill wind that doesn't bring someone some good". Sure enough, the Main Street Wastewater Treatment plant was flooded and did not operate for three days after Hurricane Ivan.   Raw sewage was sloshing through the streets of downtown Pensacola. But FEMA help was on the way. Of course, this didn't happen immediately. But Hurricane Ivan had energized and eventually got FEMA funding for moving the downtown plant.   Eventually, a $134 million FEMA grant would help offset the estimated $300 million cost to move it. In the final environmental assessment done by FEMA in March 2008, the plant was going to move to a 330-acre site in an isolated part of the county which had formally been owned by the chemical company, Solutia. The plan called for all the domestic wastewater to be used by Gulf Power in their cooling towers. Water reclaimed from the cooling towers (about 6 MGD of the 17 MGD, the remainder evaporated) would then be returned to the ECUA wastewater treatment facility for land disposal. The 2008 FEMA report did not mention sending effluent to IP.

When we were finally able to get back into our house several days after Hurricane Ivan and call some of our Friends of Perdido Bay members, we realized that many of our members were either not living in their houses because of the destruction or just too busy to worry about an IP permit. We called the DEP and told them they should postpone the hearing on the permit. The News Journal ran an editorial recommending postponement of the hearing, but to no avail.   The hearing date was not going to change, but the location had. The hearing had been originally scheduled for the Pensacola High School auditorium; however, it had been damaged by the hurricane. At the last moment, DEP moved the meeting to the University of West Florida's Main Stage Theater. We hurriedly sent out a flier to our members with some pertinent information which the IP draft NPDES permit contained and an announcement with the change in venue. We were pretty certain none of our members had probably read or seen the draft permit. The October 13, 2004 hearing on the IP/ECUA draft NPDES permit was held irrespective of Hurricane Ivan damage. My husband and I had decided to set up a Friends of Perdido Bay "information booth" in the back of the theater lobby and give our reasons for opposing the draft permit. Our "information booth" was a little card table we could easily transport. The DEP had their large display present touting all the "good" things about the permit. As I recall, IP did not have an information booth present. They let DEP run interference for them.

One of the people we talked to at the pre-hearing session was Congressman Jeff Miller's representative. Jeff Miller had been elected our federal representative several years before. The first thing he did when he took office was insert money in the Federal budget for training planes for the Navy. The Navy hadn't even requested these planes. I figured Jeff Miller's campaign had been funded by people who benefitted by a big defense budget. Of course, Jeff Miller's representative was all for the IP permit. We were just nothing but "rabid environmentalists." Tom Jorling, IP's old Vice President for the Environment was also there. We got into a heated discussion with him. We told him IP needed to control their solids (TSS) better. He told us, "You pay for it". In the end, all property owners on Perdido Bay did pay for it. As we expected, we saw very few of our Friends of Perdido Bay members at the permit hearing. DEP spent about half an hour explaining the permit, and then there was a 3-hour public comment. Public comments were limited to 3 to 5 minutes. I thought it was interesting, in reviewing the IP/ECUA draft permit and Consent Order, DEP failed to mention some important facts. DEP was going to have to give IP variances for discharging their wastes to wetlands because IP's effluent did NOT meet standards. And DEP was allowing IP to have nine years once the Permit and Consent Order were issued to try and get alternative criteria for meeting state standards in the wetlands. These important facts were left out of DEP's explanation and discussion, mainly because DEP was giving people and politicians the false impression that this plan was going to bring IP into compliance with state standards. What the proposed IP NPDES permit did do was give IP more time to operate. It did not bring IP into compliance. But few people realized this. I thought the DEP logo - "More Protection, Less Process" should have been changed to "Less Protection Through Process." The Secretary of DEP was Colleen Castille. The past Secretary David Struhs was now Vice President for the Environment at IP.

Because of the devastating effects of Hurricane Ivan, very few Friends of Perdido Bay and others attended the hearing to speak against the permit. It was an IP show. Most spoke in favor of the permit, even though I suspected few, if any, had actually read any of the 240 pages. All the Florida politicians and IP employees thought the plan was great. Tom Jorling was sitting in front of us. I could tell he was very pleased with the comments. IP took out a full-page ad in the Pensacola News Journal the next day thanking everyone for attending the meeting and for their support. The ad said "...*An overwhelming majority, including area business and governmental leaders, independent scientists, our own employees and others, spoke strongly in favor of the project's approval.*" Hurricane Ivan had definitely tilted the opinion at the meeting in favor of IP. The meeting surely would have been more contentious if our Friends of Perdido Bay and local homeowners had been able to attend.

My husband and I made critical comments at the hearing and sent in pages and pages of comments to DEP citing deficiencies in the plan. One interesting comment letter came from Rivera Utilities, the Utilities Board of the City of Foley, Alabama. We were sent a copy of the letter which was addressed to Florida's DEP. It was written November 8, 2004, and blasted the draft permit. The letter from Rivera Utilities said the comments from the public hearing were mainly from IP employees and consultants and were centered on the economic benefit to International Paper. Environmental impacts were not considered. The monitoring protocol contained in the draft IP/ECUA permit would only consider the future condition of Perdido Bay as it relates to the present condition, and the present condition is not good. The letter stressed improvements should be made to environmental conditions in the bay. The letter also pointed out that *"...relaxed standards are a bad environmental investment."* I thought it hit the problems of the proposed permit perfectly. I wondered what could be the impetus behind this letter. Maybe it was one of the Alabama politicians who did not want to look like they were opposing "big business" or the timber interests in the state.

Alabama Congressman, Jo Bonner, who was sent a copy of Foley Utilities report, sent a letter to DEP. In the response to Jo Bonner, DEP's District Director, Dick Fancher, sent a reply letter (February 23, 2005) saying that

"...One point of emphasis in the Utility Board's letter is that the permit serves to relax existing water quality standards. The basis of this premise is not clear and is absolutely incorrect. DEP has determined that IP provided reasonable assurances that all applicable standards will be met for this project." Here again is DEP lying to an Alabama Congressman. The Foley Utilities' letter did not say that Florida was relaxing their water quality standards, but that the permit allowed more relaxed standards. IP had not provided reasonable assurances that all water quality standards would be met, unless IP interpreted the Florida rules for applying low energy wastewater to wetlands as giving them a blanket exemption from meeting water quality standards. Later at the administrative hearing, DEP would clarify the exemptions given by this rule. IP had to apply for variances for various water quality standards it could not meet in the Class III wetlands.

On April 11, 2005, Friends of Perdido Bay sent a letter to Jo Bonner pointing out the inaccuracies in DEP's response.

"...While the permit says that IP will be in compliance with all state standards, the Consent Order OGC No. 04-1202 allows IP to violate state standards. Specifically Table 3, on Page 17 of the Consent Order OGC No. 04-1202 allows IP to violate state standards for pH, specific conductance, turbidity, color, and dissolved oxygen for nine years and then apply for a variance for these parameters from state law." We also pointed out to Mr. Bonner that we had discovered high levels of dioxin and arsenic in the sediments from Perdido Bay which had washed onto our properties after Hurricane Ivan. Understanding permit requirements is complex and often beyond the understanding of politicians, so the politicians must rely on the explanations given by the environmental agencies. As can be seen above, the explanations are not necessarily truthful or only partially truthful.

The muck that was washed onto Bayfront properties from Hurricane Ivan also became a matter of concern. People were shoveling and sweeping this material out of their houses and driveways. Was it hazardous? With money from the Perdido Bay Foundation, approximately seven samples of this muck from different properties around the upper bay were tested for dioxin and heavy metals. Dioxin values were approximately three times higher than the recommended soil cleanup value and arsenic values were 16 times higher than the recommended soil cleanup. Yes, the "muck" was hazardous. On March 30, 2005 Friends of Perdido Bay put out a press release about the hazardous muck. We noted in the "Press Release" that the new IP permit would allow 2008 pounds per day of AOX (chlorinated organic compounds of which dioxin is one such compound). We sent letters to DEP and EPA about this hazardous muck. On April 15, 2005, we got a reply from Sally Cooey, Public Outreach coordinator for DEP. She said the most recent dioxin testing indicated that dioxin in International Paper's discharge was not detectable. We understood why this was so. Dioxin is

201

found in the TSS or sludges of the paper mill effluent. The EPA rule which had been passed in the mid-1990's for dioxin in paper mill effluent, only required dioxin testing of the whole effluent, not the sludges. In whole mill effluent, the dioxin in paper mill sludge is diluted to such low levels that it cannot be detected. Sally Cooey also informed me that the DEP had issued its "Intent to Issue" the IP permit documents on April 12, 2005. The fight would begin.

We heard nothing from EPA. Perhaps the agency was just overwhelmed. In 2000, a Pensacola News Journal article (June 12) had the headline:
"EPA: Dioxin 10 Times More Deadly." "Besides increasing the risk of cancer tenfold, the EPA is reporting the substance is linked to other health problems, including birth defects, learning disabilities, and decreased thyroid and liver functions." While the EPA ignored the bottom of Perdido Bay and even allowed more dioxin-like compounds to be released into Perdido Bay, a different industrial site in Pensacola had been declared a "superfund site" due to dioxin contamination. The EPA had agreed to move 358 families from the area.

The dioxin in sediments of Perdido Bay would also be discounted by lawyers in Ester's lawsuit, proceeding at the same time. On June 12 2006, attorneys for class members on Perdido Bay would stipulate that there were no claims for diminution of property values, there was no claim for contamination of shoreline properties above the mean high water line, and there was no claim for damages arising out of any claimed deposits owned by any putative class member. This was shocking because our lawyers should have seen the health risks arising from sediments contaminated with dioxin from the only industrial entity, International Paper, on Perdido Bay.

CHAPTER 11 ~ Ester's Lawsuit

The second-class lawsuit on Perdido Bay began
innocuously enough. The first-class action lawsuit had been
filed in Baldwin County Alabama in 1992 and had been settled
in 1995. But the outcome of that lawsuit did little to clean up
Perdido Bay: the bay was still polluted and dioxin was still an
issue. On March 16, 2000, an attorney, Steve Medina,
representing long-time activist on Perdido Bay, Ester Johnson,
filed a lawsuit in Escambia County Circuit Court to try and get
the Florida Department of Environmental Protection to fine
Champion for years of water quality violations. Ester and her
husband were in their eighties. They had spent their lives raising
a family while living on Perdido Bay. Her husband, Weldon,
was a fisherman and much of the food they had eaten had come
from the bay. The Florida DEP was doing nothing and Perdido
Bay was still lifeless with contaminated sediments. Steve
Medina also was working for the Clean Water Network which
was run by Linda Young.

Prior to filing of this lawsuit, Ester, my husband and I
had been having an administrative battle with DEP over a
Consent Order No. 98-3089 which had been issued to Champion
in 1999. Did the Consent Order act as a permit and did it solve
all issues on Perdido Bay, as the DEP attorney claimed? We
certainly did not think so. We had filed for a Florida
administrative hearing in January 2000 claiming that the few
violations which were cited in the Consent Order did not fine
Champion for all the years of violations to water quality
standards which had been occurring. Champion had taken no
action and the DEP was trying to transfer the expired permit to
the new owners of the mill, International Paper (See Chapter 10
International Paper Years). When I heard about the lawsuit, I
also decided to file one. Originally, the first lawsuit or
Complaint had four counts - citizen enforcement of agency
action using one of the Florida Statues, negligence, negligence
per se and nuisance. The lawsuit filed by Steve Medina was a

combination of administrative and civil complaints. The case was assigned to Circuit Court Judge, Michael Jones. As I interpreted the intent of the lawsuit, the main thrust of the suit was to get the DEP to fine Champion for the violations they were causing in Elevenmile Creek and Perdido Bay. Given the years of violations, the sum would have been substantial (in the millions). Perdido Bay citizens had lots of data to show the violations. For the violations in Perdido Bay, we were going to use Dr. Livingston's study of Perdido Bay. However, there was a risk involved in using the Florida Statute we used to file the lawsuit. If we were ruled against in a court proceeding, we could not come back and file any more complaints against the company. This is the legal theory known as *res judicata*. The violations would have been forgiven. But we figured we had a lot of data and it was worth a try. Instead of pursuing my own suit with the same issues, I decided to intervene in Ester's suit. In June 2000, I wrote a Motion to Intervene. As an intervenor, I was entitled to participate in hearings but could not file any of my own complaints. It is easier to intervene than to run a whole separate lawsuit, especially if the issues are the same. I was becoming more adept at writing legal motions, mainly by copying motions and legal documents I had received from Champion's attorneys. I also ordered a book of legal procedure.

Therein began the long legal process generating mountains of papers and CD's full of "evidence". Right away, Champion made a motion to dismiss the suit, and dismiss my Request to Intervene. We had to answer all their filings and present evidence supporting our position. Originally, Segundo Fernandez from a Tallahassee Florida law firm was Champion's attorney. The first hearing in this case was October 31, 2000. The judge entered an order on June 13, 2002 granting my request to intervene. By this time, the first complaint had changed to a second complaint. I spent many hours writing and reading legal documents. The Court granted Champion's Motion to Abate certain counts in the lawsuit. The Court agreed with Champion that administrative remedies had to be pursued through the environmental agencies before cases in civil court could be considered. Of course, the environmental agencies did nothing. Maybe "nothing" is too harsh. The DEP would usually send letters and "Notices of Violation". These were their responses. The fight with the state over the Consent Order #98-3089 had ended with us accepting DEP's legal statements that the Consent Order was just a method for fining the mill only, and did not constitute a "permit". The DEP re-wrote the Consent Order to make it a "fine only" for a few violations. We did not have standing to challenge the fines. The fight with the DEP over the Consent Order was finished, but the civil complaints in the original lawsuit filed by Steve Medina sprang back to life.

On August 27, 2002, Jones Day law firm from Atlanta entered the fight on International Paper's side. The mill was no longer owned by Champion but had been taken over by International Paper in 2001. This was a big change. No longer was it just a few local attorneys filing papers and making motions. Jones Day is a large, wealthy law firm, representing all types of clients in 42 offices throughout the world. Steve Medina filed a third amended complaint on September 24, 2002. The Levin, Papantonio firm had entered the lawsuit on our side and Steve Medina had become part of that big local law firm. I think that the Levin, Papantonio firm would be considered the biggest law firm in Pensacola. They were also politically active. Now we had two law big firms battling it out.

I decided after IP got a prestigious law firm, I had better get some legal representation. I was still just an Intervenor. I called around and several people suggested a plaintiff's firm in Tallahassee, FL. We contacted them. They said they were very interested. We sent them the important documents which showed the damages to the bay and to our property. The lawyer said they were going to contact one of the other firms which were in the case and talk to them. After that we heard nothing. I tried calling the attorney several times and she never returned my phone calls. Finally, I got to talk to her. She told me her law firm could not take the case because "the players were too big". She already knew about International Paper being the defendant. Who else was involved with this law suit? Because I could not find legal representation, I was forced to continue on my own.

On December 26, 2002, Judge Jones ordered mediation. I remember going to a lunch at the Pensacola Grand Hotel where all the parties had gathered. I think the Levin firm footed the bill. We all had a very nice lunch and then I had to leave because I was not invited to negotiate. It turned out that negotiations did not lead anywhere. The Judge called an impasse in February 2003. After the impasse, the case languished.

I thought perhaps our attorneys were undecided about which direction to take. The Levin firm was talking about turning the case into a class action lawsuit. I know they were having meetings with certain people on Perdido Bay, but I was not part of those discussions. Third and fourth amended complaints were added as "class action" lawsuits. But there was little legal action. I became worried that no papers had been filed since October 2003 and filed a "Motion for Pretrial Conference" on September 30, 2004. According to Florida law, if no papers are filed for one year, the case is dismissed in favor of IP.

While the lawsuit was languishing, IP was moving ahead with their plans to pipe their effluent to a wetland adjacent to Perdido Bay. They had gotten the local utility, Escambia County Utilities Authority (ECUA) which is a public utility, to partner with them on building a pipeline to this wetland using Florida's revolving loan fund. The ECUA was going to build and own the 10-mile pipeline and IP was going to pay the ECUA rent for using the pipeline. The details were very sketchy.

Hurricane Ivan hit Pensacola on September 16, 2004, and people were preoccupied with cleaning up their homes.

206

Many homes, including ours, were without power for over a week. The 15-foot tidal wave generated by the hurricane, had damaged many homes along Perdido Bay and downtown Pensacola. One of the structures damaged was ECUA's domestic wastewater plant in downtown Pensacola. FEMA money was pouring into the area and looked like it was going to be used to move the wastewater treatment plant to a new location. Several of the ECUA board members were suggesting piping all of Pensacola's domestic sewage to Perdido Bay.

Suddenly in mid- 2005, Ester's lawsuit came back to life. New attorneys were added to the plaintiff's (our) side. The local firm of McKenzie and Taylor, and the largest law firm in Alabama, Beasley, Allen, were added along with members of Bobby Kennedy Jr's firm, Kevin Madonna and Daniel Estrin. On June 30, 2005, a motion for "Class Certification" was filed. All properties along the shoreline of Perdido Bay were included as class members, except my husband's and mine. Our lawyers had gone out of their way to exclude the Interveners (me) from the class action. On September 16, 2005, IP's attorneys filed a Motion asking the Judge to reconsider the order permitting me to intervene. IP's attorneys argued that since I was not a member of the class, I did not have an "interest in the litigation". The original purpose of the lawsuit - to fine the paper mill for water quality violations - had evolved into something else. In their motion, IP's attorneys seemed particularly worried that my participating in the discovery phase would lead to using the information for an improper purpose. They cited my letter to the editor dated, August 28, 2005 as proof. My letter to the editor concerned arsenic and dioxin in the coal IP used. The Judge never ruled on that motion. Our attorneys were also trying to get me out of the lawsuit. In one of their trips to Pensacola, Kevin Madonna from the Kennedy firm asked my husband and me what it would take to get us out of the lawsuit. I said I was staying in the lawsuit as an Intervener.

One reason for trying to get us out of the lawsuit, it seemed, was that our interests were counter to those of both groups of attorneys. My husband and I had filed for an administrative hearing on the proposed permit which Florida DEP had issued to IP on April 12, 2005. The permit permitted IP to use a wetland adjacent to Perdido Bay for discharge. This was just two months prior to the filing of the Class Action Lawsuit which excluded us as members. My husband and I had challenged the permit because we felt there were too many loose ends and unknowns. Our environmental group, Friends of Perdido Bay, could see that the new proposed IP/ECUA plan was not going to bring IP into compliance with state laws. IP had been operating on a NPDES permit which was supposed to expire in 1995, 10 years before. Permits are only issued for five years.

In the Motion for Class Certification, we could see that the Levin firm had spent a lot of money. Scientific studies, a marketing study of peoples' attitudes about pollution on Perdido Bay, and a technology study about what IP could do to improve the quality of their effluent were some of the documents in the Motion for Class Certification. One of the experts which the Levin firm had hired, Neil McCubbin, was a professional engineer from Canada who had worked for nearly 40 years as a consultant to paper mills. He understood what could be done. He examined the IP mill in Cantonment and listed many changes that could be made to improve the effluent. But all these changes cost money, which I am sure IP did not want to spend. He indicated that new mills were more efficient and produced cleaner effluent, but even some older mills were more efficient than the IP mill in Cantonment. He showed that burning coal/wood in the boilers produced an ash which contributed to heavy metal and dioxin contamination in Perdido Bay. By simply going to natural gas as fuel, this source of contamination could be eliminated. One of the changes which Mr. McCubbin recommended was changing the treatment basin to an "activated sludge" basin. This technology included pumping some of the sludge which came out of the treatment pond back into the treatment pond, to maintain a constant supply of treatment bacteria. This technology helps to remove nutrients from the effluent. IP would later adopt a modified version of this technology when they finally got their NPDES permit. The only problem with this technology is that it required a very large basin to work properly. The sludges which this technology produced did not settle well and therefore needed a longer time to settle, i.e. bigger basin or maybe a wetland.

IP's attorneys took the deposition of Mr. McCubbin in Atlanta. I attended the deposition. The deposition took place in the United Industries building on Peachtree Street in Atlanta. The building was identified by the letters "UI" on the outside. On the outside, the building was low key; on the inside, it was extremely rich. The walls were paneled in mahogany with marble floors. The theme was Japanese. I don't think I had ever been in a more impressive building. Compared to the federal government buildings in Atlanta, where I had gone several times, the United Industries building spoke enormous wealth. I didn't really learn anything new from attending the deposition.

Another report which had been commissioned by the Levin Firm was a study of the fine sediments (muck) in Elevenmile Creek and Perdido Bay. The report was done by Wayne Isphording, a professor at the University of South Alabama. As we had found in our previous sampling, Perdido Bay sediments were high in certain heavy metals, and dioxin was found in certain areas. The levels of these contaminates were many times the levels recommended for residential areas by the EPA guidelines. Dr. Isphording's analysis showed that these heavy metals came from the boiler ash washed from the power boilers into an ash pond and then into treatment ponds. IP estimated that in 2002, they generated 17,000 tons of ash per year; some being fly ash and some being bottom ash.

The Motion for Class Certification also included various documents and notes which were gleaned from IP files. These papers had been given to our attorneys as part of the "Production of Documents" during discovery. One handwritten page of notes (IP-107502), are minutes from a meeting about the new IP permit which eventually was issued in 2010. From the notes, it is apparent that IP personnel knew that bleaching with chlorine dioxide could produce dioxin. IP personnel wanted sampling for dioxin in fish limited to one time per permit cycle (supposed to be every 5 years) or as little as possible. The issue of dioxin had faded away as a public issue. The permit which Florida DEP eventually issued did not contain a requirement for sampling for dioxin. It should be noted that Friends of Perdido Bay found dioxin in the sediments of Perdido Bay in November 2004 and again in 2014. The EPA had established a dioxin standard in the water but not in the sediments or sludges of the paper industry. Those agencies seemed unimpressed when given the data. Global warming was becoming the new environmental concern and Al Gore was leading the advocates.

The Motion for Class Certification also did a census of the residents living on the bay. According to Exhibit 13 included in the report, there were approximately 1,000 parcels in the proposed class, with 545 parcels lying on the Florida side and 455 parcels on the Alabama side. One thousand was not a lot of density. The Levin firm also had a marketing study done about people's attitudes about the pollution of Perdido Bay. The results of this study were not mentioned in the Motion for Class Certification; however, they sent me a copy of the report. Only about one-third of the people seemed concerned about the pollution - some didn't know about it, others didn't really care or think it was that bad. In the end, only about 300 parcels, or people, thought the bay was polluted enough to do anything about. I have always thought that the lack of numbers was a problem with our cause.

The Motion for Class Certification contained some good information. I was very hopeful that we would win. The previous class action in the 1990's did not generate enough money to compensate each member for damages to their property, so I was not expecting much. I intended to live on Perdido Bay the rest of my life. To be able to swim and fish in clean water was my dream. But besides the obvious damages that must be proven, our lawyers had to convince the judge that a class action was justified. There are legal rules which must be satisfied for the judge to enter an order establishing a "class". Those prerequisites for Class Certification are: Numerosity, Commonality, Typicality, and Adequacy. In the previous class action filed in 1992, our lawyers were successful in arguing that the class action followed these prerequisites. But this was a different group of lawyers, in a different state with a different judge.

I was also skeptical about the motives of our attorneys, and as far back as 2002, I had voiced my concern. In a letter I wrote to Steve Medina dated July 9, 2002, who was by then affiliated with Levin/Papantonio, I asked him why he had not informed his client, Ester Johnson, about the fact that the Judge had dismissed sections of his suit, specifically the ones dealing with the violations to water quality standards. I had talked to Ester and she did not know anything about it.

In another public letter to the editor dated July 16, 2003, I question the motives behind the lawsuit. I mentioned that Levin had worked for the previous owners of the mill, which should have precluded him from representing anyone on Perdido Bay. In addition, Mr. Levin's good friend, W.D. Childers, always seemed to be protecting the paper mill behind the scenes. W.D. Childers was a powerful, local politician who had been a state senator.

Between the time the Class Action was filed in June 2005 and the time a hearing was finally held on the matter in

211

October 2006, approximately 190 legal papers had been filed with the Clerk of Court in Escambia County Florida. The filings became contentious with plaintiff's (our) lawyers filing requests for documents which IP contended were privileged information. A special master had to be hired to determine if the documents were privileged. IP lawyers wanted to take depositions of Class Members; our lawyer objected. Class Members were deposed. To anyone looking at the file, both sides were fighting hard for their side.

Before the actual hearing on the Motion for Class Certification, two stipulations were filed which confirmed my fears that our attorneys were working on their own agendas. The attorneys in class action lawsuits have a way of doing what is best for them, and not necessarily what is best for their clients. Of course, the attorneys might have interpreted what was best for their clients in their own way. Most of the time, the clients didn't seem to know what was going on. This is especially true if, like the Levin firm, they had spent a lot of money. Stipulations are issues which attorneys from both sides agree upon. The first stipulation was filed May 18, 2006. It basically said that the Hearing on the Motion for Class Certification should be cancelled and the attorneys would submit written arguments and evidence and another stipulation. When the second stipulation (Stipulation for Class Certification Hearing) was filed on June 12, 2006, I was shocked. Our attorneys had given up their right to a "Class Action" lawsuit. They basically admitted that damages were individual. This statement knocked out some of the requirements for a "Class Certification" - commonality and typicality. This was it, no more lawsuits. But the stipulations went further. Our attorneys stipulated that there were no claims for diminution of property values, there was no claim for contamination of shoreline properties above the mean high water line, and there was no claim for damages arising out of any claimed deposits owned by any putative class member. I couldn't believe it. The issue of contamination of our properties by dioxin and arsenic laden muck during Hurricane Ivan was

212

serious, and obvious. This was an obvious rejection to us. At this point, I was glad that I had been left out of the class or was not a class representative. I filed an objection to these stipulations, but to no avail.

The actual hearing was held October 27, 2006 before Judge Jones. The court room was packed with the Class Representatives (seven in all) and most of the lawyers. Bobby Kennedy's firm attended by telephone. The mood was tense. I looked over at Ester and she looked tired. She was a "trooper" who had attended meeting after meeting, speaking about the pollution on Perdido Bay. She always wore her "Save Perdido Bay" t-shirt which the long-since abandoned Perdido Bay Environmental Association, had printed. She never trusted me after my husband and I had agreed to work with Champion in 1987. She figured we had been "bought out". I am not sure that any of the Class Representatives knew that their attorneys had basically given up. The hearing on the Motion for Class Certification was just a formality. The Judge said he would take all the arguments into consideration and issue a ruling. It took nearly a year before the Judge's ruling on Class Certification came out. On July 18, 2007, the Judge's Order denying the class certification came out. On Page 16 of the Order Denying Class Certification, the Judge explains his reason for denial.

"As explained below in the analysis of predominance, however, a class action is inappropriate where the presence of individual issues of fact predominate over these common issues. These common issues will not materially advance this litigation, as the common issues will tend to fragment over time, resulting in the need for individualized proof again and again. This makes class treatment of Plaintiffs' claims inappropriate." A lot of paper and a time had been generated. What had it produced?

Just before the second stipulation on June 12, 2006, the administrative hearing had begun on my husband's and my challenge to the proposed permit DEP was trying to issue to IP (See Chapters 12 and 13 - Administrative Hearings for more detail). We spent two weeks in June 2006 fighting the proposed IP permit to go to a wetland. Previously (August 2005), IP decided to stop making all bleached paper and went to making mostly brown paper. But they also were going to increase production. Another interesting aspect was that David Struhs, who had been Jeb Bush's Secretary of DEP, had become IP's Vice President for Environmental Affairs. Someone was going to make sure that the wetland discharge was built.

For me, the Judge's order denying class certification was pretty much anti-climactic. I don't know how many of the class representatives knew what was going on. I am sure Ester was disappointed. The previous "class action" lawsuit in Baldwin County, Alabama, had been ruled a class, but not this one. This basically killed the lawsuit. Plaintiff's lawyers do not want to spend money and time litigating for each individual member, when the monetary awards to each member are low. After the Order denying class certification, I lost track of what was happening in the lawsuit. My husband and I were busy filing legal documents in the administrative challenge to the new NPDES permit for IP to go to a wetland discharge along Perdido Bay.

From the Court docket in the lawsuit, I learned that Ester had filed an appeal. Next I received a letter, from the First District Court of Appeals in Tallahassee, Florida, announcing that both the case in the local circuit court and the First District Court of Appeals had been dismissed with prejudice. With prejudice means you cannot re-appeal or try this case again. This was a "stipulated" dismissal, meaning both sides agreed to it. That was it. At the time, I did not delve into the "settlement". However, I was disturbed with the outcome. I filed a complaint against Mike Papantonio with the Florida bar about the outcome in this case. He was the one who had spent money running T.V. ads about the toxicity of the IP effluent, which kept IP, originally Champion, from transferring their effluent to Escambia Bay. He was known nationally and worked closely with Bobby Kennedy Jr's firm. The Florida Bar dismissed my complaint as I expected.

A year later, I found out the terms of the settlement. In 2008, I heard from several class members that they had been threatened with lawsuits if they did not give up their claims against IP. But the claims which they gave up were for damages up until December 2008, and not for future damages. The Ramsey Beach Homeowners however gave up a lot more. I contacted the Association president who had represented the small group of homeowners living nearest the IP outfall into Perdido Bay. He told me that the Homeowners' Association was given $10,000, which they subsequently donated to Friends of Perdido Bay. In return for getting the money and dropping the lawsuit, the Ramsey Beach Homeowners agreed to "never again" sue International Paper. To me this was outrageous; they were the most impacted properties on Perdido Bay. Once IP went to their "wetland" treatment (2012), the pollution (foam, dark smelly, turbid water) from the IP effluent was worse than it had been previously. I kept thinking that the attorneys must have known this when the settlement was made (2007). Those people had given up their right to sue and I am sure, their property lost much of its value. I also found out from the Ramsey Beach Homeowner president that IP's attorneys had agreed to pay expenses of our (plaintiffs) attorney, even though the "Stipulation for Dismissal said that all parties would bear their own cost. It sounded like a "sell out" to me.

I had originally suspected that there may have been some collusion between our lawyers and the paper mill or their suppliers. Events several years later made me even more suspicious. The Levin law firm, headed by Mike Papantonio with Steve Medina as the lead attorney, had won $155.5 million in a law suit in West Virginia against the Dupont Company in October 2007. The lawsuit against Dupont had been filed in 2004. While it was not known locally, Dupont owned the St. Joe Company, which at one time was the largest land owner in

215

Florida. The St. Joe Company owned most of the land in North Florida. (The company sold much of its land to the Mormon Church in 2013). The St. Joe Company grew pine trees for pulp in paper making and for lumber and sold a lot of pine chips to the paper mill in Cantonment. They were politically very powerful and a supporter of many important Democrats. Charlie Crist, the ex-Florida governor, was on their Board of Directors. Dupont, owners of St. Joe Company, also made chemicals used in paper making. The St. Joe Company had donated land for a new building for the First District Court of Appeals in Tallahassee. I kept thinking that maybe this was the pay-off. It would be next to impossible to prove, but the dates of all the events were too close to just be a coincidence. The Levin firm has not filed any lawsuits recently on Perdido Bay even though the paper mill is still pumping out dioxin and heavy metals and an effluent toxic enough to kill almost everything in Perdido Bay. Lawsuits don't seem to get us anywhere.

As I write this book, I still believe that there may have been some point to the lawsuit, and that deals were made of which the public was totally unaware. Perhaps, forcing the mill to convert from bleached paper to mostly brown linear board was the object of the suit. This would have made the mill more economically viable and have kept the mill open. This may have been the point of the lawsuit – to keep the mill open. Many people felt that manufacturing brown paper was more environmentally friendly. It also may have allowed the mill to increase production, and use more wood. At about this time, the mill announced that they were going to use 100% pine instead of hardwoods which were becoming scarce. The St. Joe Company would have benefitted from this.

CHAPTER 12 ~ First Administrative Hearing

The ability of Friends of Perdido Bay to challenge Florida's attempt to give IP a proposed NPDES permit we believed faulty and not in compliance with Florida law, was allowed because of a Florida statute. This statute is found in Chapter 120 Title X and is called the Administrative Procedures Act. It governs how state government is run and how citizens may challenge actions of the government. Florida's government operates under a set of rules. Each state agency must adopt rules following the Administrative Procedures Act. The declaration of policy (FL Stat § 120.515 (2014)), states

"This chapter provides uniform procedures for the exercise of specified power under Article IV of the State Constitution or the legal authority of the appointing authority to direct and supervise those appointees serving at the pleasure of the appointing authority." Anyone who is affected by government's decision may use the Administrative Procedures Act. This includes teachers, industry and any citizen. It is a mechanism whereby persons may seek redress for perceived government wrongs.

As citizens on Perdido Bay unhappy with our government allowing our bay to be terribly polluted by this paper mill, we have used the Administrative Procedures Act many times to try and change the situation. Jim's and my challenge in 1987 to the Champion state permit (later dropped), was done using the Administrative Procedures Act. Seven or eight times over the 30-year period, we have tried to stop our government from issuing permits which we believed harmed Perdido Bay and our right to enjoy our waterfront property. We have spent huge amounts of money and time trying to fight the decisions of our government in administrative challenges.

The first thing that must occur to enable citizens to use the Administrative Procedures Act is that the government must do something - an Agency Action. The "administrative continuing of Champion's and then IP's permit" was not considered "agency action" and citizens could do little except wait for the government to act. "Minor permit revisions" are not considered "agency action" either. The issuing of the permit to build a pipeline to wetlands adjoining Perdido Bay which was going to affect the water in Perdido Bay was considered "Agency Action." Since issuing of the permit was affecting the people on Perdido Bay, the part of the statute (FL Stat § 120.569, Decisions which affect substantial interest), was applicable. We had to be "substantially affected parties". If you are a substantially affected party, you have "standing" to challenge the agency action. There is a huge body of law which defines standing. In several previous attempts to use the Administrative Procedures Act, we had been denied access because the judge ruled we did not have standing i.e., we were not "substantially affected parties." Many of the air permits which DEP gave to Champion and then IP, we challenged, but the judge ruled we were not substantially affected because we did not live close to the mill in Cantonment Florida that pipes its effluent to Perdido Bay. In one case, I even got a person who lived close to the mill to challenge the proposed permit along with me, but we were still not allowed to enter the hearing process.

Once deemed to have "standing" and allowed to enter the administrative proceedings, either by the head of the agency or by an administrative law judge, one must have a "disputed issue of material fact". This means you must say that the agency erred in its decision because it used the wrong information. One must specifically state what the wrong information was. The challenge to the agency action must also follow certain time limits. After the agency issues their action in a legal notice, one has 15 days to seek a hearing. If deemed a substantially affected party and the "disputed issues of material fact are considered truthful with merit, one is then permitted to enter the process which the state has set up. Typically, what happens is the agency head will transfer the dispute with the agency to the Division of Administrative Hearings for an 'administrative hearing." The division will assign an "administrative law judge" to hear evidence presented on both sides and then weigh that evidence. These administrative law judges are lawyers hired by the state.

The Rules of Civil Procedure are used in these trials, with one or two variations. The administrative law judge will listen to the witnesses and evidence, weigh all the evidence, and write an opinion called a Recommended Order. This Recommended Order will then go back to the Agency which makes the Final decision. The Head of the Agency may accept, modify, or deny the administrative law judges Recommended Order. That agency head issues the "Final Order" which may be appealed to Florida's Appellate Courts.

Do you get a fair hearing? Many people do not think so. Linda Young of the Clean Water Network was one who thought that politics affected how the judges weighed the evidence. In big cases like the IP permit case, both sides have experts which "testify" to the merits of the side paying them. So, the administrative law judge is going to have conflicting testimony. He then must weigh this testimony. Which side is more believable? What did the rebuttal evidence show? What were the requirements of the law? But in the end, an administrative hearing is the only recourse citizens have to challenge the actions of their government, besides direct violence. Even demonstrations conducted peacefully would likely have little impact. Citizens may have their day in court if they meet the rules, but often at great expense. When your government does not follow its own rules, and is obviously on the side of business, the situation becomes unpredictable.

The DEP issued the IP permit documents to build a pipeline to wetlands along Perdido Bay on April 12, 2005. The Friends of Perdido Bay's requests for an administrative hearing began arriving at DEP headquarters on April 20, 2005. This was well within the 15-day deadline. The proposed permit and supporting documents were long (240 pages) and confusing. Most people who are not regulators or involved with the regulatory process, such as industry engineers and attorneys, would not understand the intricacies of the process. Since we had been doing this so long (18 years or since 1986), we somewhat understood the process. The first document was the proposed permit. Since the environmental agencies can not issue a permit if standards are not being met, the permit says, "Standards are being met". However, in the case with IP, water standards were not being met, so the state (DEP) had to issue a Consent Order spelling out corrective actions to be taken and a time frame within which these corrective actions shall be completed. One provision in the Consent Order allowed IP to violate certain water quality standards, including dissolved oxygen, pH, saltiness, turbidity and color, in the receiving wetland for 9 years after the Consent Order went into effect. Another Consent Order provision allowed IP to stay in Elevenmile Creek for two years. 36-months after issuance of the Consent Order, IP had to cease discharging to the creek and had to be discharging to the wetlands. IP had to monitor the impact of the effluent on the wetlands. They were also supposed to monitor Elevenmile Creek and Perdido Bay. Eight years, after the Consent Order had been formally approved by the Secretary of DEP (after all our challenges to the Consent Order, the Secretary of DEP formally approved the Consent Order in March 2010), IP had to submit "*to the Department a final report on whether there have been significant adverse impacts in the wetlands and lakes.*" If there had been no "adverse impacts", IP could then petition for alternative criteria in the wetlands. To determine adverse impact, IP had done a "before effluent" sampling in the wetlands and marsh lakes and then would compare the results at the same locations after effluent had been applied. The problem with this approach was that the wetlands were far from pristine, even before the effluent had been applied. The wetlands had been logged and ditched over several years which had caused a degraded habitat. A large wild fire had burnt a portion of the wetlands in April 2001. The Tee and Wicker marsh lakes, prior to effluent being applied, had been impacted by paper mill effluent flowing in from Elevenmile Creek. Those lakes were far from "pristine."

About the only thing the before-and-after studies would show was whether the situation had deteriorated. As written in the draft Consent Order, *"the present Consent Order requires corrective actions to bring the Facility into compliance with the Department's applicable water quality standards and criteria."* This was the same statement that was made in the Consent Order issued in 1987 which DEP had obviously not enforced, since in 2005 the paper mill was still out of compliance with Florida rules. The terms of the 1987 Consent Order had not been fulfilled or enforced. Considering the 9 years IP had to seek alternative criteria in the wetlands in the current permit, the Department was allowing the paper mill to violate standards for 25 years. After our challenges to the permitting documents, it would be even longer. Not only that, there were no assurances that IP could show that they were not harming the land and life in the wetland and lakes. We were certain IP's effluent would harm life in the wetlands since the effluent had harmed Perdido Bay and Elevenmile Creek. Fines for any violations to the high permit limits were only $500.00 a day. This is extremely low fine.

Part of the permitting package also contained an application for "Experimental Use of Wetlands for Low-energy Water and Wastewater Recycling". The rules for this application were found in Florida Administrative Code 62-660.300(1). This rule had been written for applying tertiary-treated domestic wastewater to wetlands. Tertiary-treated domestic wastewater was required to have a BOD concentration of 5 mg/l; TSS (total Suspended Solids) of 5 mg/l; Total Nitrogen of 3 mg/l and a total phosphorous of 1 mg/l. Paper mill BOD concentration was running about 25 to 30 mg/l and the TSS concentration was even higher. Total Nitrogen and Phosphorus was about the same as domestic wastes; therefore, I considered using this rule for

221

application of paper mill wastes inappropriate. Furthermore, there were seven provisions which had to be met for this rule to be used. One was that the effluent would "not be expected to have a significant adverse impact on the biological community in the receiving water or to adversely affect the designated use in the wetlands or the contiguous surface waters." The Department assumed that IP met this provision of the rule; however, IP was supposed to demonstrate no significant adverse impact by their studies. The reasoning was circular and absurd. There were two provisions in the rule which IP did not meet. IP was supposed to prevent the public from entering the experimental wetland. This would include the Tee and Wicker marsh lakes. The state would not allow IP to block off these little lakes since the public liked to fish there. IP had to get a waiver from meeting these two provisions. The waiver was also part of the permitting package. Another justification for allowing IP to use the wetland rule was that they had already experimented with wetlands in the 1990's. Although it was not mentioned in the permitting documents, the early experimental wetlands had turned into monocultures of one type of plant, cattails. Only 2% of the planted trees had lived. The DEP made all types of false assumptions so that IP could use this rule. IP should just have applied for variances in the wetlands.

My husband and I decided to include our five children in the hearing. I wrote petitions for each child seeking a hearing. I was planning on representing our children and myself at the hearing. My husband had decided to hire attorneys to represent him and Friends of Perdido Bay. Because Friends of Perdido Bay was a group of people, it had to have qualified legal help, i.e. an attorney or attorneys. After much searching and speaking with attorneys, we settled on Marcy LaHart of West Palm Beach, FL and Howard Heims from Stuart, Fl. Both were environmental attorneys who had been successful in arguing previous administrative cases. International Paper was represented by Terry Cole and Pat Renovitch from a Tallahassee law firm. IP also had a corporate attorney, Steve Ginski, present.

DEP had its attorneys, Doug Beason, David Thulman, and Stacey Cowley. Terry Cole had been Champion's and was IP's attorney. He was very good. Donald Alexander was the administrative hearing officer.

In big cases such as this, the actual hearing begins after a lot of legal arguments and lots of papers have been written. Both sides try and get the issues focused on their strong points. Because you must follow the rules of civil procedure, there may be a long "discovery" process. You must identify who your witnesses will be and what they will be testifying about. You must also list all the written documents you intend to present as evidence and give the other side copies. Either side may then decide to take depositions of the other side's witnesses. Rebuttal witnesses and documents do not have to be disclosed. The whole pre-trial process can be lengthy. As in most of our other proceedings with the paper mill and Terry Cole, IP made a motion (request) to dismiss our petitions or sought a more definite statement. This was the usual start of the administrative process with the paper mill. In some cases, our petitions for a hearing were dismissed (thrown out) such as the air permits. However, in this case, DEP opposed IP's Motion to Dismiss our Petitions. IP claimed that we didn't really have standing because there was going to be a net overall improvement in the environmental conditions of Perdido Bay. DEP, in opposing IP, said that a "net overall improvement" could not be used as a test for standing.

The hearing officer allowed our challenge to the permit to proceed. We amended our petitions. I was named a qualified representative for our children. To proceed with discovery, we made a request for documents and entry on IP property. IP objected. IP wanted to hurry to the hearing. And so the legal battle went. IP would make motions and we would answer those motions. In July 2005, Marcy LaHart and Howard Heims made a Motion to continue the Final Hearing saying that IP's continual motions had not allowed enough time for preparing for a hearing. The hearing was postponed until January 2006. On July 25, 2005, IP gave notice to all parties that it was changing one of its bleach lines to brown Kraft. They said that there wouldn't be much change to the wastewater treatment system. They were going to submit a minor permit revision. It was hard for me to understand how changing a process would not affect the nature of the effluent.

An article in the Pensacola News Journal on July 20, 2005, alerted us to the fact that IP was changing processes and cutting jobs. The article said IP was going to invest $100 million in converting the paper mill to making mostly brown linerboard. A small amount of bleaching would continue but with the changeover to producing linerboard (cardboard), total production at the mill would increase. According to the article,

"The conversion was one in a number of changes announced Tuesday as part of a sweeping restructuring plan that will dramatically shrink the world's largest paper company to boost profits and cut debt." "The strategy involves selling $8 billion to $10 billion in assets, including millions of acres of forestland around the nation, closing mills and possibly relocating its headquarters. Substantial job cuts are expected." IP did relocate its headquarters from Stamford, CT to Memphis, TN. *"The move is the latest effort to cope with weak demand and higher costs in the paper industry."*[1] According to the article, IP had a loss of $35 million in 2004 and was warning that its second quarter profits in 2005 would not meet Wall Street expectations. At that time, IP's stock was trading at $32.22 per share on the NYSE. As of July, 2016, a little over ten years later, IP stock was up $45.00. On August 26, 2005, Chris Read, the Pensacola Mill Manager wrote a "Viewpoint" in which he stressed that although IP was committed to its mill in Cantonment, Florida, there would be job cuts.

In the end, IP cut its workforce substantially. Today the mill employs 400 people as opposed to 1200 employees during the Champion years. The mill has several unions and union jobs.

While the mill was cutting jobs, they were increasing production and replacing hardwood fiber with 100% pine. On October 22, 2005, a legal notice appeared in the Pensacola News Journal announcing this change. But as in previous increases in production, the change was done through an air permit. IP was planning on increasing bleach softwood pulp to 1000 air dried tons per day. And yes, the increase in production was going to increase certain pollutants in the air - mainly sulfur and fine particulate matter. We immediately sought an administrative hearing on this air permit. To try and get standing, I recruited a neighbor of the mill who lived about a mile down the road. No luck. Again, IP claimed we did not have standing to challenge the air permit. The hearing officer agreed. We went back to focusing on the IP/ECUA pipeline wetlands plan.

To increase production, more energy had to be made at the mill. IP produced most of the energy it used in the manufacturing process in five power boilers. Originally (in 1992), these power boilers were supposed to use natural gas. However, over the years, a different fuel had been adopted - a mixture of coal and ground-up wood. Some of this wood was excess produced from the manufacturing process. But some of this wood came from local tree trimmers who would take trucks filled with mulched wood to the mill and sell it for fuel. The increase in air pollutants would be captured in scrubbers on the smoke stacks. The problem was that the scrubbers using sodium hydroxide were being dumped into the wastewater treatment ponds. Also, power boilers which burned a mixture of coal mixed with mulched wood also produced an ash. This ash was washed out of the power boilers into an ash pond and collected. But the "sluice water" went into the wastewater treatment ponds and then into Perdido Bay. I was sure that this "sluice water" was a big source of arsenic, dioxin, and other heavy metal contamination in Perdido Bay.

Instead of taking the ash from the power boilers to their own landfill, IP was taking the ash to Escambia County's

225

Landfill, where it was being used as a "landfill cover". This was a public landfill not too far from the paper mill. IP and the County had an agreement where IP would use the landfill gas and the County would accept IP ash at no cost. I was sure the ash also contained heavy metals and perhaps could be toxic, but apparently, the DEP had approved this arrangement. I had inquired about this arrangement several times. The last time was in 2011 when I had contacted a County Commissioner. According to the County spokesperson, the contract between IP and the County had expired in 2009. IP had not been using landfill gas, but the landfill still accepted IP ash, usually 300 cubic yards a day, at no charge. To be allowed to dump this ash for free was just another perk the county was giving to IP.

Because of the change in production at the mill from 100% bleached paper to mostly brown linerboard, we thought that a new permit should have been issued. We argued that the old permit was moot or "not applicable". IP countered that with less bleaching, there was going to be less BOD. However, we knew that TSS (Total Suspended Solids) would increase, as would saltiness, color, and sulfate from the smoke stacks. TSS was no longer an issue with the regulators. We were also concerned that all the modeling and "assurances" which had been used to issue the permit documents were no longer applicable. The modeling had been down on a bleach effluent. The effluent was changing to unbleached (with a bleached component) but with an increase in production. The minor permit revision which IP was going to present to us in August 2006 had not yet been filed in October 2006. Our attorney, Howard Heims, asked that the proceedings be abated (postponed) until IP had filed their "minor permit revision" and the DEP and EPA had time to review the change. A new judge was assigned to the case in September 2005. His name was Bram D.E. Cantor.

On October 14, 2005, IP filed their "minor permit revisions" with the Division of Administrative Hearings.

Production was going to increase from 1500 air dried tons of bleach pulp to 2000 air dried tons of bleached and unbleached. But the mixture of bleached to unbleached was different than what had been filed in the air permit. IP was anticipating making 1,570 air-dried tons of unbleached pulp and 441 tons of bleached pulp. Later during the deposition of Mike Steltenkamp, Environmental supervisor at the mill, we would learn that IP planned to increase production to 2,500 air dried tons. This increased production was going to increase BOD (Biological Oxygen Demand) and TSS (Total Suspended Solids) in the mill effluent and other chemicals, but the environmental agencies seemed unconcerned. We anticipated dissolved oxygen in Perdido Bay would be worse, not better. To calculate the amount of BOD and TSS which would be allowed using these production figures, IP had gone to using "categorical" limits. These were the limits, which under the Clean Water Act had been termed technology-based. The Clean Water Act has two types of limits for "conventional pollutants, BOD (biological oxygen demand) and TSS (Total Suspended Solids). Technology based limits were calculated for BOD and TSS from what the EPA considered the best performing mills. The amount of BOD and TSS allowed was based on paper mill production. The environment into which the mill discharged was not considered. The Clinton EPA, under Carol Browner, had re-evaluated the paper mills' technology in the early 1990's and set new "technology-based limits". The paper mill in Cantonment Florida had been considered in the top 20 % of the best performing mills. The problem in using this method to set limits is that it does not encourage industries to do better than their peers. You might be able to increase your performance by using a new technology, but then you would put your peers in a bad light. Using this method for establishing limits is basically encouraging "technology fixing".

The other set of limits which the Clean Water Act uses is "Water Quality Based Effluent Limitations (WQBELs). According to the Clean Water Act, if technology-based effluent limits are not stringent enough and result in violations to water quality parameters, especially dissolved oxygen, then modeling had to be done to establish the correct limits. This had always been the case on Perdido Bay where for years it was known that the BOD and TSS in the paper mill effluent had caused oxygen depletion especially in the deeper waters. The Champion people had been ordered to do a full water quality model on Perdido Bay. However, the modeling was faulty. The modeler, Tom Gallagher from Hydroqual, ignored the oxygen consuming properties of Total Suspended Solids, which settled to the bottom of the bay. He only looked at the 5-day BOD and did not consider the long-term oxygen consumption which the paper mill fibers were having on the bottom of the bay. His model didn't even have the thousands of pounds of solids which IP sends to the bay, settle out in the bay. He claimed in court hearings that the solids just disappeared or went to the Gulf. According to his models, the bay was not going to meet the water quality standards for dissolved oxygen, especially in the deeper waters, with or without IP's solids contribution.

The bay was already polluted; what it would have been like without the sludge deposits of the paper mill was impossible to determine from this modeling exercise. With the faulty modeling, Gallagher found that IP's effluent would only depress the dissolved oxygen "a little bit". Livingston also never identified the carbonaceous (BOD and TSS) sources from the paper mill as causing problems. He kept emphasizing nutrients, nitrogen and phosphorus. So, with the increase in production, the DEP and EPA were allowing the mill to argue that "technology-based" limits applied in the wetlands and Perdido Bay. According to DEP's permitting expert, the effluent was no longer going to be limited by the low flow in Elevenmile Creek. It was another "whitewash". For IP to make paper using "water quality-based effluent limits" would have made paper more expensive to produce. Perdido Bay was not a good location to discharge oxygen consuming products, as George Crozier from Dauphin Island had pointed out.

228

Nevertheless, DEP and EPA who are supposed to review the limits, agreed with IP. The limits which were in the proposed permit were stringent enough to *"protect the flora and fauna in the wetlands and contiguous waters"*, according to the environmental agencies. On November 21, 2005, IP announced that they and DEP were going to file small changes to the permit and Consent Order, but did not say what they were. On November 29, 2005, our attorney, Howard Heims, asked the judge to abate (stop) the proceedings until we were informed about the changes to the permit and Consent Order. We still had to find our witnesses and plan our case. A list of questions (Interrogatories) which I had sent to IP as part of discovery had come back with IP objecting to every single question. They did not answer any of them. We had tried to oblige IP and answer their interrogatories and requests for documents.

On December 1, 2005, Judge Cantor granted the continuance and put the case in abeyance (on ice) until January 13, 2006. On January 11, 2006, DEP filed amendments to the proposed Consent Order, Draft permit and Fact Sheet. We then amended our petitions for a second time. Part of the amendments included the use of 5 million gallons a day of water from ECUA in the IP process. With an increase in production, IP was going to need more water. ECUA's effluent did contain nutrients and BOD, but there was no calculation of how this was going to change the characteristics of the combined effluent which was going to the wetlands. The plan to build a 2.5 MGD wastewater treatment plant on an IP site had been scrapped. IP was going to use 5 MGD from the new Central Reclamation Wastewater Facility which was being built on Escambia Bay near the Monsanto (now Solutia) Plant. Post-Hurricane Ivan FEMA money had helped move the old Main Street Plant to a new site.

On March 17, 2006, the judge filed the Order of pre-hearing instructions. We were getting ready to begin the hearing

229

May 31, 2006, over a year and a half since we had filed our petitions. With the change in process, the characteristics of the effluent had to change, even though IP's attorneys said the effluent was similar to the old effluent. There were probably less chlorinated by-products because there was less bleaching, but unbleached effluent with pine has its own toxic resins and acids. Perhaps less dioxin would be produced, but we were not sure. Dioxin in rather high quantities had been found in the paper mill sludges washed onto people's properties after Hurricane Ivan in 2004. IP was reporting that dioxin was not detectable in their whole effluent but dioxin was associated with the TSS (sludges) and diluted sufficiently in the whole effluent. We knew that dioxin-laden sludges would be deposited in the wetlands. I wondered if the attorneys in Ester's lawsuit, which was on-going, had any influence on IP's changing processes. I knew the Levin and NRDC attorneys wanted the mill to stay open, but did not want the effluent going to Escambia Bay.

All sides handed in their witness lists, opinions, and documents which would be presented at a hearing. I noticed that two of DEP's witnesses were EPA administrators who we had been writing all these years to try and get some help. The rats were going to testify against us. My husband and I made a trip to Stuart, FL so we could take all our documents and the documents which we had copied from DEP's files to Howard Heims. We discussed the strategy in the case. Howard Heims and Marcy LaHart were going to present the case for my husband and Friends of Perdido Bay. I was going to present the case for our children and myself. I had decided to concentrate on the high levels of BOD and TSS which the mill was putting out and the detrimental effect this was going to have both on the wetlands and Perdido Bay where we were raising our children. Right away IP filed a motion to eliminate certain witnesses which we had deemed experts.

Two of the witnesses which we had listed, were experts which the Levin Firm had hired to study Perdido Bay.

Unfortunately, the two witnesses would not testify for us unless the Levin firm agreed to let them testify. The Levin firm never agreed so we had to drop those witnesses. Several of our witnesses were the biologists who were working for DEP. Even though they had stopped testing the bay, they were aware of what had happened to Perdido Bay over the years. The permit limits had not changed since the 1983 permit so the damage would be the same. Howard Heims and Marcy hired an environmental expert, Barry Sulkin. He had read all the permitting documents and was going to testify that the permit limits were not protective of the wetlands, the receiving waters of Perdido Bay, and Tee and Wicker marsh lakes. But for some reason, IP was incensed that we had a long list of witnesses. Some of our witnesses backed out at the end, but we figured we had enough to prove our case.

The hearing began on May 31, 2006. It ran discontinuously for 11 days. Twenty-one volumes of hearing transcripts were produced with 3077 pages. The hearing cost us (the Petitioners) approximately $184,000. Nearly $150,000 of the costs came from the Perdido Bay Foundation which was established through settlement of the lawsuit against Champion Paper Company in 1995. The remaining $35,000 came from donations of Perdido Bay citizens ($11,000) and from the Lane family ($23,000). Most of the costs were attorney's fees ($95,000), although our attorneys tried to be frugal. They even stayed at our house for the first couple of days. Our expert witnesses usually charged approximately $2,500 for their testimony. The hearing transcripts also were expensive.

IP presented its case first. They had five witnesses including their modeling expert, Tom Gallagher, the biologist, Dr. Livingston, and the wetland expert Dr. Nutter. DEP had one expert, Bill Evans who had reviewed the permit. Our side had ten experts and five fact witnesses. The fact witnesses testified about the terrible drift algae blooms we had during the 1990's and the general decline in the bay. Col. Howell, one of our fact

231

witnesses, testified about the dangers of swimming in the bay and how he gotten infections. The DEP biologists who testified described how Perdido Bay was overwhelmed by the organic matter coming from the paper mill. They said that the bay was the most polluted and had the lowest species diversity of any bay in the state of Florida. They testified that most of the solids deposited occurred in the lower bay but that the high BOD caused oxygen depletion in the upper bay. Bill Chandler, the DEP chemist, said that he had run long-term BOD tests on the paper mill effluent and that the BOD after 100 days was often ten times higher than the BOD after five days. The permit limits for BOD are for a five-day limit only. To refute the argument of Dr. Livingston that high BOD which caused low dissolved oxygen was coming from the Gulf, the biologist, Glen Butts described how he and other biologists went out and measured BOD and Total Organic Carbon throughout the bay. The highest BOD (oxygen consuming material) was found in the upper bay, not the lower bay. Glen Butts also testified that he thought toxic substances were involved in the paucity of life in Perdido Bay.

Most of our case focused on the harm which IP's effluent was having and still would have on Perdido Bay after discharging to the wetlands. We also tried to show that the same problems which IP was having in Elevenmile Creek would also occur in the wetlands and the small streams. According to state law, IP had to affirmatively demonstrate that they would not have an "adverse" effect on the flora and the fauna of the wetlands. Don Ray, a Florida state biologist who had sampled the IP wetlands and the small streams there, testified that IP's effluent would have an even more adverse effect on these little streams than it was having in Elevenmile Creek. This caused a serious difference of opinion between IP's expert, Dr. Wade Nutter, and Don Ray (our expert). According to Dr. Nutter, whose team of biologists, geologists and hydrologists had designed the IP wetlands, no streams existed on the site. When Mr. Ray pointed to the "stream" on a map, Dr. Nutter claimed it was a fire break. A large fire had occurred on the wetlands in 2001.

Dr. Livingston, who was continuing his study of Perdido Bay along with Tee and Wicker Lakes, stuck to his story that toxic algae blooms caused by excessive nutrients released by the mill were causing the detrimental effects in the bay. His latest studies confirmed that life in the bay had declined still further from 2000. He also stuck with his story that salt water on the bottom of the bay was responsible for the low dissolved oxygen. Dr. Livingston also maintained that if IP achieved the limits for soluble nitrogen and phosphorus which he had proposed for the permit, then the chronic blooms of toxic algae would cease. The only problem was - the mill had already achieved these limits, but the bay continued to decline. The limits for nitrogen and phosphorus which Livingston was proposing came from what Livingston termed as "good years" in Perdido Bay. The "good years" were 1988 and 1989 when Livingston claimed Perdido Bay had a healthy population of plankton. Another of our expert witnesses, Lawrence Donelan, testified that he had gotten complaints from citizens on Perdido Bay about algae blooming along the bay in the years 1988 through 1990. The bay, in the years 1988 and 1989, appeared to be over fertilized.

Dr. Nutter, whose team had designed the wetlands, had done a modeling exercise to determine the fate of nutrients in the wetlands. He found that nitrogen and phosphorus would be removed in the wetlands. We all expected this to happen. His modeling did not show if plants in the wetlands would be harmed by IP's effluent. In court testimony, he opined that the plants would not be harmed. There might be a small change in the flora, but over all things would be O.K. According to state law, the IP effluent was not supposed to have an adverse impact on the flora and fauna of the wetlands.

Occasionally during the testimony of witnesses, some interesting facts will emerge. One piece of information caught my attention. It seemed IP (or previously Champion) had shut down their tall oil extraction plant at the mill in 1999 and allowed this substance to remain in the effluent. Tall oil comes from pine trees and is very toxic. Tall oil is used to make paints, glues and other products. I thought, at the time, that tall oil present in the effluent could explain the toxicity of the effluent. Bill Evans, Florida DEP permitting engineer, did testify that IP's effluent was toxic about 37% of the time, i.e., it did not pass the toxicity tests. IP had not been required by EPA to ascertain the nature of this toxicity as EPA should have done. Another piece of information, which also came from Bill Evans, was the "public interest" requirement in the Florida environmental rules. When the DEP looked at "public interest", they only considered IP's interest as public and not citizen's interest as "public interest".

Dr. Livingston was not the only one doing studies in the bay. During the summer 2005, biologists from DEP had come to Perdido Bay to measure life in the bay for a program started in 2000 called "Total Maximum Daily Load" (TMDL). Bottom sampling was done at stations throughout the bay. One of the biologists was alarmed and called me to tell me that there was so little life, especially at the bay stations in the upper bay, that it looked like something toxic was being dumped. This information was presented at our hearing. From the testimony in Court:

"studies conducted by the Department as part of the Total Maximum Daily Limit analysis found an alarmingly low biodiversity in Perdido Bay. Only one species was found and that was a worm whereas significantly more would be expected in the Bay. Only one worm was found in the sediment compared to 36 organisms such as shrimp, arthropods, and worms, found in Escambia Bay next to an industrial outfall during the same time. The Bay was as bad if not worse since prior studies were conducted by the Department in 1988. There were low numbers of and very poor quality of animals in the sediment in Perdido Bay as recently as November 7, 2005." Later, when I tried to

get the DEP to use this study so that Perdido Bay could be put on the list of bays which did not meet aquatic life standards, the study had been "lost".

After the hearing ended July 28, 2006, all parties wrote "Proposed Recommended Orders," summarizing their arguments and presenting the evidence from the transcripts which supported their arguments. These Proposed Recommended Orders were sent to the Administrative Hearing Officer and due October 27, 2006. Our side felt good about how our case had been presented and we were hopeful that we would win. We certainly didn't want our bay to continue to be in such bad shape.

The Proposed Recommended Order of Friends of Perdido Bay and James Lane written by Howard Heims, was especially good at pointing out the flaws in DEP permitting and enforcement of the paper mill's discharges. Mr. Heims addresses the failure of the DEP to enforce the past Consent Order which issued in 1987.

"It was determined that the consent order (1987) as proposed by the department, with time constrains mandated therein, was a reasonable exercise of the Department's discretion under Section 403.151. The Department and the paper mill were ordered to comply with the compliance schedule in Paragraph 14 of the consent order. The compliance schedule in the Consent Order was not followed and the paper mill did not complete corrective action and the paper mill has still not come into compliance with all applicable standards and criteria as required by Paragraph 14F. No documentary evidence of a modification was submitted into evidence in this proceeding which would constitute a valid modification to the terms of the Consent Order. (Paragraph 34 of the Consent Order). 136. Accordingly, this Court cannot ignore, and is bound by its prior ruling, that the paper mill must be in compliance with all applicable water quality standards as of this time. The proposed permit under review in this case and associated agency actions authorize the continued violation of water quality standards

indefinitely in violation of this Court's prior Order." Mr. Heims writes: *"International Paper is currently operating without a valid permit. Rule 62-620.1000(2) (I), F.A.C. (Florida Administrative Code), mandates that the expiration of the facility's most recent permit is the date the 1983 permit expired. The Department claims that International Paper Company is operating under a 1983 permit yet on its face, the 1983 permit expired on January 3, 1988."*

In August, 2006, a public hearing was held before the Escambia County Commissioners to issue pollution control bonds to IP so they could proceed with their "improvements". All IP needed was the permit. All parties had timely submitted on October 27, 2006, the Proposed Recommended Orders. Normally, administrative law judges can read the all documents and issue a Recommended Order in six to eight weeks. The Final Order would be issued by the Secretary of DEP. Most of the time the Final Orders were issued about one month after the Recommended Order. These Final Orders could be appealed in the First District Court of Appeals. However, our case was big with complex issues and 11 days of testimony.

On January 10, 2007, we got a notice from Judge Canter informing us that he had been given extra duties which delayed his Recommended Order. The local community, i.e. Pensacola, was getting impatient. A Sunday January 28, 2007 edition of the Pensacola News Journal featured a two-page article about the conversion of the IP paper mill from white paper to cardboard. The headline read: *"From white paper to cardboard. International paper cuts back on paper production as its demand decreases."* Actually, this headline was misleading. From the hearing testimony, IP planned to increase total production; only white paper production was going to decrease. The side bar explained the new product. By April or May,
"IP's Cantonment plant is expected to stop producing uncoated paper - the kind used in copy machines. By September, it will begin producing 500,000 tons a year of lightweight brown

linerboard. Linerboard paper, used in cardboard, is faster and more efficient to produce than copy paper and does not require the use of imported hardwood. It will help the plant remain competitive for the foreseeable future, plant officials say." The article said that the linerboard produced at the Cantonment mill will be shipped to 10 International Paper box plants, including the plant at Bay Minette, Alabama, just north of the mill. The various articles also mentioned that the conversion to brown paper will result in a decrease in the number of employees: 421 compared to 650 two years ago[2].

At its height in the 1970's, the mill employed 1,200 employees. According to the Pensacola News Journal, the conversion cost the company $220 million. The equipment was being purchased in Germany and shipped over by ship. According to the article, Chris Read, the mill manager, hoped the change to linerboard would change the fortunes of the mill. *"I would like to get on a growth path."* As the article explained, *"For the past decade, the paper industry has struggled, in part, because of overcapacity, and in part because of low prices".* The headline of the article on the second page was *"Paper plant is Cantonment's lifeblood".* Paper mill officials predicted that the permit could be approved as early as late February, 2007.

Since IP had gone ahead and ordered the equipment for conversion to brown paper, the project was going to proceed, with or without a permit. IP had gotten their air permit approved for the conversion to unbleached paper and for the increase in production in the Fall of 2006. We had challenged this air permit but were denied standing. I doubted IP was going to send the equipment back if they didn't get their permit. But, the administrative law judge was going to make people wait.

On February 26, 2007, all parties to the administrative hearing got a request from Judge Canter to help clarify a legal issue in the use of the "experimental wetland rule." In his order, Judge Canter wanted to know why the exemption order was necessary and whether the wetland exemption could be issued before IP affirmatively demonstrated which standards more appropriately applied to the wetland tract. We had until March 16th to answer the Judge's questions. All parties argued that the wetland exemption was necessary. I thought Howard Heims arguments were particularly succinct and to the point.

"Failure to set water quality criteria and standards prior to issuance of the permit and Exemption creates an enforcement impossibility. Without specific and identified water quality standards and criteria, there can be no enforcement. There are not any assurances that no harm will happen to the environment." (Page 3). He further writes: *"IP is in an untenable predicament. They have acknowledged that their background monitoring has not yet been completed. They have not yet determined or quantified what a "healthy biological community "is. They have also established only interim limits based on monitoring that has yet to be concluded." (Page 5). "12. The Department seems to take the position that a Consent Order can be used to delay the need for an applicant to set standards and criteria or provide reasonable assurances that all water quality standards and rules will be met." (Page 6). "13. What the Department fails to recognize is that it cannot exceed its delegated authority by attempting to circumvent the rule-making process through issuance of consent orders and exemptions. The Department fails to recognize that it is not authorized to legislate by consent order." (Page 6).*

In agreement with Mr. Heims remarks, I had thought the hearing was premature. I did not think that IP was well-prepared to defend the position that they were not going to cause damage to the wetland fauna and flora. However, the hearing did one thing; it postponed the date that the permit and Consent Order finally went into effect.

The Judge finally issued his recommended order on May 11, 2007. Two years had passed since issuance of the permitting documents in April of 2005. I am sure his ruling shocked many people. Judge Canter denied the permit, the Consent Order, the authorization for the experimental use of wetlands and the IP's petition for a waiver. It was a blowout. I was shocked as well. This was the first time we had won anything in the administrative hearing process. In his 94-page Recommended Order, Judge Canter agreed with much of IP's case at the hearing, however he wrote:

"IP did not provide reasonable assurances that the proposed permit would not cause the Perdido River to be significantly degraded. 205. IP did not provide reasonable assurances that the mill's effluent would be assimilated so as not to cause significant adverse impact on the biological community within the wetland tract." Further, the Judge determined that IP did not make a sufficient showing that the project was in the public interest. The contingency plan allowing IP to go back into Elevenmile Creek if the wetlands were harmed was pre-authorized in the permit, but without any reasonable assurances that this plan would be appropriate.

Despite our victory, I was troubled by many of the hearing officer's findings of fact and conclusions of law. Judge Canter gave more weight to IP's evidence than to ours. He accepted all of Livingston's evidence and statements, even the argument about the streams in the wetlands being firebreaks and not steams (Page 94). The Judge agreed with Livingston's expert opinion that the BOD from the paper mill had little or no impact on the bottom dissolved oxygen in the bay (P. 49). The BOD and TSS limits in the permit were O.K. The Judge accepted Livingston's determination that the nutrient levels in 1988 and 1989 were "good years for nutrients." In Finding of Fact 105, the judge writes:

"Petitioners dispute that 1988 and 1989 are appropriate benchmarks years for developing the WQBELs (Water Quality Based Effluent Limitations) because Petitioners claim there were high nutrient loadings and algae blooms in those years. Mr. Ray testified that the Department received citizen complaints about algae blooms in those years. Dr. Livingston's analysis was more

persuasive, however, because it distinguished types of algae blooms according to their harmful effect on the food web and was based on considerably more water quality and biological data." We had also presented nutrient data from 1971 to 1994 to show that the nutrients in 1988 and 1989 were higher than in previous years. Livingston had started sampling Perdido Bay in 1988 and 1989. The Judge just discounted all our data and testimony.

The Judge went into a lengthy summary of the Regulatory History of the Mill. According to Judge Canter's interpretation, the mill still had a valid permit, as opposed to Howard Heim's interpretation that the permit had expired. In Finding of Fact 40, the Judge opines:

"Over 14 years after the deadline established in the 1989 TOP (Temporary Operating Permit) for the mill to be in compliance with all applicable standards in Elevenmile Creek, IP is still not meeting all applicable standards. However, the combination of (1) Consent Order terms that contemplated unspecified future permit requirements based on yet-to-be-conducted studies, (2) the wording in the TOP that tied the deadline for compliance to the expiration of the TOP, and the administrative extension of the TOP, kept the issue of Champion's and IP's compliance in a regulatory limbo. It increased the Department's discretion to determine whether IP was in compliance with the laws enacted to protect the State's natural resources, and reduced the opportunity of interested persons to formally disagree with that determination."

According to state law, permits are only supposed to be issued for five years. The Judge was giving the environmental agencies an excuse for not enforcing the 1987 permit and Consent Order.

After the Recommended Order, all parties can rebut the findings in the Recommended Order. Typically, Exceptions to the Recommended Order correct or rebut each numbered paragraph in the recommended order, which is considered in error. If findings in the Recommended Order are not based on

240

evidence presented at the hearing, then the Judge's Findings are not based on competent substantial evidence and can be challenged in the District Court of Appeals. The Exceptions to the Recommended Order were due May 29, 2007. Howard Heims exceptions written for Petitioners James Lane and Friends of Perdido Bay were especially good. Mr. Heims continues to assert that the paper mill should have come into compliance with all state laws after the 1989 Consent Order expired. He said they should not be allowed to "experiment" without meeting state rules for another 108 months. Further, establishment of nutrient water quality based effluent limits (WQBELs) for Perdido Bay, based on nutrient data from 1988 and 1989, as Livingston proposed, was not supported by any substantial or competent evidence presented at trial.

"...Mr. Ray testified that there were algae blooms in those years. It is undisputed that there were algae blooms in those years. Years in which there are algae blooms could not possibly be used for establishing such important Water Quality Based Effluent Limitations. The paragraph should state:

Petitioners dispute that 1988 and 1989 are appropriate benchmark years for developing the WQBELs because Petitioners claim there were high nutrient loadings and algae blooms in those years. Mr. Ray testified that the Department received citizen complaints about algae blooms in those years. Photographs were introduced into evidence by Petitioners showing foam and scum in Perdido Bay at the time. This foam and scum was a nuisance and violated water quality standards. These facts establish that 1988 and 1989 were not appropriate benchmark years for determining the WQBELs. The Department should have followed its practice of requiring a Chlorophyll A analysis when setting WQBELs."

As far as IP's effluent not causing low dissolved oxygen in the bottom waters of Perdido Bay, Mr. Heims rebuts this. He wrote that the evidence which Livingston used to determine IP's contribution to the bottom sediments was based on research and a paper which was never presented at the hearings and was hearsay. Furthermore, Mr. Heims writes,

"...the Administrative Law Judge applied the wrong test. The test is not whether the mill effluent "is the primary source of the sediment and low DO in Perdido Bay. The test is whether IP failed to provide reasonable assurances that it will not contribute to a reduction in water quality standards. The Paragraphs should be replaced with a single paragraph which states:

IP failed to provide reasonable assurances or to make a prima facia showing that its mill effluent will not contribute to the sediments and low DO (dissolved oxygen) in Perdido Bay and cause violations of water quality standards."

The mutagenic effect of paper mill effluent on certain fish species in Elevenmile Creek had been well documented by researchers. Certain female fish exhibited male characteristics and behavior when exposed to high levels of effluents pulping with pine. The issue had died away; nevertheless, it was brought up at the hearing. IP's engineer, Kyle Moore, confirmed at the hearing that there was a problem with the changing sex of fish in the past. There was an exhibit, entered into evidence by DEP, which helped support the problem. *"IP cannot fail to investigate the matter and then claim that there is no evidence that there is a problem. "Paragraph 129 should be replaced with: IP failed to provide reasonable assurances that mutagenic compounds in the mill's effluent will not cause adverse impacts on aquatic life in the future if the permit is approved."*

The issue of Klebsiella bacteria which was found in paper mill effluent in Elevenmile Creek, but dismissed by Judge Canter as no longer an issue was also raised by Mr. Heims. He wrote"

"IP must provide reasonable assurances that there will not be a violation of water quality standards and a public health concern. The paragraph should state:

242

IP failed to provide reasonable assurances that the presence of Klebsiella bacteria will not create a public health problem." Mr. Heims also pointed out that the same argument should have been made for coliform bacteria (*Klebsiella* is a coliform) in Tee and Wicker marsh lakes which were going to be used by the public for recreation.

International Paper and DEP also wrote exceptions to the Judge's recommended order. I agreed with many of DEP's exceptions. As the DEP's attorneys wrote, the Judge denied the permitting documents on rather minor points. The Judge made his rulings as "Findings of Fact" from the evidence presented at the hearing when they really should have been conclusions of law. Findings of Fact are not appealable unless not based on evidence from the hearing; conclusions of law are appealable. DEP pointed out that a "deference" rule recognizes that policy considerations are left to the discretion of the agency and may take precedence over findings of fact given by the administrative law judge. In the end, DEP sought more hearings (remand) so the administrative law judge could correct the problems with his recommended order. All parties wrote responses to the other parties' exceptions. It was now June 8, 2007 and we were waiting for the Final Order to come out of the Secretary of DEP, who was Michael Sole. Michael Sole had replaced David Struhs who was now Vice President for the Environment at IP.

Someone had forwarded on to us a comment that David Struhs had made to the news media. He had said that *"in any other part of the world, International Paper's efforts to clean up would be celebrated and win awards."* I answered him in letter dated May 31, 2007. I said first, we did not trust promises by the paper mill.

"Thirty-five years ago, St Regis Paper Company, then owners of the Cantonment mill, took out a full-page ad in the Wall Street Journal saying they were going to turn the mill into a completely closed system - no wastewater at all was going to leave the mill. That never happened. Eighteen years ago,

243

Champion International bought the mill from St. Regis and promised to come into compliance with all state regulations by 1995. That never happened. After International Paper took over the ownership of the mill in 2000, most of the grass beds died, the clams in the upper bay died, and bottom life in the upper bay declined to near zero. We were told it was a drought, but today things haven't improved. And International paper is still violating the same regulations which Champion promised to fix." I am not sure what effect these letters had on David Struhs, but I always felt better after writing them.

While we had been busy fighting IP's plan in Court, several other events had occurred. IP was not the only paper mill seeking to build a pipeline. Two other paper mills in Florida, Buckeye Cellulose in Perry, Florida, and Georgia Pacific in Palatka, Florida, were seeking to build pipelines to larger bodies of water. Buckeye wanted to build a 15-mile pipeline to the Gulf of Mexico thereby bypassing the small stream they were in. Georgia Pacific wanted to pipe their effluent to the Indian River on Florida's east coast and bypass the small stream they were in. Both were probably bad ideas. Buckeye's pipeline plans had been approved by DEP the year before. Sierra Club and other environmentalists had taken this ruling to Federal Court in the District of Columbia. The judge in Federal Court had ruled against the pipeline. This meant that the EPA would take over the permit and hopefully not allow the pipeline to the Gulf. Linda Young, who was director of the Clean Water Network, said she would fight in court until Buckeye was required to clean up their effluent. The response from Buckeye was the standard response which all paper mills give: *"There is no other combination of technologies that would bring the river to fishable and swimmable standards."*[3] There were, but the paper industry didn't want to pay for them. The mills were determined to try and block any advancement in clean-up technologies. I was wondering if we should have gone to Federal Court instead of trying to fight our pipeline in

244

Florida's administrative Court. But there was always the issue of expense.

Much of the news about IP's plans to convert to brown paper came from news in the Pensacola News Journal, and not from documents presented in court. On January 10, 2007, an article appeared: "Paper Mill to Switch Production This Spring"[4]. The article said that IP planned to discontinue producing white office paper in April or May 2007. IP was going to start producing cardboard in the fall (2007). They were also going to continue making bleached "fluff" pulp for disposable diapers and related products. The company had announced their conversion to brown paper in 2005. The article said: *"The company is realigning its North American mill system to increase operational efficiencies and provide capital to the most-competitive lowest-cost facilities"*. I thought that this shouldn't be the case with the mill in Cantonment. This mill should cost more to operate because it discharges into a small bay which would require more treatment. IP also announced the sale of one of their subsidiaries, Arizona Chemical, to Rhone Capital. There was an Arizona Plant in Pensacola which took the Tall Oil from the papermaking process and turned it into usable chemicals for paint, chewing gum. IP was also selling their lumber mills to West Fraser.   There was a lumber mill about 5 miles north of the IP paper mill. We also found out that IP had sold their paper mills making glossy paper to Cerberus Capital Management.

On August 8, 2007, the Final Order of the Secretary of Florida's DER (Department of Environmental Protection) came out. We were elated. The Secretary, Michael Sole's Final Order, (it is written by DEP attorneys) had upheld the Administrative Law Judge's ruling to deny the permit and related documents. It was a real victory for our side. However, there were still problems with the Final Order. While we had agreed with the outcome, the acceptance of the water quality based effluent limits (WQBELs) for nutrients based on

245

Livingston's "good years" was not good. We had written exceptions to limits based on these years, but as the Secretary said in his order, if there was any "competent substantial evidence" presented in court, he could not overturn the ruling of the administrative law judge. "Competent substantial evidence" could be any evidence. Even though we had presented contrary evidence at the hearing, the administrative law judge, as a trier of fact, agreed with Livingston. The Final Order acknowledges the weight the administrative law judge placed on the Livingston studies.

"In the RO (Recommended Order), the ALJ (Administrative Law Judge) acknowledged that IP has sponsored a comprehensive study of the Perdido Bay system by an independent team of scientists. The team was led by Dr. Robert Livingston, an aquatic ecologist and professor at Florida State University. Dr. Livingston's studies developed a chemical and biological history of the Bay with the aim of correlating the impact of the paper mill's discharge on the health of the Bay. The ALJ described the Livingston Studies as 'perhaps the most complete scientific evaluation ever made of a coastal ecosystem.'"

"The ALJ gave great weight to the Livingston Studies and concluded that the proposed permit would significantly improve the Perdido Bay system. However, the ALJ ultimately concluded that additional evidence was necessary in order for IP to demonstrate compliance with all applicable Department standards and rules."

Friends of Perdido Bay had sent out press releases announcing our "victory" to all media outlets. As far as we knew, none of the media had announced the results of the hearing. In his Final Order, Mr. Sole, went through all parties' exceptions and rejected most of them. He rejected DEP's request for remand (more hearings). He did grant IP's exception which said that the ALJ did error when he found that IP had not made an adequate showing concerning the Perdido River. The Perdido River was listed as a Florida Outstanding Water in 1979

and had special protections. IP had to show that they were not
going to impact the river. With these rejects, I wondered what IP
was going to do. Operate without a permit? IP had told us that
they were not going to start the conversion to brown paper unless
they had a permit by April 2007. I wondered what was
happening at the paper mill. IP had already spent $200 million
on the project. Had they started to make brown paper?

The answer to my question came the very next day. IP
appealed the decision to the First District Court of Appeals in
Tallahassee on August 10, 2007. They also sought a stay of the
Final Order from DEP pending the outcome of the appeal. DEP
granted the stay of the Final Order on August 22, 2007 saying it
would be a hardship for the mill to shut down. The paper mill
was back to operating on a temporary operating permit and
consent order which had been issued in 1989 after the very first
administrative hearing 18 years previously, or 1983, (for the
federal permit). It was difficult to know on what permit IP was
operating, but it was absurd, nonetheless. A Florida statute, i.e.,
Statute 403.088, does allow for non-compliance with Florida's
water quality standards for a short time (five years) so that
problems can be fixed and a discharger can come into
compliance with state laws. However, the extended period of
time which this mill had to come into compliance, was
extraordinary. However, I had to remember that the
environmental agency which had oversight over this permit and
this mill was EPA. Back in 1995, the EPA and DEP had a
Memorandum of Understanding which forbids DEP from
changing the limits in the permit without EPA approval. So
ultimately EPA was the culprit. At this time, the president of the
U.S. was George Bush and the Governor of Florida was Charlie
Crist.

After IP gave Notice of its intent to file an appeal, our
attorney, Ms. LaHart, also decided to file a cross appeal. Since
we had "won" the hearing, we could not appeal any issues we
did not agree with, such as the ruling that IP was without impact

on Perdido Bay, or the years of 1988 and 1989 were "good" years for nutrients on Perdido Bay. Marci LaHart wanted to challenge the constitutionality (Florida Constitution) of the Statute 403.088. She thought this statute was internally inconsistent. In one part, the statute requires compliance with water quality standard to get a permit but then in another part, allows dischargers to operate even if they are violating standards, if they are fixing the problem. Ms. LaHart's cross appeal was filed shortly after IP's Notice of Appeal on August 29, 2007. I thought her challenge was an unnecessary expenditure of our money since it did little to correct the unfavorable rulings in the Final Order.

Several weeks before the Final Order came out, the Judge ruled in the big lawsuit which was proceeding in Circuit Court called Ester's suit (see Chapter 11 "Ester's lawsuit"). The Judge ruled that the lawsuit could not proceed as a class action. At the time, I was not aware of the stipulations which had been made between the attorneys for both sides nearly a year before saying that this was not a class.

The appeals process in our administrative hearing with IP began with the losing party, IP, arguing why the ruling of the ALJ was wrong. This was called the initial brief and was filed December 18, 2007. IP argued that the ALJ's rejection of the permitting documents was based on narrow issues and was not supported by competent substantial evidence. Further, IP's attorney argued that we hadn't raised the issues of harming the wetlands in our petitions for a hearing. We, then, had to answer IP's arguments in an Answer Brief. To save expenditures, I was now doing the legal work for the Petitioners, which included my husband and Friends of Perdido Bay. In my responding brief, I could only answer IP's arguments from its Initial Brief. I could not bring up new issues which IP had not raised in its Initial Brief. It was frustrating, because I could not raise the issues in which the ALJ had ruled against us such as nutrient levels in Perdido Bay.

While we were waiting for the appeals process to wind its way through court, researchers from University of West Florida (UWF) published several studies on contaminates in seafood in local bays. The researchers had looked at dioxin and PCB levels in oysters, mullet and bass in the local bays and rivers. While the mullet in Perdido River were not as contaminated as mullet in Escambia Bay, the measured levels of dioxin/PCB's in Perdido River were above the recommended safe levels for eating. Elevated mercury was also found in the Perdido River bass. Fish from Perdido Bay were not tested and oysters could not be found in Perdido Bay. The researchers attributed mercury found to the burning of coal by the local power utility. IP also used coal/ wood for its power boilers. Although we have no oysters in most parts of Perdido Bay (They occasionally show up in lower Perdido Bay, but quickly disappear.), Friends of Perdido Bay decided to test the marsh clam from Perdido Bay for dioxins and heavy metals. A few clams had settled on the bottom since a mass mortality in 1986. (See Chapter 2. The Mass Mortality of Clams). Our tests of the clams showed that dioxin levels were five times higher than the safe level for eating recommended by UWF researchers. The heavy metals arsenic, mercury and chromium, were higher in clams from Perdido Bay than oysters from Escambia Bay. One is not supposed to eat the shellfish from Perdido Bay, but some people do. As I write this book, clams in the bottom of Perdido Bay are few to none, and if you do find some, eating them is not recommended.

Supposedly IP was now (in early 2007) producing mainly brown paper with some bleach. Only pine was being used to make the fiber and no hardwoods. I could see no improvement in life in the bay. Foam looked worse, especially after heavy rainfall. Years before, a Champion employee told me why the paper mill could not go to 100% unbleached product. They still had to do some bleaching. The chemical companies which sold sodium for pulping also produced chloride by splitting sodium chloride. If the paper mills bought only sodium, then there would be an excess of the chloride product. If the paper companies wanted to get a discount on the sodium product, they would have to use some chloride (for bleaching) product as well. So, the paper companies had to do some bleaching to get their discount on sodium. It sounded reasonable to me.

DRIFT ALGAE DURING SPRING, LANE'S BEACH

CHAPTER 13 ~ Second Administrative Hearing

Bad news came in December, 2007, when International Paper applied for another permit, the second one. The permit was basically the same as the one reject by the Administrative Law Judge and DEP secretary. There were no changes in the permit limits. IP was requesting a few more exemptions to certain water quality standards in the wetlands. The only change from the first situation was that IP's researchers, Drs. Nutter and Livingston, had completed their studies on the background sites in the wetlands and on the Tee and Wicker marsh lakes. How this data was going to show that IP's effluent was not going to have an "adverse" impact on the fauna and flora of the wetlands was not apparent. But it seemed we were going to have to do the hearing all over again.

Once International Paper's second permit application was submitted to DEP, the permitting process went a lot faster than the first. When I read some of the new documents, my heart sank. The new documents made it appear as if IP was no longer discharging to Perdido Bay because they were discharging to a wetland. IP was no longer a "point "source discharger according to the permitting documents. The BOD limits in the permit were no longer limited by the small creek into which IP discharged; it stated they were discharging to a wetland. I wondered how the DEP could discount the small streams in the wetland. The wetland was not going to absorb any of IP's effluent except during very dry periods, but rather add fresh water to the effluent. Added water from the wetlands, plus IP's 23 million gallons a day of effluent, was still going to enter Perdido Bay, about 70 % through the little marsh lakes, Tee and Wicker, and 30% through the lower part of Elevenmile Creek. IP was still requesting to stay in Elevenmile Creek for the first two years until the pipeline to the wetlands was built. IP was going to set up a committee to evaluate the studies which were supposed to come out of the wetlands (It was being touted as "experimental") to determine if harm was being done to the wetlands. Background stations inside and outside the wetlands were set up and had been sampled for several years. Unfortunately, most of the background stations had already been impacted by the discharges from the paper mill. The reports, coming out were titled, "Non-Significant Adverse Impact." If the reports showed "Significant Adverse Impacts" would they be renamed? I was worried that the fix was in; this time we were going to lose. But we still had to oppose it. Our attorneys were still fighting the appeals from the first hearing and the legal bills were still coming in.

The Florida Department of Environmental Protection (DEP) scheduled a public hearing for IP's second permit for May 13, 2008. Although the U.S. Fish and Wildlife still opposed the project, we were unable to get an official O.K. to allow their experts to testify. Just before the public hearing, on Friday May 9, 2008, IP paid for a full-page ad[1] in the Pensacola News Journal. Their ad called this project *"A Water Quality Improvement Project."* It touted the amount of money IP had spent. *"In order to remain an important part of the local economy for years to come, we have committed $60 million to improve water quality and eliminate direct discharge of water into Elevenmile Creek. This is in addition to the $250 million IP spent in 2007 to convert it main production line to protect 500 local jobs for the foreseeable future...Once there (in the wetland), the treated water will be slowly distributed over 1,400 acres, eventually restoring part of the land to its historic hardwood wetland ecosystem. This wetland will naturally absorb and filter the water, and create a welcoming habitat for many native plants and wildlife."* After reading the ad, I wondered who could oppose this wonderful project? Certainly, not the Chamber of Commerce or the local politicians. There was a website set up to convince people further: www.protectourecosystem.com. Nothing in the ad said anything about meeting water quality standards, however, or about bringing the mill into compliance with state laws after nearly 20 years. David Struhs, DEP's ex-secretary of DEP, was still IP's Vice President for the Environment.

The next shock came on the Sunday preceding the public hearing on Tuesday May 13, 2008. The Pensacola News Journal carried two Viewpoint articles - one by geologist Peter Dohms who was the chair of Pensacola Area Chamber of Commerce's Environmental Committee, and the other was by Marcy LaHart, our attorney. She had not said anything to us about writing an article. I winced when I read Ms. LaHart's article. Peter Dohms' article was what you would expect from the Chamber of Commerce. He said the permit was great, claiming that IP could go with a direct pipeline to Perdido Bay and meet all Florida standards. This statement was untrue since a discharger had to prove that the effluent would not harm Perdido Bay and that would be very difficult to prove. Marcy LaHart's article was titled *"Winners have gained nothing."* I thought that this was a rather negative and discouraging perspective. According to her viewpoint, the hearings were gaining us nothing. This would make it more difficult for us to raise additional money for a new hearing. She pointed out that we would have to again spend thousands of dollars to fight the new permit while IP continued polluting. The new permit was basically the same as the denied permit. She pointed out IP closed a mill in Terre Haute Ind. because it was not competitive. *"Obviously, when it is in IP's economic interest to close a mill, it does so."*[2]

I wrote a Viewpoint article for the Pensacola News Journal in reply to Marci LaHart's letter. In mine, I pointed out the importance of Perdido Bay's citizens' involvement in the permitting process. If we had just trusted our environmental agencies to do the right thing, the paper mill would have had permits to pollute Perdido Bay long before this. I also pointed out that IP had never been able to meet standards and still would not. The wetlands plan was nothing more than an overland flow to Perdido Bay. My viewpoint was never printed.

The public hearing for the second IP permit was held at the University of West Florida Main Stage Theater Building on May 13, 2008, from 6 - 9 PM with the information session held two hours prior. As we did at the first hearing, my husband and I set up a booth to explain the flaws of the permit. As with the first permit, there were four parts: the permit, the Consent Order, the authorization for the experimental use of wetlands, and the waiver for not meeting two of the conditions in the experimental wetland rule. We advised our people to write letters as they would be as effective as addressing live a hostile crowd. We did expect a hostile crowd of local, bought-off politicians, as well as Chamber of Commerce people, mill workers and a few people from Escambia Bay who did not want this toxic stuff polluting their bay. There were approximately 12 people who stood up and spoke against the permit. I noticed that Tom Jorling, IP's old Vice President and creator of the plan, was there. The turn-out was not very large for either side.

Several days after the public hearing on May 18, 2008, the Pensacola News Journal ran an editorial agreeing with us - *"IP plan: Not the Best."*[3] The gist of the article pretty much summed up the situation. Nobody wanted the mill to close and jobs to be lost. The economic impact of tree farming to the area was important, but Perdido Bay was not an ideal recipient for millions of gallons a day of industrial wastewater because of its sluggish tidal flushing., but it was already degraded. International Paper supposedly was going to improve the effluent by running it through a wetland, but probably that was probably not going to be enough. The editorial ends with *"A better treatment plan (for IP) is the best solution."* But despite our and the Pensacola News Journal's attempts, IP had too many political allies. They didn't want to spend more money on treatment of its wastewater. We also knew they would not operate the mill at a loss. They would cut corners and DEP probably wouldn't do anything.

To encourage IP to remain in the area and "give them a

break", on May 1, 2008, the Escambia Board of County Commissioners enacted an ordinance granting a 10-year tax exemption to them. This was $1.4 million annual savings in property taxes for IP which would last until December 31, 2017. This essentially was corporate welfare. Beside the tax break, Escambia County was allowing IP to dump ash waste from burning of coal/wood, at the Escambia County landfill without cost. Then there was also the free use of 35 million gallons a day of high quality ground water creating a zone of depression in the groundwater of the area and in addition, the free use of pouring thousands of pounds of toxic pollutants into the local air, making Escambia County Number 18 in the country in toxic air pollutants (Other local industries contributed to this number as well)[4]. Finally, was the free discharge of their wastes into Perdido Bay making the bay unfit for recreational activities and lowering property values of people living there? If IP had to pay the local utility for treating the wastes properly, the corporation would be out of business.

Our biggest problem was the dishonest science which IP kept funding. Dr. Skip Livingston came out with his final report on his 19 years of work on Perdido Bay. It was titled *"Perdido Project: Final Report River, Bay and Marsh Analyses December 2007."*[5]
The report was honest in his analysis of the condition of Perdido Bay. *"The overall trends of the combined species richness index was down in all parts of the bay with lows reached during the final 3 years of sampling." (P. 155). "In some ways, the biological impacts were subtle; there were no fish kills or obvious signs of the plankton blooms. The bay simply slipped away without any observations by local residents or state and federal agencies. There was almost a complete collapse of the bay trophic organization that was associated with nutrient loading and plankton blooms. Infauna, invertebrates and fish numbers and species richness in various parts of the bay plummeted to levels never seen before in the 18-year sampling period." (P 264)* But Livingston continued to blame the decline

on the bloom of toxic algae, not on paper mill chemicals. We could see that life in the bay had declined and we continued to call this to the attention of the environmental agencies to no avail. Livingston admitted that since 1999, the paper mill had significantly reduced its discharge of nutrients, ammonia and orthophosphate. So why hadn't the decrease in nutrients helped to restore the bay? He completely ignored the chemicals International Paper was discharging. I kept wondering why EPA was not doing anything about this disaster since Livingston had documented the decline in life of the bay.

Tom Gallagher of Hydroqual also contributed to the false information through mathematical modeling of certain environmental parameters. Paper mill effluent, because of its high levels of suspended solids, is very turbid. This turbidity reduces the transparency of the water so that light does not penetrate. What we did not know at the time of the hearing, was the new, activated sludge treatment which IP was installing was going to increase the turbidity of the effluent. Solids coming from the activated sludge do not settle well. They are very fine, almost colloidal. Perhaps this is the reason IP took out its third and fourth settling ponds and decided to use a wetland. They hoped that the solids would be filtered out in the wetland. But the wetland had to meet Florida Standards for Class III waters: swimmable and fishable. Because turbidity was going to be worse, Gallagher's modeling was used to "hide" this fact. IP's models showed that turbidity was only going to increase "slightly" over background conditions. But background conditions were Elevenmile Creek and Perdido Bay as existed in 1990. State rules do not allow polluted bodies of water to be used as "background". I don't know if DEP ever accepted this modeling report, but IP was ready to use it during the hearing to show "no significant adverse impact to the wetlands".

The public, Chamber of Commerce, and the local politicians believed these reports that IP put out over the years beginning in1992. IP touted them as "independent, third party"

256

reports, but the funding came from IP. In later years, IP hired more "honest" experts and fired Dr. Livingston. Wade Nutter, who designed the wetlands and continued to monitor the wetlands after the effluent discharge began, was far more honest. Even though some of his "background" stations were a little suspect, overall his science was good and his evaluations correct.

About two months after the public hearing, on July 18, 2008, the DEP published its "Notice of Intent" to issue the permit, Consent Order, and related documents. The permit had not substantially changed from the first denied permit. Two hundred acres had been removed from the wetland area, and the berms which were going to be built in the wetlands to slow the flow of water were going to be lowered. At that time, the estimated travel time of the effluent across the wetland was three days. By the time the wetland was finally built, the travel time from release to the edge of the swamp lakes was less than 12 hours. In another addition to the plan, IP was going to set aside 1200 acres of forest land adjacent to the wetland as a conservation area to offset any damage they were going to do to endangered species in the wetland. I failed to see how 1200 acres of forest land was going to atone for the damages from this effluent. Furthermore, the statute under which IP was getting their permit (Chapter 403) did not recognize mitigation. IP was also seeking Water Quality Based Effluent Limits for nutrients into Perdido Bay based on Livingston's reports of good years in 1988 and 1989 when he said there were no toxic algae blooms. The limits for Biological Oxygen Demand (BOD) and Total Suspended Solids (TSS) were assumed to be O.K and not harm the bay.

The permitting packet contained some additional calculations and written assertions. One aspect of the first permit which had been turned down by the Administrative Judge was the antidegradation review. For this second permit, IP wrote that they were not required to do an "Antidegradation Review" because: "... *As a result of considerable improvement in wastewater quality and further passive treatment in the wetlands this project will provide an overall improvement of ambient water quality in Elevenmile Creek, Upper Perdido Bay and Lower Perdido River."* Therefore, according to IP's thinking, *"...an antidegradation analysis is not required for Elevenmile Creek, Perdido Bay and Perdido River, since water quality will be improved, not lowered."* I wondered: improved from when? I noticed these documents had been revised in March, 2008. Also, included in the packet of documents was IP's environmental policy for its Pensacola mill. The first and second points were: *"Protection of the environment is an essential and integral part of our overall business strategy"* and *"100% compliance with all environmental laws, regulations, and permits as required."*[6] This second, proposed permit was so open-ended that it was hard to know with which regulations IP had to comply. DEP was just allowing IP to disregard standards in the wetland.

The benefits of the proposed project included in the permit package sounded to me as if written for a travel brochure. *"The site will be planted with native wetland hardwood species in order to discourage invasion of opportunistic and exotic plants and trees. Residual nutrients in the effluent will have a beneficial effect on biological diversity and productivity. Maturation of the planted trees will return the site to a forested wetland environment.....The recovery of Upper Perdido Bay will be enhanced as nutrient loads to the Bay are significantly reduced and better dispersed......Construction of ECUA's new Water Reclamation Plant will allow the utility to serve growth in North Escambia County, reducing the use of septic tanks while avoiding a new surface water discharge to state waters."* It just sounded like paradise; unfortunately, none of it turned out to be true[6]. But maybe this was what it would take to win over the Judge's mind. It was a written document which would be considered as evidence in court documents.

I immediately applied for an administrative hearing. My objections to the permit were the same as in the original permit:

258

it was going to cause damage to the wetlands and the effluent would not be sufficiently treated to prevent damage to Perdido Bay. My husband and Friends of Perdido Bay also sought a hearing on the second proposed permit. He decided to use Marci LaHart as his and Friends of Perdido Bay's attorney. I was serving as my own attorney. However, we were faced with the fact that the hearing was going to cost money. The Friends of Perdido Bay had $3,000 in the treasury and the Perdido Bay Foundation had disbanded. Despite a shortage of funds, Friends of Perdido Bay's Board of Directors voted to go to the hearing and we began to solicit funds for it. I was hoping to stop the hearing in its tracks. There is a legal doctrine called *res judicata* which has been used many times. The doctrine is: you cannot be tried twice for the same crime. In our case, the issues were the same and the parties were the same, although I did not include my children this time. The permit application was also the same and the judge had already ruled on the issue. So, in this case, how was the argument new? IP had collected more data, but more data didn't really answer the question whether or not IP's effluent was going to harm the wetlands. I started to look for cases dealing with *res judicata* in the law library at the court house. In most cases, the courts had not permitted a permittee to make a second application if it had been turned down the first time. If the party failed to present sufficient evidence supporting their side, they could not try to reverse a decision by presenting more evidence at a new trial. There was only one case in which the DEP had allowed a person to return, collect more data and then reapply for a permit. I had hoped to stop this most recent permit and let the Appellate Court rule on the challenge to the first hearing.

Before the DEP relinquished the case for hearing to the Division of Administrative Hearings, IP had already petitioned for an expedited hearing. All their motions required answers on our part; otherwise, the motions went unanswered and were usually granted. As I argued in my Motion in Opposition to IP's request for a hurry-up hearing, IP had had four years to collect their data. They knew the rules, had lost and that should be it. Now the Petitioners (us) had to go out and collect more data. DEP did not rule on my Motion to dismiss due to *res judicata*, nor rule on IP's Motion for an Expedited Hearing, but instead sent the case to the Division of Administrative Hearings. Their request was filed August 12, 2008.

Realizing that their permitting situation was rather tenuous since DEP was trying to issue a new permit and their old permit had been denied, IP applied for a Stay of the denial in the First Hearing in the First District Court of Appeals on August 7, 2008. I immediately wrote a motion opposing the stay in the Appellate Court. In their Motion for a Stay, IP wrote that their chances of success in the second hearing were very good. I countered that IP's success in the second hearing was unlikely. Evidence provided in the first hearing showed that their effluent would harm the wetlands. The pilot wetlands which Champion had built in the 1990's showed that the effluent was toxic to trees. Only 2.5% of the trees lived and the wetland had turned into a monoculture of cattails[8]. One requirement to obtain the stay from the First District Court of Appeals was that the effluent could not harm public health. I provided three affidavits from people who had been harmed by swimming in Perdido Bay. In the affidavit of one resident, he testified that his neighbor had died three days after swimming in Perdido Bay with a cut, having gotten blood poisoning. The affidavits were not enough to stop the District Court of Appeals from issuing the stay.

In August 2008, Friends of Perdido Bay again began our fund-raising efforts. Ramsey Beach Homeowners who had "settled" with IP in their law suit (Ester's suit) were given $10,000 in exchange for dropping past damages. The homeowners gave Friends of Perdido Bay $5,000 for our continual legal battles. Before that donation, we only had $3,000 in the bank. My husband decided to again hire Marcy LaHart on a limited basis to represent him and Friends of Perdido Bay. We were amid an economic downturn. The subprime mortgage debacle had erupted. IP had also just acquired Weyehaeuser's linear board mills for $6 billion. Everyone was broke. We held a fund raiser at the famous Flora-Bama Beach Bar on Perdido Key in November, 2008. We also collected items for an auction and had no problem raising them.

The preparations for an administrative hearing raged on. At the end of August, 2008, IP made a motion to limit the issues in the case. They said the issues in the second hearing should be limited to only those which the judge had ruled against them. All other issues, such as compliance with the permit, or validity of the water quality limits for nutrients, or change in the manufacturing process from white paper to brown, or any increase in production should be barred from litigation again. IP used a doctrine called collateral estoppel. We opposed IP's motion to limit the issues to the ones they had chosen. The Administrative Law granted IP's request to limit the issues in the second hearing. The Administrative Law Judge was Bram Canter, the same judge who had presided over the first hearing. (As an aside note, as of 2016, this judge has ruled against environmentalists and for industry in recent cases). The hearing was scheduled for January 14, 2009. We were trying very hard to prepare for it and present new information not presented at the past hearing. The list of witnesses which DEP presented revealed three new experts on wetland biology. DEP was loaning their experts to IP's case. I wondered how much influence Davis Struhs, IP's Vice President for the Environment who had been Secretary of DEP, was having on DEP; possibly a lot.

In December 2008, our attorney filed a challenge to three of DEP's rules used to approve the IP permit. She argued that these rules were an "invalid exercise of the authority the legislature had granted to DEP". I thought her chances of winning and stopping the hearing were slim. But I was hopeful that the EPA might step in and do something. George Bush was no longer president. Barrack Obama was now president and maybe his EPA would stop what I considered a disaster for Perdido Bay. No luck. Charlie Crist was still governor of Florida. Also, we had been appealing to some of the larger environmental organizations to help us. Once again, no luck. The local university, University of West Florida, was founded by one of the founders of the paper mill, John Pace. The Pace Family was still active in university affairs and we thought that no help would be coming from that direction. We also felt certain that everyone knew about the problems on Perdido Bay, but were unwilling to come to our aid. We were doing this by ourselves.

We were madly getting ready for the second hearing supposed to start January 14, 2009. We obtained several new experts to testify. Dr. George Crozier, director of Dauphin Island Marine Lab, and Dr. Wayne Isphording, a geologist who had studied the sediments in Perdido Bay for the Levin firm, agreed to testify for us. We had also hired a University of South Florida hydrologist, Dr. Mark Rains, to testify. Although there were still some questions about what the issues were going to be at the hearing, we were pretty much concentrating on the damage the IP effluent would do to the wetlands.

To counter the argument that the paper mill effluent had killed the trees in the experimental wetland, DEP wrote in their new "Fact sheet" that the 2.5% tree survival was due to the shading effect of invading cattails and not to any problem with the water quality or sediment conditions. DEP was also using several of their wetland experts to testify about the effluent's impact on the wetland (or lack of impact). Again, in the Fact Sheet, the DEP writes: *"Pursuant to the land management plan for the Wetted Effluent Area, one of the primary land management objectives for the wetted effluent area is to establish and maintain forest species appropriate to the hydrological regimes and provide for further nutrient uptake of the applied effluent. The land management plan requires that exotic and nuisance plant species to be identified, controlled and eradicated.* "[9]   In the Fact Sheet, DEP also commented about the potential harm due to flooding of tree and plant roots. DEP did agree that some plants would be damaged by the flooding of the wetland behind the berms. IP reengineered (lowered) the berms so that 103 acres would not be flooded. They were giving 1,188 acres of land adjacent to the wetland to mitigate for the harm going to be done to some rare and endangered species due to flooding. The Florida Statute being used to give IP a permit did not recognize mitigation. Supposedly this could not be included in the wetland analysis. IP's expert testified that it would plant wetland trees on hummocks so that flooding of roots would be minimal.

The question about whether the water quality based effluent limitations (WQBELs) were going to be addressed at this hearing was still up in the air. There had been some changes in the WQBEL information from past hearings. Mainly, ECUA's contribution to the nutrients was now included. IP did not want this issue addressed again.

We were going to concentrate on the effluent's damage to the Elevenmile Creek as an example of what would happen to small freshwater streams in the wetlands but first, we had to counter IP's testimony from the first hearing that there were no small streams in the wetlands. We took the deposition (sworn statements) of Don Ray, a DEP freshwater biologist who currently was sampling freshwater streams. We had used him in the previous hearing. Don Ray testified that on March 21, 2006, he and another biologist did a biological analysis on a creek in the IP wetlands for a state program called TMDL (Total Maximum Daily Load).   The biologists called the stream Wicker Creek because it drained into Wicker Lake.   They did an Eco summary of Wicker Creek and published a report to DEP's website. The report had been reviewed by a supervisor. Later a supervisor called him and told him to take the report off the website and change it. When Don Ray asked why, the administration in Tallahassee said it was not a creek but a firebreak. During the deposition, I asked Don Ray if he thought the stream was a firebreak. At this question, the DEP attorney, Doug Beason, who was listening to the questioning on the phone, objected. *"Mr. Beason: I just want to be clear, are you asking him if it's personal opinion or his capacity as an employee of the Department?"* I answered that my questions will be personal opinions. I did not want to get Don Ray in trouble with his job. These biologists had already been censured once and paid the price for testifying truthfully. Mr. Ray testified that the stream was not a firebreak but a freshwater stream. Mr. Ray had brought the report with him. (I submitted the report to the Court Reporter, but it was not a part of the deposition returned to me. It had been lost). We then went through the parameters which the biologists had measured in the stream. It was typical of many freshwater streams in this area. Mr. Beason, and IP's attorney, objected to every question I asked Mr. Ray. When I asked Mr. Ray if the stream currently had a healthy population of freshwater animals, he said "No". It had failed the biological test. When I asked why, Mr. Ray said it was because the stream had been damned up by all the earthmoving IP was doing to prepare the wetlands for the new project. He said that he had reported this alteration of the stream to the Corps of Engineers, but they had ignored the problem. When I asked Mr. Ray, what in his opinion would happen to the wetlands if IP's effluent was applied, over much objection from the other attorneys, he responded that the wetland would turn into a cattail marsh. He stated, *"...most of the wetland trees in that area can't take smothering of roots by heavy sediments."* Don Ray said he thought the whole wetland would change. He testified that there were other freshwater streams on the wetland site that would be affected as well.

Dr. Rains, our expert witness/ hydrologist, also told us stories about IP's sludges in Ticonderoga, N.Y. He had worked at Cornell University. IP's Ticonderoga mill discharges to Lake Champlain where it has covered the lake bottom with a huge layer of sludge. Prior to discharging directly to the lake, IP had discharged to a wetland which then discharged to the lake. The wetland filled up with paper mill solids. IP was fined by EPA for filling the wetland with its solids and had to do remediation of the wetland; nevertheless, the filling was termed "unintentional". In the wetland IP was constructing along the banks of Perdido Bay, I doubted that much of their solids would accumulate. The slope was too great and the flow too rapid. Also, the IP solids were much finer than with the previous treatment system. Only behind the berms would sludge accumulate, and that would probably be washed out in a rainfall.

Friends of Perdido Bay and I (the Petitioners) were ready to go to a hearing by mid-December, 2008. All parties had submitted our witness lists; however, I was still not sure what issues we could raise at the hearing. I kept filing motions attempting to determine what issues the Judge had eliminated ("estopped") from the new hearing, and amended my petition for a hearing accordingly. The Judge denied my request to amend my petition, saying the time to a hearing was too short. He implied we also could not raise the issue of Wicker Creek as being a creek and not a firebreak as he had already ruled in the first hearing that it was a fire break. Judge Canter, in his December 22, 2008, order, said the only issues which remain to be litigated were compliance with the requirements of the wetland rule (Florida Administrative Code 62-660.300). It seemed to me as if the Judge was allowing IP to present new evidence on the same old subject which had been litigated at the first hearing, but was not allowing us to present new data. We took the testimony of DEP's witness, Eric Hickman, who was DEP's wetland expert. He testified that the small streams in the IP wetlands were not considered wetlands but Class III (swimmable, fishable) waters. These small streams had to be protected. IP opposed all my requests to amend. Then on Christmas Eve, the DEP attorney called to see if I would oppose postponing the hearing set for January 14, 2009. It was annoying that IP had been in such a hurry and was now stalling. The reason which DEP gave for postponing was the rule challenges which our attorney, Marci LaHart, had submitted. The DEP said that these rule challenges should be resolved before the hearing. The new hearing dates were May 4 through May 8, 2009.

Since we still had time to collect more information before the May, 2009, hearings, our expert in hydrology, Mark Rains, wanted to visit the IP wetlands. In April, Dr. Rains, my husband, Mike Steltenkamp, the mill's Director of Health, Safety and the Environment, and I drove around the wetlands taking pictures and scientific readings at different sites. It was very apparent where IP had damned up the little streams, but overall, the wetland looked pretty and green.

On April 9, 2009, DEP and IP filed a Motion to revise the Consent Order. The "new" Consent Order withdrew the necessity of using the wetland exemption rule (F.A.C. 62-660.300). It said that IP could apply for alternative criteria for dissolved oxygen, specific conductance (saltiness), and turbidity in the fresh water wetlands 97 months after the Consent Order had been issued. The Consent Order allowed IP to violate Florida Standards for 108 months (9 years) without showing this would not harm the wetland. Further, the DEP had just changed its rules since the first hearing to allow alternative criteria for these three water quality standards. During the first hearing, alternative criteria were not allowed for these standards. To me, the whole thing seemed ludicrous. The DEP was going to allow IP to discharge to the wetland and they were changing their rules to make it easy. Prior to DEP issuing the new Consent Order, the Judge had changed the dates of the hearing to begin June 22, 2009.

I opposed issuance of the new Consent Order. DEP was giving IP a permit only good for 5 years and a Consent Order allowing them to operate for 9 years without complying with Florida law. The new Consent Order did not require proof that IP was not harming the wetland. It was a total farce. The change to the Consent Order made the issues for the hearing even murkier. I asked for the hearing to be postponed. The Judge denied my request to postpone the hearing, but we could amend our petitions because DEP and IP had changed the Consent Order. Two weeks before the hearing was supposed to begin, on June 2, 2009, the Judge issued an order defining the issues. Re-reading that Order today, I cannot determine what is required. Judge Canter ordered *"...that the factual issues in these cases are now limited to the following:*

1. Whether the revised Consent Order and proposed permit are valid with respect to the effects of the proposed discharge on the wetland system, including Tee and Wicker Lakes, and with respect to any modifications to the effluent distribution and treatment functions of the wetland system following the Final Order issued in DOAH (Division of Administrative Hearings) Case No. 05-1609; and

2. Whether the December 2007 report of the Livingston team demonstrates that the WQBELS are inadequate to prevent water quality violations in Perdido Bay."

It was unbelievable. In his orders in Fall 2008, Judge Canter said we could not discuss water quality issues in Perdido Bay. Now he was saying WQBELs were at issue. We were not prepared to discuss WQBELs. We had planned on showing the damage which IP's effluent would have on the wetlands. It was a true curve ball. IP had made a Motion to Dismiss our petitions which was denied by the Judge. Now, Marci's challenge to the wetland rule was dismissed as not relevant since IP and DEP were not using it for the permit. IP had withdrawn their request to use the Experiment Use of Wetlands Rule (FAC 62-660.300). It seemed like Marci's rule challenge had backfired on us. At this point, I thought we had very little chance of winning. I had hoped the Obama EPA would come to our rescue. But things only got worse. Because of Judge Canter's June 2nd order, we sought to amend our petitions again and asked for more clarification. We also asked that the hearing be postponed until a later date. No luck. We were heading toward disaster.

267

The hearing started on June 22, 2009, as planned. There were a few new witnesses. The DEP seemed to go out of their way to beef up their case. Eric Hickman, a DEP wetland expert, testified that while the wetland would change somewhat, the changes would not significantly alter the function of the wetland. Another DEP biologist from Tallahassee had gone to the old experimental wetlands which had been constructed at the mill and did sweeps with nets through the cattails looking for aquatic insects. He found a healthy population of insects in the cattails. This was to counter the evidence that 98% of the trees had died in the wetlands and the effluent was toxic to wetland trees. After five days of testimony, IP had presented their case and DEP had presented their witness. We, the petitioners, still had to complete our case. The date was July 1, 2009. It was getting difficult to schedule our witnesses because we didn't know when we would resume. It appeared to me that we were again litigating the same issues which had been litigated in the previous hearing. IP's wetlands expert, Mr. Bays, testified that the wetlands would become a restored hardwood swamp. Eric Hickman, DEP's wetland expert, testified that the wetlands would turn into a pine tree, swamp forest, more open. Dr. Rains, our wetland expert, testified that there would be a profound change in the wetlands. Don Ray, the DEP biologist who testified for us, said in his opinion, the wetlands would become a cattail swamp. Our expert, Dr. Isphording, testified that dioxin and heavy metals would be deposited in the wetlands, especially the Tee and Wicker Lakes. IP and DEP presented no evidence to counter this argument. We introduced evidence through Dr. White, our engineering expert and the head of my husband's engineering department, about mills like the IP mill which were a lot less polluting. The technology existed to reduce the use of water and pollution. There were many arguments in court about whether the testimony given had already been given in the previous hearing and found not persuasive or whether a subject had been barred from testimony. During the hearings, however, the Judge softened his stance on what could or could not be mentioned. The Judge ruled that we could talk about small streams in the wetlands, including Wicker Creek. He said information about what harm IP's effluent had done to Elevenmile Creek would be relevant. Even though he allowed this testimony at trial, he did not consider it in his Recommended Order. An unusual moment occurred in court when the Judge called all parties to his front table for a conference, off the record. Judge Canter said he was going to have a hard time ruling in favor of IP. Did they want to continue? IP's corporate attorney, Steve Ginski, said yes. It gave me some hope, but I was still doubtful.

After five days of testimony, the Judge could plainly see that the project had not changed. The berms had been lowered sufficiently so that the effluent, once released from the pipe, would only take 12-hours before it reached Perdido Bay. It was nothing more than an overland flow to Perdido Bay. On July 13, 2009, I ask the Judge to give a Summary Final Order and rule in our favor. Removal of the Experimental Wetland Rule had simply been a legal change. All the evidence was the same. The project was the same. The Judge denied my request. The hearings resumed on July 20 and 21, 2009. The hearings ran late and we tried to finish. Our attorney, Marci LaHart had gone home after the first part of the hearing concluded. We had to pay her airfare back to Pensacola. We also had a law student from the University of Miami staying at our house. He had gotten a stipend from the U.S. Bar Association to be Marci's paralegal. He stayed in our spare bedroom. His help did not cost us anything.

However, the hearing was costing more than we had anticipated. In the spring, Friends of Perdido Bay had an auction/fund raiser. Not many people attended and some auction items were not bid on. When the hearing concluded in late July, 2009, Friends of Perdido Bay had only been able to raise about $20,000. The hearing costs were probably going to run $50,000 to $60,000. We had to be able to buy the transcripts so that we could write our Recommended Final Orders and pay our experts. Marci said we could pay her over a period of time. The hearing ended up personally costing my husband and me about $40,000. He cashed in his life insurance policies to pay for it. In 2012, my husband died without any life insurance policies.

Financially, IP was not hurting. In spring, 2009, they had reported first quarter net earnings of $257 million. Part of the profit was due to a tax rebate from the U.S. Treasury for an "alternative-fuel tax". In 2005, Congress passed a transportation bill which included a variety of tax credits for alternative fuels and fuel mixtures. There was a $0.50 per gallon credit for the use of fuel mixtures which included combining "alternative fuel" with a "taxable fuel" such as diesel or gasoline. For years, the paper industry burned their black liquor (a mixture of cooking chemicals and left over organic material from pulping) mixed with diesel for capturing and regenerating their cooking chemicals. The heat also produced steam for cooking wood chips. In Fall, 2008, IP applied for this rebate. In March, 2009, IP received its first check from the U.S. Treasury for one-month period, November through December 2008 - a whopping $71.6 million dollars. Analysts projected that the tax credit, would net IP, $1.27 billion before it expired at the end of 2009. Congress did close the Black liquor loophole in December 2009, but another loophole arose - "Cellulosic Biofuels Credit". The IRS ruled in mid-June, 2010, that black liquor would qualify for the biofuels tax credit. Other paper producers were also using this alternative fuel tax credit to boost their profits. This was the time when our economy nearly collapsed because of the subprime crisis. Financial institutions and the auto industry were also getting bailouts, presumably they had to pay back.

The hearings seemed to end abruptly on July 21, 2009. We didn't know if IP was going to call rebuttal witnesses or not. If IP had called rebuttal witnesses, at least one more day could have been added to the hearings. As we walked out to our cars, we said goodbye to all the attorneys and a few members of

Friends of Perdido Bay who had attended the hearings. One of the DEP witnesses, Eric Hickman, who had been attending with Doug Beason, turned to us before he left and told us how much he admired third party groups like ours. He said if it wasn't for us, DEP would not have been able to get IP to donate the 1,100 acres for conservation. I hoped we got more than that.

All parties submitted our Proposed Recommended Orders to Judge Canter by mid-October, 2009. I thought that it was easier to write this Order because the issues at the hearing were more focused. However, because of the ambiguity of the Judge's Order on June 12th, I still wasn't sure what the issues were. Also, the hearing was not as long as the first hearing had been. The seven days of hearings had only produced 12 volumes with 1669 pages. We were urging our members to write the EPA as we hoped the new Obama EPA would be more sympathetic to our cause. Global warming seemed to be EPA's main focus. The appeal of the first hearing was still ongoing before the First District Court of Appeals. Our attorney, Marcy LaHart was continuing her cross appeal challenging the Florida Statue 403.088. IP was continuing to get extensions on their Motion to Stay the last verdict. When IP filed their original Motion to Stay on August 7, 2008, they claimed "...*a final order on the second application will, absent unforeseen circumstances render the issues on appeal moot.*"

IP's 2008 prediction about the outcome of the second hearing came true on January 27, 2010. Judge Canter issued his Recommended Order recommending approval of the permit and Consent Order. My husband did not say anything but I could tell he was extremely disappointed, as was I. It was hard to believe that the whole process had not been rigged. We had spent all Friends of Perdido Bay's money and some of our own, and we had lost. In his Recommended Order, Judge Canter praised the "Livingston Study".

"18. The Livingston studies represent perhaps the most complete scientific evaluation ever made of a coastal ecosystem.

271

Dr. Livingston developed an extensive biological and chemical history of Perdido Bay and then evaluated the nutrient loadings from Elevenmile Creek over a 12-year period to correlate mill loadings with the biological health of the Bay. The Livingston studies confirmed that when nutrient loadings from the mill were high, they caused toxic algae blooms and reduced biological productivity in Perdido Bay. Some of the adverse effects attributable to the mill effluent were most acute in the area of the Bay near the Lanes' home on the northeastern shore of the Bay because the flow from the Perdido River tends to push the flow from Elevenmile Creek toward the northeastern shore. "[10] I wondered where the Judge got this information. He didn't get it from testimony at the hearing.

The Judge went on *"19. Because Dr. Livingston determined that the nutrient loadings from the mill that occurred in 1988 and 1989 did not adversely impact the food web of Perdido Bay, he recommended effluent limits for ammonia nitrogen, orthophosphate, and total phosphorus that were correlated with mill loadings of these nutrients in those years"*. We thought that nutrient limits and WQBEL's were "off limits" in this hearing, hence we did not present any contrary evidence. But the Judge seemed to be reaffirming that these limits were valid and seemed to completely ignore any evidence we presented. DEP's wetland expert had done an evaluation and projected the overall wetland function would increase by six percent. This information was important to the judge. Ours apparently was not. In his Findings of Fact, the Judge writes: *"...IP proposes to achieve compliance with all proposed water quality standards and permit limits by the end of the schedule established in the Consent Order...."* I thought that this was another erroneous "fact" the Judge dug up. IP was going to try to get alternative criteria in the wetlands. There were no assurances that IP was going to achieve compliance. The paper mill had promised to achieve compliance at a hearing in 1988 and had yet to do so. The Livingston Study cost IP a substantial sum of money, so they reaped the benefit in a favorable ruling.

272

All parties can write exceptions to the Recommended Order. I was the only one who wrote exceptions. IP and the DEP agreed with all the Judges findings. To save money, my husband and I decided that I would write the exceptions, not Marci. All her challenges to the rules had been dismissed. I complained that the Recommended Order had two main flaws: 1) The Judge allowed IP to present evidence on the same subject litigated in the first hearing. Petitioners were barred by collateral estoppel from presenting any evidence. It was extremely prejudicial. 2) IP was being allowed to violate state standards in the wetlands without any relief mechanisms. I went on to show that most findings of Fact and Conclusions of Law had either been litigated at the first hearing or not supported by any evidence given at trial. Apparently, my arguments did not hold much weight. On March 11, 2010, the Secretary of DEP issued the final Order granting the permit and Consent Order. It had been a long fight, nearly five years since the first permit had been issued.

But I was not ready to quit. The second hearing was obviously prejudicial and unfair to us. I decided to appeal this decision to the First District Court of Appeals. I filed my Notice of Appeal on April 9, 2010. In July, 2010, I filed my Initial Brief with the First District Court of Appeals. I had thought that IP would not begin construction of any pipeline until the appeals process was complete. In my Initial Brief, I used the same arguments with which I had opposed the Recommended Order, that the Judge allowed IP to re-litigate but barred us from litigating; the DEP was allowing IP to violate rules without issuing any relief and Findings of Fact were not supported by testimony from trial.

This area had become preoccupied by another environmental disaster - the BP oil spill. On April 20, 2010, the BP oil well off Louisiana, the Macondo well, started spewing oil. It was a horrible disaster and coated the Gulf beaches in this

273

region with massive amounts of oil. All summer, people were glued to the news about the oil spill. While we only saw a slight sheen on the water where we lived, people in the lower part of Perdido Bay were seriously affected. The picture of the boom trying to hold back the oil at the mouth of Perdido Bay was numbing. The tourist business that summer was decimated. Before the well was capped on July 15, 2010, it had spilled 4.9 million barrels of oil (government figures). The well was finally sealed on September 9, 2010. Nobody was worrying about Perdido Bay's problems. The oil spill had consumed our attention. Friends of Perdido Bay tried to provide information on where to get help, especially legal. I was sure the settlements would be massive. There were many, many attorneys running around the area. Because we had only seen a small sheen at our beach, our property was not affected but the bay looked pretty much like it had before – dead. We did not qualify for any legal help. Any news about Perdido Bay seemed minor.

In the fall of 2010, my husband and I became preoccupied with a dangerous skin cancer that he had developed. We spent a lot of time visiting doctors in Mobile and Pensacola. On one of our trips to Mobile, I saw what I thought looked like a pipeline being installed under Interstate 10. I checked with DEP who said "yes" the pipeline was being built. IP had not even waited for the legal situation to finalize - they must have been sure of the outcome. I heard that David Struhs had left IP in the summer of 2010. He had done his job. From DEP on November 17, 2010, I immediately sought a Stay of the Permit pending appeal. The DEP denied my request on December 28, 2010. I should have given up, but the thought of a permanent pipeline being built to Perdido Bay was alarming. On January 10, 2011, I asked for a Stay of the Permit Pending Outcome in the appellate courts. Request denied. My husband's skin cancer would not go away and was getting worse.

Meanwhile, the proceedings in the appellate court were also moving along. The Stay of the Permit denial which had been issued in the first hearing to IP was no longer needed because the permit had been approved in the second hearing. IP had requested that the appellate court voluntarily dismiss its appeal in the first hearing on July 30, 2010. On August 5, 2010, the appellate court had dismissed IP's appeal of the denial of its permit in the first hearing without making any decision on anyone's arguments. Marci's cross appeal on the constitutionality of Florida Statute 403.088 was still pending in early 2010, but according to the docket records "...*FOBP (Friends of Perdido Bay) had doubtful standing because the Administrative Law Judge had ruled in favor of FOPB by finding that "the public interest showing in this proceeding was insufficient."*[11] In September 2010, her cross appeal was dismissed by *per curiam* opinion. No reasons given. To this day, I still believe that this Florida Statue 403.088 is unconstitutional. It has been used to allow Perdido Bay to be grossly degraded for 30 years and counting. There are too many loopholes in the statute to make it an effective deterrent against pollution. This is not what the Florida constitution allows.

A slim chance still existed that the First District Court of Appeals would overturn the Final Order giving IP its permit. It didn't. On March 24, 2011, the appellate court upheld the final order in the second hearing by a *per curiam* decision and it was now official. The effluent was being piped to the wetlands. It has been a long wait and a big fight, especially since my husband was now battling skin cancer. We would have to wait and see if Perdido Bay would revive, but I had my doubts. It should be noted that the primary judge in our appellate case was C.W. Hawkes, who had been implicated in a conflict of interest dispute in a lawsuit against St. Joe Paper at the same time our case was dismissed.

CHAPTER 14 ~ The Wetlands

The official date the permit and Consent Order went into effect was March 15, 2010. According to state law, permits are only issued for five years, so the expiration date would be March 15, 2015. Terms in the Consent Order lasted longer. IP had 108 months to comply with the limits in the Consent Order or until March 15, 2019. Maybe the point of the entire hearing process was to allow IP to operate without compliance as long as possible and hope that Perdido residents would lose interest or die. As it turned out, one Perdido Bay resident did die – my husband, Jim, on August 3, 2012. It was a blow since he and I had fought the paper mill together for 26 years. In 1986 we began the fight by pointing out that the paper mill did not met standards and probably had not before then, but continued to operate. He had been my stalwart partner in life and it would be an adjustment to fight the paper mill without him.

We managed to pay our attorney, Marci LaHart, the rest of the money we owed her. I filed an injunction in Escambia County Circuit Court trying to stop the building of the pipeline. But an injunction requires a bond to offset the damage if the injunction is granted. I figured a bond would cost hundreds of thousands of dollars. The pipeline was going to be impossible to stop. The condition of the bay had not changed – it was still dead. Occasionally, a red fish or a sea trout could be caught, but not like in the 15-years previously. One could see that the bay water was herbicidal. We had groins at our beach built by my father-in-law many years before. Those groins used to be covered in green algae, but no more. Little snails used to eat the algae, but they had disappeared. For years, I had done research on the feeding of those snails. I had also studied the marsh clam which were still present, but few in number. Occasionally in the spring, I would find small, recently settled clams among the sand grains in the bottom, but only if spring weather had been rainy and paper mill effluent diluted sufficiently. When we went into a dry spell in late spring, the little clams all died. I continued to use the bay for swimming. Sometimes we were wading past big globs of foam and the bay was turbid - but the green trees surrounding the bay were beautiful.

In the summer months, I measured bacteria in the bay. I bought a bacteriological test kit for measuring coliform bacteria. Coliform bacteria are the type of bacteria which live in our intestines. These bacteria like environments organically rich. They tolerate low-dissolved oxygen. According to the reference book, "Standard Methods," these coliform bacteria are often associated with paper mill and sugar cane effluent.[1] I did not incubate the bacteria, therefore I could not say with certainty that these bacteria were just from human or mammal fecal material. But every summer, I found thousands of these bacteria growing in the bay water, especially after rains. Rains would wash the solids out of the ponds or off the wetlands and become food for them. These coliform bacteria, of which E. coli and Klebsiella are members, can cause infections. Friends of Perdido Bay had documented several cases of those infections from swimming in the bay.

After 2010, we followed the work IP was doing. They had to submit progress reports and a detailed study of the wetlands once a year to DEP. Dr. Livingston was no longer working for IP. Even though he had been honest about the condition of the bay, continuing to blame the deterioration on toxic algae and too many nutrients was dishonest. I keep wondering why he would have done such a thing. IP also had to submit monthly discharge reports to DEP. From DEP reports I knew the effluent was occasionally acutely toxic and almost always had an effect on the growth of minnows and reproduction of water fleas. The local utilities authority (ECUA) did not build a plant on IP property. After Hurricane Ivan and the large grant from FEMA, a new sewage treatment plant, called Central Reclamation Plant, was built in Northern Escambia Bay. The domestic wastes formerly treated by Pensacola Main Street

277

Sewage Treatment Plant were being piped to this new plant. Gulf Power, the local power company, was using some of the effluent and also IP. An eleven million gallons per day (MGD)-pipeline was built from this new sewage plant to IP. The ECUA discharge permit was different from IP's. Initially, IP had planned to use five MGD in their industrial processes. A DEP permit writer told me IP was NOT going to use any of the reclaimed sewage for dilution. But soon after they began transporting the effluent to the wetlands, IP began diluting their effluent with five MGD of domestic wastewater. The effluent must have needed this dilution.

As long as IP discharged to Elevenmile Creek, we were able to go and take samples. I took them to a certified lab for analysis. We calculated that IP was discharging 100,000 pounds a day of sulfur to the bay. The level of sulfur had been steadily going up through the years. In the 1970's, the owners of the paper mill had a limit for sulfate in their permit - 6,300 pounds per day. But that limit had been quietly removed so today IP could discharge whatever it wanted. Throughout the 2000's, the levels of arsenic and lead seemed to be going up as well. As I write this book, Florida is proposing on raising its limit for arsenic in water. The onslaught of weaker standards continued through the 2016 US presidential election, and upon the confirmation of President-elect Donald Trump, support for the environment looks pretty bleak. As of 2015, there was no improvement in IP's solids or BOD. For the average daily solids, IP was discharging close to the permit limit of 8000 pounds per day. We also made periodic flights over the mill and the treatment ponds. You could see that IP had turned down the aerators in their ponds as compared to pre-2000. This had been one of the selling points to the judge in the hearing. IP was going to increase the aerators to 2900 horsepower. But you could see that they were not. In 2012, I asked DEP personnel why IP had turned down their aerators. The DEP spokesperson asked IP and they said they were achieving limits without using all the horsepower. While IP said they may be achieving BOD

278

limits, aeration is important to remove toxicity. However, by not running aerators at full horsepower, IP was saving money and producing less pollution from burning of coal.

After my husband died of his skin cancer in 2012, I began to look back at the long time we had spent trying to clean up the polluted condition of our bay. We didn't realize the power and influence of the opposition. At first, we thought it was only us vs the paper mill; but there were many players, - chemical companies, timber companies, labor unions, and the local people. These were all beneficiaries of paper mill production. And most of the "big players" controlled the politicians who in turn controlled the environmental agencies. We were just small voices with no power or leverage. Many people who had worked so hard to clean up Perdido Bay had also died: Jim Murray, JoAnn Allan, Ester Johnson, and more. Maybe this was the plan of the power lobby in North Florida. If everyone who remembered Perdido Bay as it was before pollution by the paper mill died, then there would be no memory of how beautiful Perdido Bay could be. People would come to accept the foam, turbid water and lack of fish and shrimp as normal. My sisters-in-law and brother-in-law remember, but don't live here anymore. The "old timers" who are still around support us. But whether we will ever see Perdido Bay without paper mill effluent is questionable. As long as making paper is profitable for IP, they will continue. The environmental agencies are not going to force the large companies into cleaning up so that they become unprofitable. But people continue to support Friends of Perdido Bay, sending in donations and dues. If we continue to point out the damage and remind people of how beautiful Perdido Bay could be, International Paper may decide to 'clean up' or close.

In July 2012, shortly before my husband death, DEP held a public hearing in Pensacola to establish nutrient limits for the bays in this area - Pensacola, Escambia and Perdido Bay. Public hearings are required by EPA and most federal laws to get "public input". However, most of the time public comments have little or no influence on the outcome. DEP, with EPA's blessing (See the Chapter on Nuisance Algae), decided to set different values for each bay. I thought it was ridiculous as most local bays should have similar limits and similar response to nutrients. In the past, the DEP biologists had used limits which were a rule of thumb for all bays in this region. DEP biologists had recommended a total nitrogen value in the marine waters of 0.36 milligrams per liter of water and a total phosphorous value of 0.05 milligrams per liter of bay water, but these were not enforceable. These numbers were not just pulled out of the air, but were based on significant research. Of course, the industries and domestic wastewater treatment companies, many of whom were public utilities, said these nutrient values were too strict. It would cost them millions to clean up.

At DEP's public hearing on the nutrient limits in 2012, I finally understood why the judge in our administrative hearing in 2009 had allowed us to re-litigate WQBELs in Perdido Bay. Our administrative hearing was the due process for establishing nutrient limits for Perdido Bay. The limits recommended by Livingston for 1988 and 1989 were the limits which would be used for in Upper Perdido Bay. They were 1.27 milligrams/liter for total nitrogen and 0.102 milligrams/liter for total phosphorous, much higher than the old recommended limits and much higher than limits for other bays. These limits were set high to accommodate paper mill discharge. It was disgusting to me. In other local bays the regulators had used past historical limits taken over many years; but in Perdido Bay, the limits were restricted to only two years, 1988 and 1989. In the power point presentation on setting nutrient limits in Perdido Bay, the DEP spokesman had included Judge Canter's glowing report on the Livingston Study. But they wouldn't have to worry about outbreaks of algae or plankton blooms as we had seen in the 1980's and 1990's - the herbicidal influence of the IP effluent would keep them under control. Perdido Bay was being managed just like a swimming pool.

IP easily met all the time limits for construction of the pipeline to the wetlands and for construction in the wetlands. On Sunday, August 12, 2012, the Pensacola News Journal ran an article about IP stopping the pollution of Perdido Bay. The title of the article was *"At Long Last, Relief."* The subtitle was *"But will IP's $60 million treatment project work?"* The article began by quoting Bob DeGraaf, a longtime resident of Ramsey Beach on Perdido Bay. Bob was also a board member of Friends of Perdido Bay and not in good health (Bob died July, 2016). *"We've tried over the years but we've not been able to stop the paper mill from polluting the bay.......They have too much money."* It went on to call the project *"...one of the most innovative pollution-control systems ever built for a U.S. paper and pulp manufacturer."*[2] As with past articles, the $60 million which IP spent to build the wetlands and change to a slightly different treatment system were mentioned. *"It employs more than 460 workers and has an estimated economic impact of $300 million annually."* The article described the wetlands before the effluent arrived and the article contained a beautiful diagram of the wetlands and what they hoped would happen. However not everyone was optimistic. Keith Wilkins, director of Escambia County's Community and Environmental Department, said *"...IP is being overly optimistic about the environmental benefits of the wetlands system."* Wilkins said the wetland system will further *"...polish - reduce some solids from the treated discharge from the mill - but not actually "treat" or totally remove solids and chemicals that impair water quality."* March, 2013, was the date that IP would be completely out of Elevenmile Creek. This was the last article to appear in the Pensacola News Journal about the paper mill, the IP wetlands or the condition of Perdido Bay to date. Perdido Bay has become a dead issue, if not a dead bay. (Note: a recent explosion at the mill on January 22, 2017 has been in the news)

When IP did finally switch all their effluent over into the wetlands (2012), the bay was especially horrible - black and turbid. It was as if the effluent was just washing all the fine sediments off the wetlands and into the bay. The closer you were to the wetlands, like Ramsey Beach, the worse it was. I got a note from Bob DeGraaf, who lived up at Ramsey Beach. He said it was the worst he had seen it. He sold his house and was moving. Elevenmile Creek, now free from paper mill effluent, was clear. I went up to see the creek and was struck by how small the flow was without the effluent. IP was still allowed to discharge their storm water to the creek. When their effluent exceeded the capacity of the pipeline which was 47.5 million gallons a day, the overflow would have to go back into the creek. ECUA was sending approximately 10 million gallons a day (MGD) of domestic wastewater to the mill - 5 MGD for use in the mill and 5 MGD for dilution water in the wetlands. This left IP with little extra capacity, as their normal discharge was 27 MGD. The previous owners of the mill, Champion, calculated that with a 2" rainfall, the flow of the effluent would exceed 50 MGD.

Over time, the washing effect from the effluent was not as bad. Only when heavy rainfall occurred, did the bay look black. We were seeing duckweed, a small plant, after rainfalls. This duckweed must have been growing in the ponding water behind the berms in the wetlands. We saw it several times in the fall of 2013 and spring of 2014, but then it stopped. How IP controlled this duckweed is unknown. It appeared to me that the foam was better, but the biology of the bay was worse. The schools of anchovies we used to see in the summer were missing. Blue crabs had disappeared. We did a survey of members of Friends of Perdido Bay. By consensus, members of Friends of Perdido Bay thought the foam was a little better, but there was less life. Several members of Friends of Perdido Bay did a crab survey one summer and found that the number of blue crabs was down. Nobody was doing biological sampling of the bay. The IP consultant, Wayne Nutter, was only required to take samples of phytoplankton in the Upper Bay. We continued to follow his reports.

At the end of 2013, IP applied for a change to their air permit. As in the past, IP was going to increase production through an air permit. DEP announced the issuance of the permit in a legal notice on March 20, 2014. The air permit put a limit of 950,000 tons of black liquor solids a year and limited one of its power boilers to 5,000 tons per year of coal. No wood products were to be used in this power boiler. IP still had three other power boilers which used coal/wood mixture. I wondered if paper mills were still getting a tax break by claiming their black liquor as "cellulosic fuel". This year (2016) that tax break ended.

On October 30, 2014, the Pensacola News Journal ran an article about IP spending money on the mill. The article titled *"International Paper Allots $90 M for Mill"* stressed the amount of money IP was investing in the mill and the number of people it employed - 400. A quote from Florida Senate President, Don Gaetz was included. *"Northwest Florida's business-friendly environment and initiatives continue to attract strong, innovative businesses.....Just last year, International Paper's Pensacola Mill had a local economic impact of nearly $330 million."* Every five to ten years, paper mills must refurbish their equipment. This expenditure probably meant that IP did not plan to shut down any time soon. In fall 2013, the enormity of timber producers to the economy of North Florida was demonstrated in a newspaper article[3]. The largest timberlands owner in North Florida, the St. Joe Company, sold 383,000 acres of timberlands to AgReserves, a "tax paying affiliate of the Mormon Church". The Mormon Church already controlled 290,000 acres in Central Florida called Desert Ranches. With the purchase of timberlands in North Florida, Ag Reserves would be Florida's largest land owner. The other large landowners in Florida are the Perry-based Foley Timber and Land company with 562,000 acres and Plum Creek, a Seattle-based real estate trust with 448,000 acres. Previously, the St. Joe Company founded by Edward Ball, a brother-in-law to Dupont, had closed its paper mill in Port St. Joe and tried to reinvent itself as a big scale developer in North

Florida. At its peak, the St. Joe Company owned over a million acres of land in North Florida, much of it in timber. However, in 2011 when the real estate business in Florida went bust, the St. Joe Company lost $330 million. It did retain 184,000 acres of strategic developable land in North Florida and was a powerful player in politics in Florida. The past Governor, Charlie Crist, was on their Board of Directors. The St. Joe Company donated land in Tallahassee Florida on which a new District Court of Appeals building was constructed. The building was so costly and elegant that it had come under fire from tax payers who paid for the building. Apparently oversight of the construction of building by Tallahassee lawmakers was lax[4]. One of the judges who had ruled against us in the First District Court of Appeals, C.W. Hawkes, was implicated in the lavish spending. Jeb Bush, an ex-governor of Florida, was on the Board of another large Florida land owner, ITT Rayonier. According to Wikipedia, this company, based in Jacksonville, Florida owned a pulp mill in Jacksonville, Florida and 2,191,000 acres of land in the Southeastern U.S. It is the seventh largest private timberland owner in the United States.

Eight years previously in 2006, International Paper had sold most of its U.S. timberlands. IP sold 5.1 million acres for about $6.1 billion to several investment groups[5]. 2006 was a time when real-estate was selling very well. This was a trend among paper manufacturers who also owned vast tracts of timberlands. The real assets of paper manufacturers were their vast land holdings. Many turned themselves into real estate investment trusts (REITS) such as Weyerhaeuser and ITT Rayonier or into paper manufactures like IP. In this way, paper manufacturers got additional political advantage from the new owners of these vast tracts of land - the timber companies.

As the demand for paper continues to decrease because of the digital age, the demand for timber will also decrease. The large timberland owners will look for other markets for their timber and land. Recently, one environmental group sent me a request for a donation. They were warning that Congress was going to allow the timber industry to use their forests for energy production - burning trees for energy production. Development was another potential use of timberland resources. We have seen this occur, especially in central Florida. But development can only occur so fast, which is why paper mills must remain open to provide a market for trees. Generally timber companies pay very low taxes, often only one or two dollars per acre. It can also get a return on its properties by renting lands out to hunt clubs. In the South, this is very popular. Hunt clubs get leases on timber properties and then maintain and protect these properties for the companies.

Environmental groups also indirectly promote saving paper mills and their forests. This is why I believe we never got any help from large environmental organizations. If one saves paper mills, one also saves the planted forests. I recently received an invitation to attend a Mobile Bay Sierra Club event. The title of the program was "Securing the Future of Our Southern Forests" presented by a group called Dogwood Alliance. The information provided explained the rationale.

"...Southern forests are some of the most diverse temperate forests on the planet; they're also the world's biggest source of pulp and paper. But the forests' unseen assets are among the most important: they're a force against climate change, erosion and water pollution, a source of shelter for critical plant and animal species and one of the last, best places to experience the power of nature. Since 1996, Dogwood Alliance has championed this irreplaceable resource, safeguarding its environmental and economic value. Though Dogwood Alliance's mission is focused on protecting forests of the South, the work transforming the practices of major US corporations also helps improve forest conservation across the nation and around the world...."[6]

Because the existence of forests is tied to existence of paper mills, especially where privately owned, I understood the problems we were having in trying to get IP to clean up. Paper manufacturers understand their importance in maintaining these forests. I believe this is why paper mills are so polluting and have never really been made to clean up. They have allies in both political parties. Because forests are so important in protecting against climate change and paper mills are the economic reason for forests, mills have also been afforded special protections. It is not a good situation for those of us on Perdido Bay.

Once IP was no longer in Elevenmile Creek, it seemed they became invisible. I read a summary of dischargers to Perdido Bay and IP was not even listed. I am sure this was intentional and in fact, the idea. Perdido Bay's problems were no longer associated with IP. What problems did Perdido Bay have? Since the environmental agencies or IP were no longer monitoring biological life in Perdido Bay, no one could see how bad it was except for the few residents who continued to care. Much of the information which the governmental agencies put out was either not true or slanted. An example was the report DEP had written for justifying their nutrient limits that said no grass beds had ever existed in Upper and Middle Perdido Bay. This was totally false and DEP knew it. The Fish and Wildlife had done a summary of grass beds in Perdido Bay in 1990, and yes they were in Upper Perdido Bay. Perdido Bay had been listed as an impaired water body for dissolved oxygen and nutrients in the 1980's. It supposedly was no longer impaired (See Chapter on Hiding the Problems). However, if you go out and take oxygen readings early in the morning, even in shallow water, the oxygen concentration is very low. If you take oxygen readings near the bottom in Perdido Bay, it is very near zero. But this kind of data was not being taken, so having management meetings without knowing the true problems in the bay were fruitless. But they were a way to gloss over the problems.

In April 29th and 30th, 2014, Pensacola experienced a deluge of rain - 26" in 24-hours. Places never flooding before flooded. Roads and bridges were washed out. My driveway was washed out. All the prior existing drainage problems were exacerbated. An area which flooded was a subdivision on Elevenmile Creek. The subdivisions had been built in the creek's flood plain. I doubted they would normally flood, except for the fact that IP was at the headwaters. IP said it was prepared to hold water from a 25-year storm, but this storm was one which maybe occurred every 200 years. The dikes holding back storm water broke and a huge wave of water swept into homes. It was horrendous. IP denied that its dikes broke, but pictures of broken concrete dikes exist. There is a class action lawsuit still pending from the flooding. IP was not fined by DEP because this was considered "an act of God." This was the second time these subdivisions had been flooded by paper mill effluent. With IP's ponds above and subdivisions below, the situation always looked to me like a disaster waiting to happen. But it was the response of the federal government that was amazing. A special federal grant was obtained to purchase 27 homes. I am sure this made IP very happy because it reduced their risk. Furthermore, Escambia County is planning to use part of the money they get from the BP oil spill fines to restore the flood plain in Elevenmile Creek, a give-a-way to the mill.

We continued to get IP monitoring reports from DEP. Chlorine was being found in the IP effluent as early as 2011[7]. DEP rules do not allow any chlorine, but IP couldn't say where it was coming from. There was toxicity associated with the effluent. In February 2015, production at the mill had increased to 2,217 air dried tons per day - 593 tons of bleach pulp and 1,624 tons/day of unbleached. Production had increased threefold over what the mill produced in the 1970's. In testing sediments in 2014, Friends of Perdido Bay still found dioxin and high arsenic content in the sediments of Tee and Wicker Lakes at the end of 2014. I thought that these chemicals had come from the washing of ash from their power boilers.

In 2016, IP is still operating on a permit with a Consent Order. The Consent Order means that it cannot meet the environmental standards for discharging their effluent to swimmable, fishable waters. The paper mill has been operating on a Consent order ever since citizens complained in 1986. Consent Orders are issued to bring dischargers into compliance with state standards. After 30 years, this has yet to happen. This is a strike against IP because these big companies get credits for having current permits which meet all standards. This is the only mill IP has that is unable to meet standards - a black eye for the company. Under David Struhs, the Florida environmental agency had adopted a slightly different interpretation of what "compliance with rules" meant. The David Struh's DEP interpreted "compliance" to mean "at the end of the pipe" and not consider the effect on receiving waters. But the EPA and Florida rules are pretty clear about the impact on the receiving waters: they must be considered.

The plan is to get IP a legitimate permit involved getting different (reduced) water standards in the wetlands as compared with the general standards issued by EPA and the state environmental agencies. These different standards are called site-specific alternative criteria (SSAC). If a discharger is able to demonstrate (with scientific values) that a "natural" background has a naturally low (or higher) value than the EPA value, then they ask the regulatory agency for that "natural" value as their new standard. This was how Florida established the nutrient limits for total nitrogen and total phosphorous in Upper Perdido Bay. Champion had often tried to get "alternative criteria" for dissolved oxygen in Elevenmile Creek, but the science was far-fetched. There were too many streams which had dissolved oxygen values meeting state standards. At the time "site-specific alternative criteria" for dissolved oxygen was not allowed by the environmental agency. The Consent Order, issued in March, 2010, and expiring March, 2019, listed four parameters IP could not meet in the freshwater wetlands: pH, specific conductance (saltiness), turbidity and dissolved oxygen.

Its compliance plan was to demonstrate that the background stations in the wetlands or the areas without paper mill effluent had similar values to those areas with paper mill effluent. I thought they may have been able to achieve a site-specific alternative criterion for dissolved oxygen in the freshwater wetlands, but not the other parameters. Also, I did not see how they were going to get alternative criteria for dissolved oxygen in the brackish-water of Tee and Wicker Lakes. There was too much information on oxygen values in Tee and Wicker Lakes before IP started to apply the effluent to the wetlands. Our expert witness in environmental engineering, Dr. White, had calculated the dissolved oxygen in the little lakes. He testified that oxygen would probably go to zero with addition of paper mill effluent, as it contained too much oxygen consuming material. But the real reason for the nine-year Consent Order may have been hopes that the citizens would lose interest and abandon oversight, allowing the environmental agencies to again be able to freely ignore the many problems the mill was causing, thereby issue IP a permit. However, as of 2017, Friends of Perdido Bay continues to exist and is funded through donations and dues. The many citizens follow the fight through the information in the newsletters of the group.

Will IP be able to achieve this goal of long term compliance? It doesn't look like it. Just recently, I received IP's yearly 2015 report which had been done by Dr. Nutter and his Associates. There was good science which showed "no significant difference" existed between "background stations" and stations in the "effluent-applied" areas in some aspects of the wetlands. The report mentioned that 160,968 canopy trees had been planted on raised hills prior to application of the effluent. But the Executive Summary described the problem.
    "...Based upon results of vegetation community sampling, several vegetative community trends were observed in the overall project site. Increased hydroperiods (flooding) since 2012 couple with the historic presence of silviculturally established canopy species (i.e. slash and loblolly pine) within

289

the EDS (Effluent Distribution System) has resulted in a large decline in canopy species density and abundance between 2008 and 2015 due to mass tree mortality. It is anticipated that canopy species native to the area and tolerant of long periods of inundation (i.e. bald and pond cypress, swamp tupelo, sweetbay, etc.) will become reestablished within the EDS." The IP wetlands or EDS (Effluent Distribution System) was being turned into a cattail swamp. Don Ray's 2007 predictions of what would happen to these wetlands had turned out to be the correct prediction. Table 9-1[8] gave the stark results. In 2008 (before the effluent was applied to the wetlands), the average canopy coverage was 23 percent. In 2015, the average canopy coverage was 5 percent. There was a rapid decline in canopy coverage starting with the application of the effluent. Trees per acre in 2008 averaged 203. In 2015, three years after effluent started being applied, there were 21 trees per acre, a 90% reduction. These were the same results which had been found for Champion's experimental wetlands. So why was anyone surprised? Corresponding to the dramatic changes in vegetation were dramatic changes in benthic macroinvertebrate (invertebrate animals which live in the ground). In the phytoplankton (small suspended algae in the water) section of Nutter's report, one little paragraph describes the results. Nutter's team found blue-green algae at all upper bay stations except for the station right in front of the Perdido River where dilution was sufficient. Phytoplankton is the beginning of the food chain and a requirement for a healthy ecosystem. Blue-green algae are junk. A healthy ecosystem can't exist on blue-green algae. It is like eating potato chips and candy all the time. The herbicidal effect of the IP effluent was apparent in the findings of the report.

IP's monthly discharge monitoring reports found at DEP's online site were also revealing. IP must report many parameters for which there are no limits in the permit. The reporting point and compliance point is a location on its property which is inaccessible to the public. IP must also report internal values coming from the bleaching area to show "best management practices" are working. In reviewing the December 2015 monthly report, it had not violated any of its permit limits except the water flea toxicity test. But it re-ran the test and everything was O.K. This was usually what happened and the EPA has never required IP to actually try to pinpoint what is toxic in their effluent. They only have to do these toxicity tests twice a year. But some of the other parameters were shockingly high. IP reported a chemical oxygen demand (COD) value of 36,287 pounds per day. These are chemicals that remove oxygen from the water. The paper industry has no limits on this parameter. The average Biochemical Oxygen Demand (BOD) value was 3,905 pounds per day with a daily maximum of 8,598 pounds per day. These are chemicals and organic substances which consume oxygen. The BOD value is measured after five days but paper mill effluent BOD can still consume oxygen even after 100 days. If you measure the BOD of paper mill effluent after 100 days, it is usually four to five times (some researchers have found 10 times) higher than the five-day value. Total suspended solids were also near the permit limit of 8,000 pounds per day. IP reported in December 2015 an average Total Suspended Solids value of 6,931 pounds per day. I thought that between the COD (chemical oxygen demand) and BOD (biological oxygen demand), it was no wonder that waters such as Perdido Bay receiving paper mill effluent were very low in oxygen.

In March 2016, I sent an e-mail asking the DEP spokesperson about this COD and what it was. His reply:
"EPA documents that Chemical Oxygen Demand (COD) is a measure of the quantity of chemically oxidizable material present in wastewater. Sources of COD include the pulping area, recovery area, bleaching area, and papermaking area. A portion of COD is readily biodegradable while the rest is resistant to biodegradation (i.e. "refractory"). The refractory portion is derived from spent pulping liquor (i.e., kraft mill "black liquor"), thus COD biodegradability indicates the degree

to which spent pulping liquor is recovered from brown stock
pulp. Wastewater COD loads also correlate with discharges of
toxic organic pollutants that are not readily biodegraded. IP's
permit requires reporting COD both as a concentration and
pounds per day. EPA has not yet established effluent guidelines
for COD. IP's permit requires reporting COD both as a
concentration and pounds per day. EPA has not yet established
effluent guidelines for COD. IP's COD data shows an average
111milligrams/liter and 21,976 pounds per day."[9] Great! This
is a measure of the toxic components and it is high. I thought
that if COD were taxed instead of black liquor given a tax credit,
the COD number would go down in a hurry. This is the problem
with pollution control; there are no economic incentives to
controlling pollution except making the processes more efficient.
Even then, these big industries are going to cut corners. If
pollution was taxed, we might see some progress.

So, the situation in 2016 as I write this book is that the
permit for IP supposedly expired in March 2015. It had made a
timely application in the Fall 2014 and DEP has not yet acted on
it. This means we are probably in an administratively continued
permitting situation, as before. The Consent Order, which is not
supposed to act as a permit (it says so in the Consent Order) is
good until 2019. IP has not yet applied for any site specific
alternative criteria. Life in the bay does not appear to have
improved.

Several weeks ago, I was kayaking in the bay around the
corner from our beach in the bayou. In the mouth of the bayou
were lush grass beds with fronds floating on the surface of the
water. This grass bed had been growing in the bayou for years,
but this year looked especially lush. The only problem with this?
The fronds floating on the surface of the water were red. They
are supposed to be green. The last time I saw grass beds with
red fronds was in 1998 and 1999, just before all the grass beds in
Upper Perdido Bay died. At that time, I examined the fronds
under a microscope. You could see the chloroplasts (the little

organelles which contain the chlorophyll) were deformed. I supposed this was also true with the red fronds this time. It was one more indication that the bay water was herbicidal. These grass beds just happened to survive because the water coming out of the bayou provided sufficient dilution. Their lush growth showed they were getting sufficient nutrients. So, Friends of Perdido Bay continues to wait and watch.

FOAM COLLECTED AT SEAWALL

CHAPTER 15 ~ Hiding the Problems – The TMDL Rule

The poor health of Perdido Bay in 2016 can be traced back to decisions made decades ago – a time before the current global economy. But as U.S. industries began to compete on a global stage, government regulators began to lessen environmental regulation of U.S. industries. An example was the environmental policy changes made in the mid 1990's led by policy maker Ms. Chertow and Daniel Esty of the Yale School of Forestry and Environmental Studies and Yale Law School. The focus was no longer on industrial "point source" polluters which had to obtain permits but on "non-point" source polluters which did not have permits. Dirt roads, storm water runoff, and all kinds of unmeasured chemicals coming from domestic wastewater treatment, such as aspirin, were now the reasons for degraded environments. Governments had to do a better job monitoring these "non-point source" parameters. Federal monies became available to monitor storm water. Municipalities had to obtain storm water permits. According to this new policy, the Clean Water Act had accomplished the job and major dischargers had reached the goals set for them. These policies were good for American manufactures that were competing in a global world where foreign competition often lacked any rules.

As time went on I began to understand why Dr. Livingston had ignored the oxygen consuming properties of paper mill waste and concentrated on the nutrients. He was the purveyor of the new environmental policy which was being pushed by the Clinton administration and his friend Vicki Tschinkel. Biological Oxygen Demand (BOD) and oxygen consuming solids of the paper industry (TSS) were no longer considered a problem. Just as the modeler, Tom Gallagher, had ignored TSS in his models, so were government policy makers. These were the conventional pollutants which supposedly the Clean Water Regulations had taken care of, not so much by actual clean up but by policy determination. It was a gift to the paper industry and all the large land owners who sold trees to paper mills. But on a small non-flushing bay like Perdido Bay, conventional pollutants were still a big problem.

During the permit administrative hearing in 2007 making a case for non-point sources of pollution, especially in Upper Perdido Bay, was hard. As Dr. Livingston testified in 2007 at the first hearing,

"Perdido is just a very simple system where for many years we have had one major source of nutrients that were anthropogenic to the bay and upper bay, and that was a pulp mill. So that makes it very simple. We have one source. We have a very narrow, small system. We can run the entire system in a tidal period, which is very important in synotic sampling. So it makes it relatively simple to study. And to understand how it works is more complicated, of course. But it is a lot simpler than on many of the other systems that we're talking about. So the Perdido system fits into a galaxy of systems as a relatively simple system with a relatively low level of development in terms of people. It isn't like New York City; it isn't like Chesapeake; it isn't like Seattle. You know, it's a relatively simple system. It was, in many ways, natural in terms of the, for instance, the Perdido River. The loading there hasn't changed much except when the drought occurred, we had very low loading. But it hasn't changed much because it (the river) hasn't been polluted. The water is still in good shape based on our 18 years of work."[1]

Government regulators did not want to hear about BOD and TSS. They wanted to make the problems in Perdido Bay into mysterious non-point source problems which are very difficult to cure. They wanted to see dirt roads, landfills, filling wetlands, etc. as the culprits, not the paper mill. This was the "Ecosystem approach" which was being touted as the new environmental approach by the Clinton administration (See Management Plans). A lot of great sounding environmental initiatives were being proposed like the EPA's "Clean Water Action Policy, Restoring and Protecting Americas Waters"

"In his 1998 State of the Union Address, President Clinton announced a major new Clean Water Initiative to speed

*the restoration of the nation's precious waterways. This new
initiative aims to achieve clean water by strengthening public
health protections, targeting community-based watershed
protection efforts at high priority areas, and providing
communities with new resources to control polluted runoff.*"[2]
It sounded great, but we would have to see what fruits were
produced.

In July 1998, a bound, 157-page plus appendices, new
Perdido Ecosystem Management Strategies report came out.
(See Management Plans). It had cost a lot of money to print.
The report said that it had been prepared by the Perdido
Ecosystem Restoration Group (PERG) and the Florida
Department of Environmental Protection. As far as I knew,
PERG had met very few times, certainly not enough to produce a
report at this level. I was given special recognition as having
made significant contributions to the document. I never recalled
making much of any contribution except to remind the group that
the paper mill was the major problem in the bay. Somewhere in
the 157 plus pages, the paper mill is mentioned along with
livestock operations, unpaved roads, and storm water.

Besides money for this elaborate book, monies to print
up fliers to get citizens involved were also available. But the
fliers again tried to place the blame for the degraded
environment of Perdido Bay elsewhere. One of the headlines in
the flier read *"Who makes the biggest pollution contribution to
the Perdido ecosystem?" Big industry? Consider this....."*
Then the flier goes on to list the various reasons why it was not
just Big Industry. These industries were regulated. The problem
was known and solved with them. It was the other polluters -
golf courses, cleaning products, our lifestyles. In some cases,
this may be true. But as Livingston said, the Perdido watershed
was not heavily developed. It was a simple system with a big
polluter - a paper mill. Citizens were not going to be interested
in coming to meetings to hear that their life styles were causing
the problems when everyone knew it was the paper mill.

The 1998 Ecosystem Management report also mentioned two EPA reports, both required by the Clean Water Act. One report is called the 305(b) report and gives the overall water quality of all the waters in the U.S. The overall water quality is based on water chemistry, nonpoint source assessment, evidence of toxic material, and fish consumption advisories. The other report is called the 303(d) report. This report lists all the waters which do not meet all the "applicable" water quality standards. For those water bodies not meeting standards, the Clean Water Act requires that an assessment called the Total Maximum Daily Load Assessment (TMDL) be done. Total Maximum Daily Load calculations for waters deemed impaired had been a requirement of the Clean Water Act for many years; however, states and the federal government had ignored the requirement. It was not until big environmental groups such as Earth Justice began suing the EPA to implement TMDLs, that the requirement was recognized.   There were so many water bodies not meeting standards that the EPA had to prioritize the list. Only those water bodies which were listed as "poor" water quality were addressed. In 1998, Perdido Bay was listed as not meeting the water quality standards for nutrients and dissolved oxygen; its water quality was fair.

At the time, it was important to me that Perdido Bay remains on the list of water bodies not meeting water quality standards, i.e. impaired, because permits could not be issued to new dischargers if the water body was impaired and the impairment would continue because of the discharge. Any permit issued to the paper mill could not be less stringent than the past permit as long as Perdido Bay remained "impaired." As I viewed the situation in 1998, the longer pollution of Perdido Bay continued, the fewer people would realize how beautiful Perdido Bay could be. Things should get better, not get worse. The mill had to continue to meet more stringent standards than those set by the technology-based limits of the rest of the paper industry as long as Perdido Bay remained "impaired". The opposite was also true. If the paper mill discharge should cease

297

and Perdido Bay became beautiful and full of life as it once was, people would see the change. No discharger could ever again be able to use the bay as its dumping ground. The bay would be lost forever as a discharge site, certainly a boon to the property owners on the bay and to the local economy. So the stakes were high.

The states were taking over their own assessments of waters in the late 1990's. A lot of federal money was being given to implement and install storm water controls. Much of the water quality testing was being directed toward measuring the success of these storm water controls. The local municipalities would write grants to get funding for this testing. In 1999, the Florida Legislature passed a bill which authorized the Florida DEP to draft rules to implement total maximum daily loads. It had the euphemism "The Florida Watershed Restoration Act of 1999" The Florida statute was 403.067. The intent of the legislature is given in the first paragraph.

"(1) Legislative Findings and Intent - In furtherance of public policy established in s. 403.021, the Legislature declares that the waters of the state are among the most basic resources and that the development of a total maximum daily load program for state waters as required by s. 303 (d).........will promote improvements in water quality throughout the state through coordinated control of point and nonpoint sources of pollution. The Legislature finds that, while point and nonpoint sources of pollution have been managed through numerous programs, better coordination among these efforts and additional management measures may be needed in order to achieve the restoration of impaired water bodies. The scientifically based total maximum daily load program is necessary to fairly and equitably allocate pollution loads to both nonpoint and point sources...."[3] The calculation of a Total Maximum Daily Load (TMDL) was fairly straight forward; TMDL = wasteload allocation for a discharger + load allocation for nonpoint source + natural background. TMDLs were to be done on water bodies

which were listed as "impaired" or not meeting standards. This is where problems arose - identification of impairment. The statute gave the Florida's Department of Environmental Protection, the authority to

"...adopt by rule, a methodology for determining those waters which are impaired. The rule shall provide for consideration as to whether water quality standards codified in chapter 62-302, Florida Administrative Code, are being exceeded, based on objective and credible data, studies and reports, including surface water improvement and management plans approved by water management districts and pollution load reduction goals developed according to department rule."

I thought the last sentence of this statute was the "loophole".

In 1999, a Consent decree between EPA and the environmental group, Earthjustice, imposed a 13-year schedule to development more than 2,000 specific TMDLs in Florida. Often the threat that EPA would come in to Florida and establish their own TMDLs was enough to make the state regulatory agency do something. DEP had to establish their TMDLs in Florida. DEP set up a website to explain what a TMDL was.

"Section 303 (d) of the CWA requires states to submit lists of surface waters that do not meet applicable water quality standards (impaired waters) after implementation of technology-based effluent limitations, and establish Total Maximum Daily Loads (TMDLs) for these waters on a prioritized schedule. TMDLs establish the maximum amount of a pollutant that a water body can assimilate without causing exceedances of water quality standards. As such, development of TMDLs is an important step toward restoring our waters to their designated uses. In order to achieve the water quality benefits intended by the CWA, it is critical that TMDLs, once developed, be implemented as soon as possible......Implementation of TMDLs refers to any combination of regulatory, non-regulatory, or incentive-based actions that attain the necessary reduction in pollutant loading. Non-regulatory or incentive-based actions may include development and implementation of Best

299

Management Practices (BMPs), pollution prevention activities, and habitat preservation or restoration. Regulatory actions may include issuance or revision of wastewater, storm water, or environmental resource permits to include permit conditions consistent with the TMDL. "[4]

      With the legislature's blessing, DEP got busy. Even before the statute was passed, DEP was holding meetings on TMDL's. Beginning in March 1999, representatives from DEP were going around the state holding meetings to explain the program to the public. I remember going to the meeting in Pensacola but at that point it was difficult to make any decisions on the program. Generally, it sounded like a favorable program. It was a massive undertaking with 55 DEP staff members involved. Daryl Joyner was the program administrator and seemed very nice. Still, I was suspicious that government regulators would try to hide Perdido Bay's problems.
To develop a rule to define impaired waters, DEP appointed a Technical Advisory Committee. Their first meeting was August 12, 1999. DEP staff would write the rule using the federal TMDL rule as the guideline and then the TAC committee would refine it According to the statute, this rule had to be scientific and based on creditable data. I knew several of the Technical Advisory Committee (TAC) members. When I saw that Tom Gallagher (the modeler who had worked with Dr. Livingston) was on the TAC, I began to worry. From August 12, 1999 to August 28, 2000, this committee met monthly in different parts of the state. There was lots of transparency. Many public funds were spent. I had seen how DEP adopted rules, before. Generally, they would hold two or three meetings about the proposed rules and then the rule would go before the Environmental Regulatory Commission (ERC) for passage. But the Impaired Waters Rule got a real dose of sunshine; meetings were held all over the state for a whole year.

      A second technical advisory committee was formed that was supposed to deal with allocation. The first meeting was held

June 14, 2000. The fourteen members of the allocation technical advisory group were introduced. They were mostly from government organizations, but two were from big environmental groups. In the opening remarks, Daryll Joiner said

"...that the membership of the technical Advisory committee provides a broad-based representation and that DEP needs this group to provide input on how to allocate TMDL's. He added that the Department formed this TAC to help prepare a report to the legislature, which is due February 1, 2001, on the allocation process." I guessed that allocation was very important issue so that "non-point" sources did not take all the blame for the pollution. Non-point sources would include farm run-off. The big farm groups were very concerned that they would get strapped with the blame and with rules. So far, farmers only had to comply with "best management practices" which has no enforceable limits. The Florida Department of Agriculture and Consumer Services was a co-enforcer for the TMDL's for "non-point" source problems. This second technical advisory committee didn't last long. According to some accounts, the Florida Sunshine Rules were so severe that many members feared they would be in violation of the law, and be punished. The committee disbanded.

During the summer of 2000, policy meetings took place about what data was going to be important as far as being considered impaired. Nutrient (nitrogen and phosphorus) values and chlorophyll a (the green pigment in plants) was going to be important. Note: Florida did not have a numeric nutrient rule at this time. Also, taking a water body off the impaired waters list or delisting was also important. By August 2, 2000, a draft rule was already circulating. Its administrative number was 62-303 and was known as "the Impaired Waters Rule".

Once DEP drafts a rule, the rule must go before the Environmental Regulation Commission (ERC) to get a formal passage. The members of the ERC are appointed by the governor, so true independence is questionable. But most members of the ERC have some environmental credentials.

Many are developers, as that is a big industry in Florida. The Governor at this time was Jeb Bush with David Struhs as DEP secretary. I did not attend the ERC meeting when the Impaired Waters Rule was passed, however, I had sent in comments about the rule. Comments would allow me to have standing if I should decide to challenge the rule. I could see language in the rule which provided huge loopholes and which would take Perdido Bay off the Impaired Waters List. The rule passed the ERC on April 26, 2001. I was really surprised about how easily it had been adopted and passed. Usually, if the big guys (United Industries of Florida, Phosphate Council, Pulp and Paper, and the Big Agriculture Groups) oppose a rule, it is nearly impossible to get a rule passed. And once a rule has passed which the "big" players oppose, they can hold it hostage in court forever or until the DEP legal department has run out of money. DEP will "negotiate" before it runs out of money. The budgets of environmental agencies have been cut in recent years and so has their "negotiating" power. The environmental agencies are like toothless tigers. I knew the "big guys" probably supported the rule, but why?

On May 9, 2001, DEP put out a press release announcing the adoption of the new "Impaired Waters Rule". It put a positive spin on the rule:

"Florida's Impaired Waters Rule More Protective Than Federal Standard" was the headline. The press release developed a defensive tone when it said: *"...Some environmental groups have assumed that the new methodology is more lenient and will result in a shorter 303 (d) list. However, the new method is much more environmentally conservative than the Department's old methodology in many ways."* I had heard some criticism from some environmental groups, but not much. The Florida Impaired Waters Rule, Florida Administrative Code Rule 62-303, was written so water bodies had to go through two stages. First was the planning list. All waters identified as impaired in 1998 (the 1998 305(b) report) were placed on the planning list. The DEP would then go out and do an assessment

302

to determine what parameters were causing impairment. If the water body was still found to be impaired after the first round of assessments, then it was placed on the verified list for a TMDL determination to be done, depending on what was causing the impairment.

In the 1998 305 (b) list, Perdido Bay was found to not meet (impaired for) dissolved oxygen and nutrient standards. In that year, I had written a letter to a panel of citizens which the DEP had formed to examine the problems on Perdido Bay called the "Citizens Advisory Panel" or "CAP". This committee was composed of two or three citizens (I was one of them) from Perdido Bay and another ten or twelve were citizens from other areas. In the letter, I had stressed the impairment due to nutrients and enclosed photos of algae-covered crab traps and masses of drift algae at our beaches. Dr. Livingston never acknowledged that the massive amount of drift algae at our beaches ever existed. He only reported the blooms of toxic algae, *Heterosigma*, which had begun in 1995. The citizens who lived on Perdido Bay never saw any indication of toxic algae blooms, only drift algae. Perdido Bay was also not meeting the biology criteria for benthic diversity. The Livingston Studies were demonstrating this impairment, but the bay had not been placed on any planning list for impairment due to biology. At that point, I don't know of any bay that had been listed as impaired due to biology, but I figured this would change when the DEP team came out to do an assessment of the bay. At this point, Florida had not adopted a nutrient rule. All water bodies in Florida were placed in Groups 1 to 5 and the state would begin the assessments starting in Group 1. Perdido Bay was placed in Group 5. It would be one of the last basins to get an assessment.

The Florida Impaired Waters Rule, Florida Administrative Rule 62-303, had a large loophole written into it. Despite the impairments, I was very worried that this loophole was going to be used to take Perdido Bay off the impaired list. Perdido Bay would lose any special protection it had. The paper mill could be given a permit without any special requirements such as lowered BOD or Solids levels. Section 62-303.100 (5) says:

"Pursuant to Section 403.067, F.S., impaired waters shall not be listed on the Verified List if reasonable assurance is provided that, as a result of existing or proposed technology-based effluent limitations and other pollution control programs under local, state, or federal authority, they will attain water quality standards in the future and reasonable progress toward attainment of water quality standards will be made by the next 303(d) list for the basin is scheduled to be submitted to EPA. "[5]

At this time, DEP's Secretary, David Struhs, was promoting this partnership with ECUA and a wetlands treatment. According to DEP, this novel technology was going to bring IP into compliance with water quality standards in Florida, and Perdido Bay was going to meet those standards. The low dissolved oxygen in the deeper parts of Perdido Bay was considered "natural" because the mouth of Perdido Bay had been dredged early in the 1900's and salt water had entered. When salt water entered, the bay became layered with heavier salt water on the bottom and fresher water on top. This created a barrier through which oxygen did not pass. The result was oxygen was used up in the bottom layers. What was totally ignored was the 8,000 to 12,000 pounds per day of oxygen consuming materials being dumped into the bay by the paper mill. This material sank to the bottom and contributed to very low oxygen. This settling of solids in Perdido Bay was what the Gallager model had ignored. And this dumping of sludges had been going on since the 1950's. So Perdido Bay was considered historically degraded. But wasn't this rule supposed to be part of a "Water Restoration Act"? It was supposed to correct the problems.

I decided in 2001 to challenge the validity of the rule because of this glaring loophole. Did the legislature really mean to allow the Department to have such "unbridled discretion" to take a water body off the impaired waters list for some future improvement? I didn't think so. On April 9, 2001, I sent in my petition for a formal administrative hearing. In my petition, I listed the two parts of the rule which appeared to me to be glaring loopholes. I also suggested language which I thought would tighten up the rule and make it "less capricious," one criterion for denying a rule. I thought the case would be DEP versus me. A small case, where DEP might consent to the changes I suggested. Was I ever wrong! The "big guys" jumped in. These were probably the groups behind the statute and rule to begin with - the Florida Electric Power Coordinating Group Inc.; the Florida Pulp and Paper Association Environmental Affairs, Inc.; Florida Manufacturing and Chemical Council, Inc.; and Florida Water Environment Association, Inc. I understood why the rule had passed so easily. The big players were behind it. This probably meant that the rule was supposed to take waters off the "impaired" waters list rather than "restore" them. This really wasn't a "Water Restoration Act" at all. Joining me on our side (Petitioners) were Linda Young's Clean Water Network. This included the groups: Apalachicola Bay and River Keeper, Inc., Save Our Bays, Air and Canals, Inc., Florida Public Interest Research Group, Citizen Lobby, Inc., Santa Rosa Sound Coalition, Friends of Saint Sebastian River, Save Our Suwannee, as well as Linda Young. The attempt to close a loophole had turned into a full-fledged fight. Not what I hoped.

Linda Young and her environmental efforts were admirable and successful, but she also seemed to have a hidden agenda. I later found out that she had been funded by a liberal organization - the Tides Foundation. George Soros was one of the contributors. While she promoted environmental issues, and was very good at getting media attention, she never really helped us on Perdido Bay with our problems. I suspected that she wanted to prevent the paper mill from discharging to Escambia Bay, but did not want it to close. Many Democrats supported timber growing and retaining forests as a buffer against climate change, and paper mills were the market for timber growers.

Ester's lawsuit (Chapter 11) was begun by Linda Young and her attorney, Steve Medina. Sometimes I thought that her involvement hindered our efforts. The rule challenge was one time when I thought her involvement hurt our cause.

In the 2001 hearing, there were two main attorneys for the Big Guys - Terry Cole who represented the Paper Industry and whom I continued to meet in court over the next several years, and Jim Alves from the big Tallahassee law firm, Hopping, Green, Sams and Smith, P.A. Both were excellent attorneys. David Crowley was the main attorney for DEP. For our side, Linda Young had gotten Steve Medina and Jerrel Phillips to represent her groups. Steve Medina was the same attorney who had originally started Ester's lawsuit in 2001. I represented myself and usually sat behind Linda Young at the hearing table. The case had turned into serious litigation. Subpoenas were served on many witnesses. Even David Struhs and Jeb Bush were subpoenaed by Mr. Medina. Both subpoenas were quashed (cancelled by the Court). I had not really intended to have a big hearing, but it had gotten out of hand. My main witness, a law professor from the University of Florida, Joe Little, had written a Memorandum of Law supporting the fact that the rule was an invalid exercise of delegated authority to DEP. This is one of the requirements to have a rule overturned. Judge Lerner presided over the hearing and wrote the Final Order at the end. The hearing was held in Tallahassee, FL and lasted nearly three weeks - September 4-7, 10-14, and 17-21, 2001. We were in a hearing during the 2001 September 11th terror attacks on the Twin Towers. The remainder of the hearing was cancelled for that day. I lived in a motel room in Tallahassee, Florida for three weeks across from the location the hearing was held. My husband, Jim, was teaching at the time and could not accompany me. We talked every evening. I thought that a lot of the testimony from our side was rather ridiculous and tedious. I didn't think there was much point to a lot of it. Most of the parts of the rule were straight forward and pretty good. The National Resource Council had reviewed the

Florida Rule and it had passed their examination. There were still parts of the rule, however, which I found to be vague and would allow the DEP to take a water body off the impaired list for any reason. I decided to amend my petition to include those parts as well. The Judge allowed me to amend my petition at the end. I was still puzzled about Linda Young's involvement and wondered if there had not been some collusion between the "Big Guys" and Linda Young and her supporters.

The Judge's Order in this case would be the Final Order. All parties had written Proposed Orders and then responses to the Proposed Orders of the other parties. In the end our arguments were rejected. On May 13, 2002, in a thorough 465-page tome, our petitions were dismissed. The Judge found our arguments not persuasive. We appealed, but I figured that was rather hopeless since the Judge had been thorough in his analysis of the 3 -week hearing. Even though I was skeptical about what would happen to Perdido Bay with this rule, there were still some good parts to the rule which I figured would keep Perdido Bay on the "Impaired Waters" list. Because the rule stressed the importance of Chlorophyll in determining impairment, our algae blooms in the 1990's would certainly put us on the impaired list. Further, the decline in life on the bottom which Dr. Livingston was documenting would be part of the determination for impairment. Dissolved oxygen was still very low in the certain places in the bay, especially in the bottom waters. The low dissolved oxygen added to the paucity of bottom life, as Livingston had explained in his 2000 report.

Perdido Bay was placed in Group 5 which meant the TMDL assessment would begin five years after the TMDL program started. In 2004, DEP called and asked if I would be interested in doing some boat monitoring stations for dissolved oxygen for the TMDL. I knew that the DEP biologists were no longer sampling stations in Perdido Bay. I had oxygen and salinity meters which I took and had calibrated at DEP's office. Beginning in the Spring of 2005, I sampled approximately 10 stations in Perdido Bay, starting with Elevenmile Creek and going down the bay to Innerarity Island. I sampled from surface to the bottom taking a reading every ½ meter. I did this every other month in 2005. I would turn my data into the DEP office in Pensacola. They would then enter the data into the state's central data storage called STORET. STORET was not a user-friendly system so I was never able to look at the data unless I requested a copy of it. I never did as I trusted that DEP was entering the data correctly.

My sampling showed the low dissolved oxygen in the bottom waters, especially if the layering of water was present. While Dr. Livingston made a big deal out of the layering of water, this phenomenon was only present some of the time - like 25%. I was pretty sure that my data would keep Perdido Bay on the "impaired list" for dissolved oxygen as there were many samples below the state requirement of 4 parts per million. Bay water on the surface usually met the state standards, however if a sample was taken early in the morning; occasionally the dissolved oxygen fell below the state standard of 4 parts per million. Dr. Livingston's data also showed low dissolved oxygens in the deeper waters, however, I was not sure if Dr. Livingston's data was being entered in the STORET system. After 2005, I was not keeping track of the TMDL process, as my husband and I were busy challenging the permit which was being proposed for IP.

Some of our witnesses at the first and second administrative hearings spoke about sampling the bottom of Perdido Bay for the TMDL program in the summer of 2005. They all remarked about paucity of life on the bottom and how they had to continuously sample before they found even one living worm. The biologists told me it looked like toxicity was present. This information was consistent with what Dr. Livingston was reporting. Later, when I had time I followed up on this information. I requested the bottom biology data from DEP. No report existed about this 2005 sampling of life in the

308

bottom. A 2005 report on sediment data existed, but no report on the biology of life in the bottom. For this book, I continued to try to get the biology report. A report didn't exist according to the current DEP person in charge of the TMDL program as of 2016. I contacted some of the same biologists who had testified for us at the hearing and who had mentioned the 2005 testing of the bottom. One of the biologists recalled the biologists taking samples and finding very little life. He said he did remember seeing a data printout from the lab analyses showing a "severely altered biological community". He put copies in the Pensacola bio lab files. They are not there today. Perdido Bay never was listed as impaired for biology.

I continue to pursue this oversight by the state DEP. The most recent explanation that I have received from the DEP is that *"FDER does not have a specific bio-assessment method for estuaries, other than the Shannon-Weaver Diversity Index."* There is nothing wrong with using the Shannon-Weaver Diversity Index; however, the state may not want to use it because too many waterbodies may be found to be "impaired". All past (more than 10 years old) Shannon-Weaver Diversity Indices measured on Perdido Bay were less than 3 and most were less than 2, indicating a severely impaired bay. Maybe in the next round of assessments in 2017, the bottom biology will be examined. But I am not holding my breath.

The oxygen data which I had submitted to DEP had been "refined" as I later found out in early 2016. An upper level administrator had selectively chosen which data to use to determine impairment. My data, showing violations in dissolved oxygen at the lower depths, had been removed as "outliers". The result - Perdido Bay was no longer violating oxygen standards. It was removed from the impaired list for dissolved oxygen in 2009, one year prior to IP getting their permit. When I discovered this, and asked for an administrative hearing, my petition was ignored. I also learned that the local person who had entered data into the STORET data system complained to the administration. She got into trouble because she kept insisting that more dissolved oxygen violations existed in the STORET system. There are honest people working in the environmental agencies, but few will go against their bosses who have political agendas.

During 2005 to 2009, I was unaware that DEP had contracted with an engineering firm to develop a watershed hydrologic and water quality model for Perdido Bay. In 2007, DEP hired Camp, Dresser and McKee (CDM) and Dynamic Solutions to develop a watershed model which would be used by FDEP to develop TMDLs for Perdido Bay. At the time the firms were hired, Perdido Bay was still on the impaired waters list. It wasn't until 2010 or 2011, that I found out about the model. While DEP was not advertising that they had developed a model, they had not destroyed any evidence of this model either. I was able to obtain a CD with the model results. According to the authors, data for the Perdido Bay model came from the 1990's and 2000's. The model considered three "point" dischargers - the International Paper mill, Bayou Marcus Domestic Wastewater Plant and Foley Domestic Wastewater Plant. The model also looked at "non-point" sources. Some of the data was Dr. Livingston's. The model simulated the bay's flow and water quality from 1987 to 2005. The model was calibrated with data from 1993 to 1994. I thought the predictions of the model looked fairly accurate. The dissolved oxygen values predicted by the model showed that most stations in Perdido Bay were going to have minimum oxygen values below the state standard of 4 mg/liter, and some stations were very low, like 1 or 2 mg/liter. The model values agreed with measured values. So Perdido Bay would have remained on the "impaired" water list for oxygen if the model had been used. But administration at DEP did not want this information to come out.

Further, the model predicted average values for nutrients, total nitrogen and total Phosphorus and Chlorophyll a, for the entire bay. The average total nitrogen was 0.235

milligrams/liter (mg/l); total phosphorus was 0.010 (mg/l), and the chlorophyll a was 0.0023 mg/l. This was simulated values for years 1999 to 2005. The values predicted by the model were usually close to the actual average data taken from over 150 data pairs. The site specific nutrient values for Perdido Bay had not yet been established in the Florida nutrient rules. These site specific nutrient values did not get formal approval until 2014. The actual nutrient values which were established for Perdido Bay in 2014 were much higher than the values which came out of the 2007 model; in some cases, three times as high. These high nutrient values would accommodate the high nutrients put out by the paper mill and the increased domestic wastewater which was being planned for discharge to Perdido Bay. But the problem remained - how were these high nutrients not going to cause excessive algae blooms in Perdido Bay as in the past? The huge amounts of drift algae which we had seen as late as 1999 had not reappeared. When International Paper took over the mill in 2000, all plant life including seagrasses and vegetation along the shoreline had disappeared. Perdido Bay will not be listed as impaired for nutrients, not because high nutrients are not present, but herbicidal effects of the paper mill effluent will keep the algal growth under control. The red seagrasses seen in a local bayou adjoining Perdido Bay in the summer of 2016 are indications of un-natural properties of the bay's waters

The passage of a "site specific nutrient rule" in 2014 for all bays in Florida took care of the nutrient impairment problem. Perdido Bay had its own specific set of nutrient standards which had been "scientifically set" by the same group of scientists who had found blooms of toxic algae - Livingston, Gallagher, Niedoroda and several other scientists. The values established for Upper Perdido Bay are the highest in the state. The data had been taken from Livingston's good years. There were fewer data sets than the 2007 model had used. DEP ignored any attempt to challenge these limits as our "due process" requirements had been fulfilled in the 2008 to 2010 administrative hearings.

As of the close of 2016, Perdido Bay is only impaired for mercury, and per state regulators, that is soon to be removed. To me, the Total Maximum Daily Load (TMDL) rule did nothing but remove waterbodies from the "Impaired Waters List", as DEP's press release had said it would not. To date, 1,287 waterbodies in Florida have been "delisted" as impaired. Exactly how many of those waterbodies have been "restored" so that they actually meet water quality standards is questionable. Certainly, Perdido Bay is not a "restored" water body. Elevenmile Creek, the creek into which the paper mill used to dump, is certainly cleaner, but does not yet meet water standards. The "restoration" process was an illusion of government. Perdido Bay remains an unrestored bay with little life and dangerous levels of chemicals. Thanks to government agencies, the paper mill will be free to discharge its wastes and turn the bay into its own treatment pond.

CHAPTER 16 ~ Final Observations

Even though as of the close of 2016 Perdido Bay remains unrestored with little life and dangerous levels of chemicals, I continue to use it for swimming in the summer. It is warm and salty, and on a hot summer's day one can forget the chemicals while enjoying a swim in its tea-colored water. As I float in the water and look at the puffy cumulus clouds in the blue sky, I try not to think about mercury and the other chemicals that lurk there, and I enjoy the beautiful solitude of the water gently lapping at my backyard. It is a peaceful way to keep cool. I don't have to drive anywhere and I enjoy living here. I continue to monitor the bacteria in the bay, sometimes with alarming results. Some people use the bay for swimming; others don't. I still worry about the health of my grown children after swimming in dioxin-laden water for the years of their childhood. I still wonder if my husband's skin cancer could have been caused partially by the chemicals in the bay. In Spring and Fall, you may catch a stray red fish or a trout. The water in summer is too hot for fish. But you won't see mullet, anchovies, menhaden fish or flounder as we used to see in the years before the paper plant's pollution took its course. One or two blue crabs occasionally will show up. Small baby clams appear in the bottom and then disappear. A few snails show up on the groins. No seagrasses. The dissolved oxygen is low in the bay, but no one sees "low-dissolved oxygen". No one sees chemicals. Perdido Bay remains impaired going into 2017, but the states of Florida and Alabama do not list it as so. The trickery of rules and a lack of sampling have pretty much taken care of any recognized impairment. If you don't sample the waters, you will not identify the problems. And if you haven't lived here long, you won't notice the decline in bay life.

As I look back I can see that our chances of success were predictably slim. We were faced with money and power we never knew existed until we engaged in battle with the paper companies. Maybe there was even corruption. We figured if

300 to 400 people got up and complained and made noise we would prevail, but we were wrong – even with the environmental laws on our side. The Florida Rules which had been copied from the Clean Water Act stated, "...*all surface waters of the State shall at all places and at all times be free from pollution*...." (Florida Administrative Code 62-302.500 (1). But as an attorney for International Paper told me, those rules were boiler plate. They didn't mean anything in the end.

The big guys in the industry and in state politics just waited - waited for the complaints to die down. They changed the rules and environmental policy to make our case weaker and would continue in control as they had in the past. Friends of Perdido Bay still exists mainly through the bi-monthly newsletters which I continue to write, and we also have a website: www.friendsofperdidobay.com

We continue to keep the issue of our bay before the public. The local media and the *Pensacola News Journal* no longer carry stories about Perdido Bay as they once did. We who live on Perdido Bay don't want the public and our government to think it has been cleaned up and the problem solved. Friends of Perdido Bay members faithfully send in dues and donations along with occasional suggestions and encouragement. We know that as far as help from the government is concerned, we are on the losing side. We no longer write letters to our congressmen. It seems a waste of paper. More pressing environmental issues such as climate disruption are getting all the media attention. Maybe this book will help. I hope so.

While our bay continues to deteriorate, the area has been able to save the 400 union jobs at the paper mill, and the economic impact of the mill on the local economy. The mill is now operating on an expired permit. It ran out in March 2015. IP made a timely permit application, so now the DEP must make the determination on whether to give it a permit or not. IP is trying to get alternative permit standards for discharging to the wetland where their effluent has killed 90% of the trees. Maybe our government will finally do the right thing and deny the permit as they should. That should have been done 30 years ago. However, power and money kept the mill operating, hoping, that citizens would go away, shut up, or maybe just die.

Our bay is like many others around the country supposedly protected by environmental rules, but continues to decline under this questionable "protection." As Howard Ernst writes in *Chesapeake Bay Blues* (2003)[1], economic primacy will prevail in policy decisions. This local paper mill provides jobs and is an important part of the area economy. The forests which grow in the watershed and provide the raw material for the paper mills protect the water quality of the bay. To replace forests with development would certainly not be good for the bay. It seems like we must pick our poison since economic growth marches on. If the true cost of making paper, such as lost fisheries and devalued properties, was considered, paper would be much more expensive. But property owners like the people on Perdido Bay subsidize the paper-making process, thus contributing to its cheaper cost.

As for the environmental agencies, I sometimes think that the big guys keep the agencies operating to give legal validation to their pollution. These paper industries get permits to pollute. The 12,000 pounds a day of solids which IP discharges into the wetlands and Perdido Bay is legal. Of course, there are always battles about how much can be legally discharged.

The industries are continually trying to weaken the rules. But everyone has the same level of treatment (called technology based standards), so no paper-maker is stuck with extra expenses for treatment. It is pollution-treatment fixing process. If everyone must do it, then no one is at a disadvantage. The problem arises when our industries compete with industries

315

overseas which don't have the same rules or when industries discharge into little bays and the effluent is not properly diluted, such as in Perdido Bay. The close-loop technology which regulators have been pushing for paper mills is a false dream. Who is going to force paper mills to adopt this technology? Not likely the government.

Enforcement of the rules was always the major problem. Industries do their own compliance testing. It's kind of like the fox monitoring the hen house. Occasionally, the environmental agencies will check once a year with an advanced notice. It is easy to spill chemicals and ignore it. There are also force majeure clauses written into the permits for industry. Too much rainfall, too cold weather, etc. are considered acts of God. Upsets in treatment are forgiven also as acts of God. Air permits have so many days of venting allowed. Toxic air and water substances can be legally emitted. Enforcement was when citizens' involvement in the environmental process became mettlesome for the environmental agencies. We pointed out to environmental agencies that the paper mill was breaking environmental laws and most likely had been for years. The state had simply been issuing permits while ignoring the violations. It was the easiest thing to do. You don't want to make your pet industry mad. So, what did the state of Florida do? They simply stopped environmental testing. If we wanted to prove the industry was violating the laws, we would have to collect the data. If industry doesn't make too big of a mess, the public won't notice; they cannot see toxic chemicals.

So, what is the mission of the environmental agency? Well, the mission will most likely mirror what the governor and legislature want it to be. Of course, no politician is going to say they are not interested in the environment because people care about the environment. But our current governor in Florida, Rick Scott, puts jobs as the most important agenda. I am sure that most of the upper level managers at Florida Department of Environmental Protection are aware of this. Governors Chiles

316

and Bush took away most of the job protection of the civil service system in Florida. You can get fired just for going against the Governor's wishes. People like me are considered an enemy at DEP. The big money people in Florida elect politicians like this, so not everyone is going to get equal protection. The EPA, which has oversight over the state environmental programs, has been weakened by continual budget cuts and riders put on spending bills. In recent years, its actions have been very disappointing. I belong to the national environmental group, League of Conservation Voters. At least weekly I get an email warning of Congress's latest attack on the EPA. The email usually asks for money. So, it seems protection of the environment depends on the politicians we elect, and we are electing politicians who would rather see the EPA go away than protect the environment. I wonder what would happen if the EPA went away. I think it would be chaotic. Companies are going to make as much money as they can. Without rules, little bays like Perdido Bay would be polluted for profit without limit. Our air would be much dirtier. People take for granted the clean air and water we have in the U.S. Just go to Asia or India to see how unpleasant it is to live in areas with weak environmental rules. Blue sky is a luxury we take for granted.

I have heard people say, "get rid of EPA and let lawyers handle the damage caused by industry." Lawyers have their own agendas. Our experiences with lawyers and law suits were not positive. The last lawsuit we had on Perdido Bay simply allowed the pollution to continue. Lawyers must eat and the deep pockets of industry know this. This is not a solution. The public gets most of their information through the media, which frames the issues from all the others. In recent years, it seems to have focused on the latest sensational story or the latest celebrity status or sports. Job loss and industries moving overseas always grab headlines. In 2017, the latest president, Donald Trump, won because he promised to bring jobs back to this country. These are things people care about. But people also care about a clean environment even though the issue doesn't make headlines. We don't want chemicals in our water or in the fish we eat or in the air we breathe. It takes constant vigilance. Stories about how little bays are being polluted and citizens' properties are being devalued don't make the news. But ours is a story about Big Government run by Big Money trampling on the rights of citizens. So, what could we have done? Violence such as Edward Abby might have recommended? That would have made news for a week or two. Or maybe an economic impact statement which showed that rising property values were more beneficial to the community than paper mill jobs. This is perhaps a one-day news story. A representative of the paper mill once told me truth is an illusion. But maybe to some people, the truth is real. And the truth is that waterways like Perdido Bay are dying while big government and big industry continue to thrive. I can only hope this book will lead a new generation to fight for clean water before it's too late.

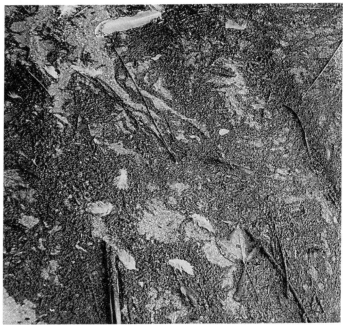

BIRD FEATHERS CAUGHT IN BLACK MILL SCUM

REFERENCES and NOTES

Chapter 1

1 There have been various documents over the years which describe Perdido Bay and River. The latest is Perdido River and Bay Watershed Characterization (draft), Northwest Florida Water Management District prepared by Ecology and environment, Inc. December 2016.

2 *Perdido River.* Outdoor Alabama, Alabama Department of Conservation and Natural Resources. 2014.

3 D. Ray, personal communication

4 Ibid. 1

5 Ibid. 1

Chapter 2

1. While the paper mill has never admitted making "soap", the paper making processes use the same chemicals which are used to make soap – sodium hydroxide and resin acids from wood. There have been many complaints from citizens on Perdido Bay dating back to the 1960's about foam as seen in early studies such as the "Effects of Pollution on Water Quality Perdido River and Bay Alabama and Florida". US Department of the Interior, Athens, GA. 1970. It has been found that "The source of the unaesthetic excessive foaming in Perdido Bay reported by residents of both Alabama and Florida is the inadequately treated wastes from the St. Regis Paper Company." P. 23.

I also have photos of foam coming from the top of the paper mill "foam suppression tower" at the outfall of the paper mill effluent into Eleven Mile Creek. Also we have reports documenting the paper mill use of anti-foaming chemicals.

Chapter 3

1. A letter from Champion environmental supervisor, D. Arceneaux, to DER permitting engineer, Steve Baisden, dated October 7, 1986, outlined how Champion had pulled the weirs on a settling pond on October 1, 1986 to lower the level of the ponds to clean out the pond. Sludge was allowed to run out into Elevenmile Creek. We knew from EPA studies that it took three days for the effluent to travel down

Elevenmile Creek and reach Perdido Bay. See Chapter 4 "The Mill" for more information.

2. Paper mills release large quantities of BOD as compared with domestic wastewater treatment plants. Much of the BOD is contained in the large amount of solids or sludges which paper mills release. The sludges and BOD may be refractory chemicals or small wood fibers which take a long time to degrade.

3. My request for administrative hearing dated October 2, 1987. The docket from this administrative hearing can be found at https://www.doah.state.fl.us/ALJ/searchDOAH/detailasp. The case number is 87-004921

4. Florida has several designations for public interest – "Clearly in the public interest" or "Not contrary to public interest". An example can be found in Florida Statute 403.061 (27) for designation of Florida Outstanding Waters.

5. Item No. 14 "Compliance Requirements" of the Consent Order 87-1398 which went into effect November 14, 1989

6. Ibid. 5

7. From *Pensacola News Journal* article dated November 22, 1988.

8. Finding of Fact #47 (Page 32). Recommended Order of Michal Ruff entered on September 28, 1989

Chapter 4

1. It was shown in studies on bottom sediments, that past accumulations of toxic material in deeper parts of Perdido Bay, were also affecting the health of the bay.

2. As part of IP's 2002 permit application, a schematic diagram of the treatment ponds was included

3. Tom Jorling, Vice president for the Environment at International Paper Company personally told me this when I asked him why paper mills did not filter their effluents

4. Letter from David Arceneaux, environmental engineer at Champion to Steve Baisden, engineer at DER, dated October 7, 1986.

Chapter 5
1. Steven Schropp et al., *A report on Physical and chemical processes affecting the Management of Perdido Bay Results of the Interstate project.* Alabama Department of Environmental Management and Florida Department of Environmental Regulation, January 25, 1991.

2. *An Evaluation of Finfish and Shellfish Resource Changes in the Perdido Bay Vicinity.* Division of Ecological Services, Panama City Field Office. US Fish and Wildlife Service Southeast Region, Atlanta, Georgia. July 1990

3. Changes in Submerged Aquatic Vegetation in Perdido Bay, 1940 – 1987. Division of Ecological Services, U.S. Fish and Wildlife Services, Southeast Region, Atlanta, Georgia, December 1990

4. Ibid. 3

5. *Site Specific Information In Support of Establishing Numeric Nutrient Criteria for Perdido Bay.* Department of Environmental Protection, Department of Environmental Assessment and Restoration, December 2012.

6. *Toxic Characterization Report for Perdido Bay, Alabama, and Florida.* Michael Brimm. U.S. Fish and Wildlife Services, Fish and Wildlife Ecological Services, Panama City Field Office. U.S. Fish and Wildlife Service. Southeast Region. Atlanta, Georgia, 1993.

7. Timothy Hall, "A Review of Recent studies in North America Using Integrated Monitoring Approaches to Assessing Bleached Kraft Mill Effluent Effects on Receiving Waters" in *Environmental Fate and Effects of Pulp and Paper Mill Effluents,* edited by Mark R. Servos, Kelly R. Munkittrick, John Carey, and Glen J. Van Der Kraak, 599-612. Delray Beach, Florida St. Lucie Press, 1996.
8. *Draft Gulf of Mexico Toxic Substances and Pesticides Characterization Report,* Science Applications International Corporation, Under Contract to Technical Resources, U.S. EPA Gulf Breeze Research Laboratory, April 30, 1993

9. Dale T. Drysdale and Stephen A. Bortone, "Laboratory induction of intersexuality in the mosquitofish, *Gambusia affinis*, using paper mill effluent", *Bulletin of Environmental Contamination and Toxicology* 43(4) (1989): 611-617.

10. My letter to B. Kriegel. "The nutrient limitation studies I view as missing the whole point about what is wrong with Perdido Bay. A quick examination of the levels of Total Organic Carbon which are put into Perdido Bay by the paper mill would certainly provide a very reasonable explanation for what is wrong with Perdido Bay. I wrote this hypothesis to Skip in the beginning and will give it again here. Perdido Bay is a carbon driven system - very much like a secondary treatment pond. The carbon which is put into this bay is food for heterotrophic organisms. These heterotrophic organisms compete with the autotrophic plants for nitrogens and phosphoresces. In the summer, with the warm water temperatures, the heterotrophs win and out-compete the phytoplankton. This keeps the plankton to rather low levels considering the amount of nitrogen and phosphorus that is entering the bay. In the winter with cold water temperatures, the heterotrophs are kept at a rather low productivity. This allows more nitrogen and phosphorus for plant growth. However phytoplankton does not occur. What does occur is a huge bloom of drift algae which "blooms" in the shallow, clear nearshore waters. For the past four winters, we have had Cladophora and this winter, Enteromorpha, blooming along this shore of Perdido Bay. As far as the nutrient limitation studies are concerned, they are not designed to show this competition between heterotrophes and autotrophes for nutrients, as they are only measuring autotrophes. Matter of fact, what I am afraid is happening here is the use of science to befuddle and baffle an otherwise obvious problem. Twenty years ago the problem in Perdido Bay was identified as too much carbon. Recently the Florida/Alabama Interstate study also identified the problem as TOO MUCH CARBON from the paper mill (about 90% of all carbon entering Perdido Bay comes from

11. Camp, Dressler and McKee and Dynamic Solutions. *A Watershed Hydrologic and Water Quality Model for Perdido River and Bay*. A Report submitted to Department of Environmental Protection. September 1, 2009.

12. *Bacteriological Survey of Champion International Corporation and Elevenmile Creek.* Wastewater Compliance Evaluation Section Division of Water Facilities and Biological Section, Florida Department of Environmental. 1999.

Chapter 6

1. House Bill 2574 was introduced by Rep. Hutton from Florida and Rep. Callahan from Alabama in 1991

2. "Opponents of Permit Argue for Environment". Pensacola News Journal, May 18, 1990

3. "Escambia No. 2 in State in Toxic Releases". Pensacola News Journal, June 8, 1990.

4. *An Assessment of Particulate Matter, Ozone, and Air Toxics in Escambia and Santa Rosa Counties.* "Phase I Assessing and Relative Risks Associated with Criteria and Air Toxic Pollutants in the Pensacola Area". *Partnership for Environmental Research and Community Health, Air Quality Study, Final Report.* Georgia Institute of Technology. December 15, 2007. Can be found at www.wfrpc.org/pdfs/perch phase I.pdf.

5. "Champion Accused of Polluting Bay Water". Pensacola News Journal October 12, 1990

6. "Letter from Harry Dail to Dick Deforio dated May 16, 1991, subject: 1990 Penalties"

7. Verified complaint from Jacqueline Lane to Department of Environmental Protection about nuisance algae. Dated May 5, 1993. Complaint contained pictures of algae.

8. Douglas Ferrell's, an EPA scientist, comment made in 1993 on the Livingston study.

9. "40 CFR Parts 63 and 430. *Effluent Limitations Guidelines, Pretreatment Standards, and New Source Performance Standards*: Pulp, Paper and Paperboard Category: National Emission Standards for Hazardous Air Pollutants for Source Category: Pulp and Paper

Production; proposed Rule". December 17, 1993, Federal Register, Volume 58, No. 241. Pp 66078 – 66216.

10. The Division of Administrative Hearing's case number of the administrative hearing on the 1993 air permit is 93-002053. The docket in this case can be seen by going to the Florida Division of Administrative hearings website: www.doah.state.fl.us, and type in the Case Number.

11. Fred Garth. In Editorial "Is Champion doing enough", Con side. June 27, 1993.

12. Modification to Compliance Plan and Application for Variances. Prepared by Champion International Corporation. September 1995.

13. EPA had provided sediment metals data to the author. Also, a study had been done on Escambia Bay in the late 2000's. This reference is: Carl Mohrherr, Johan Liebens, and Ranga Rao. *Screening of Selected Contaminates in Sediments of Escambia Bay, Pensacola, FL. June 15, 2009*, can be found at the website: www.researchgate.net/publication/267838085.

14. Scott Streeter and Dexter Chambers. *Critics scorn Champion Plan*. Pensacola News Journal July 17, 1997

15. Kevin Dietrich. *Champion to Trim Units, Cut Jobs*. Pensacola News Journal. October 9, 1997.

16. A Report of the Special Grand Jury on Air and Water Quality. Circuit Court of the First Judicial Circuit in and for Escambia County, Florida. June 10, 1999.

17. A selection from the Grand jury report - *"...We find that the Northwest District of the Department of Environmental Protection failed to properly implement and enforce environmental laws, rules and regulations. The district office succumbed to political, economic, and other pressures, allowing regulated businesses, industries and individuals to pollute the area's air and water ...."* (p 3).
"...It is clear, however, that the largest single source of water pollution is Champion's pulp and paper mill in Cantonment. It is also

clear that the largest domestic source of water pollution is ECUA's Main Street plant...." (p 20).

"...Champion's "waste treatment system removes 95% of BOD, but the effluent still has a substantial amount of BOD substances. In addition, the effluent has considerable amounts, and a high concentration of nutrients, such as un-ionized ammonia, specific conductance compounds, suspended solids, chlorinated compounds, and other harmful substances. The suspended solids absorb natural and synthetic substances and metals. When the freshwater flow of Elevenmile Creek mixes with the saltier estuarine waters of Perdido Bay, the solids fall out and accumulate in the sediment, where they consume large amounts of biological oxygen....." (p 24).

"...Northwest District of DER then (1988) stopped almost all ambient water quality monitoring in the Perdido Bay System, and elsewhere in the area, even though the mill was visibly and obviously polluting Elevenmile Creek. Biologists were assigned to other duties, the Pensacola lab was dismantled, and the task of monitoring was given to the Northwest Florida Water Management District. The water management district could not perform this work, however because of lack of funding. Monitoring was left to Champion, its paid consultants, and to volunteers from the Bream Fishermen's Association." (p 28).

"Scientists inside and outside of DEP found the Livingston Study (1992) contained numerous invalid comparisons, internal inconsistencies, and unsupported conclusions, as well as inconclusive data. DEP biologists specifically disagreed with the study's conclusions about the causes of hypoxic (little oxygen) conditions in the bay. They believed the study showed that "Champion's discharge was a major contributor to the problem in the bay" (p 29).

"In 1994, when the 1989 temporary operating permit was set to expire, Champion applied for a new operating permit. The application included yet another plan for complying with state water quality standards. The plan consisted of two phases. Phase One was a $50 million project which involved in-mill process improvements to reduce waste by reclaiming and recycling chemicals and other raw materials. Phase Two was a $50 million project which involved increasing the mill's storm water surge capacity and tertiary waste treatment system. Phase One was to start in 1994, finish in December 1995; Phase Two was to start in 1995 and finish in December 1999....Phase One was completed in 1996; Phase Two was never completed." (p 30).

"Today, four years after applying for a new permit, and twelve years after the last issued five-year operating permit was set to expire, DEP has not made a decision on Champion's application. By operation of law, Champion can continue to discharge on the basis that its application is "pending". Through all twelve years of procedural maneuvering, Champion has not complied with state water quality standards and permit conditions." (p 30).

"It was apparent by 1997, however, that Champion did not, and perhaps could not, comply with more important standards for specific conductance, in-ionized ammonia, dissolved oxygen, and biological integrity. Results of monitoring Elevenmile Creek since 1970 shows that turbidity, specific conductance, ammonia and BOD had risen." (p 31).

"...The easiest and more financially beneficial choice for Champion is to relocate its wastewater discharge to a larger receiving water, such as Escambia River or Perdido Bay.

Accordingly, we find that relocation of the discharge of mill effluent would be contrary to law and the long-term development interests of this area. DEP should not issue a permit to Champion to relocate their discharge to either the Escambia River or Perdido Bay. Furthermore, DEP should not grant Champion variances for its effluent. "(p 36).

18. Robert Livingston. *Perdido Bay Pollution 'Ecosystems approach 'needed to save bay.* Pensacola News Journal. June 27, 1999

19. Anton Caputo. *Woman to take Champion to court.* Pensacola News Journal. January 24, 2000.

20. Jonathan Hicks. *Champion sells Berkshire 300,000 shares.* New York Times. December 7, 1989.

Chapter 7

1. United States Environmental Protection Agency; Office of Water Regulation and Standards, National *Dioxin Study; Tiers 3, 5, 6, and 7.* Washington, D.C., 1986.

2. United States Environmental Protection Agency; Office of Water Regulation and Standards, National *Dioxin Study; Tiers 3, 5, 6, and 7*. Washington, D.C., 1986.

3. My article from "Tidings" about dioxin.

"Because the EPA announced that dioxin had been found in fish samples from Elevenmile Creek, I decided to write a "feature" article describing dioxin, where it is found, its toxicity to animals and man, and the relative magnitude of the values in Elevenmile fish. The following information was gleaned from The National Dioxin Study, *EPA, 1987, and from* Dioxin, *an article appearing in Scientific American, 1986.*

Dioxin is a generic term for a variety of chemicals formed from two benzene rings joined by two oxygen atoms. Chlorine atoms are found attached to the benzene rings. One of the most toxic varieties is 2, 3, 7, 8-TCDD. Dioxin is formed as a by-product in the manufacture of two herbicides, 2, 4, 5-T, which is 50% of Agent Orange and Silvex), of hexachlorophene (remember Dial soap), and of pentachlorophenol (a wood preservative). Dioxin is not removed during the manufacture and hence contaminates these above products. Dioxin is a combustion product of the ash and smoke in incinerators and wood burning stoves. Electrical transformers which are filled with PCB emit dioxin when they catch on fire. In short, dioxin is a by-product of many industries in many nations. Dioxin is soluble in fat and barely soluble in water. It adheres tightly to the organic fraction of soil and leaches very little from the soil once there. Its half-life in soil is estimated to be 10 years. The half-life of dioxin in fish is estimated to be one year. Dioxin is degraded by sunlight and a fungus (white wood-rot). In sites which have been Superfunded to remove dioxin contaminated soil, soil is sent to an incinerator and dioxin is removed by complete combustion.

Dioxin is very toxic to animals in low concentrations, although the level depends on the species of animal. Levels which have been shown to reduce survival are 0.056 parts per trillion (ppt) in coho salmon, 0.038 ppt in rainbow trout, and 1,030 ppt in a water flea. Variability in toxicity has been shown by guinea pigs which are very sensitive and hamsters which are less sensitive. Dioxin has been shown to induce reproductive abnormalities in rats at 1 to 3 ppt levels. Dioxin is a proven carcinogen in rats, causing liver and lymph-type cancers when ingested at levels of 2 ppt and above for long periods of time.

The effect of dioxin on humans is open to question. In cases where humans were known to be exposed to dioxin, no statistical evidence could prove any long-term effect (no longer than 15 years), including cancer. It is known that exposure of humans to relatively high doses of dioxin causes chloracne (a boil-like eruption on the face and buttocks), digestive disorders and flu-like symptoms. However, based on dioxin's carcinogenic activity in rats, the EPA issued a B2 level of concern for dioxin in humans. This says that eating fish containing 1ppt of dioxin could cause an increased lifetime risk of cancer of 1 in 100,000 people. The Food and Drug Administration (FDA) on the other hand, considers the risk of eating fish contaminated with dioxin much less (9 times less) than the EPA. Based on consumption of fish around the Great Lakes, the FDA recommended that concentrations of dioxin up to 25 ppt in the filet did not pose an unacceptable risk to public health. However, I must stress there is no scientific data on long term ingestion of low levels of dioxin by humans. Levels of concern of the EPA and FDA are based on data from rats.

In 1983, the EPA began a sampling program to determine the levels of dioxin nationwide. They sampled sites where they expected dioxin to appear and other sites where there had not been any previous known sources of dioxin contamination. The latter sites were essentially 'background' sites. Fish were sampled from 305 'background' sites over the nation. A fish sample constituted a whole-bottom feeding fish, a bottom-feeding fish filet, a whole predator or game-fish, and a predator or game-fish filet. The detection limit was approximately 1 ppt and standard deviation was 12% of the value. Thirty-one percent of the rivers, Great Lakes and estuaries contained detectable levels of dioxin in whole fish samples. Of those sites, which had contaminated fish, 67% had dioxin levels below 5 ppt in whole fish, and 1% of the sites had whole fish samples above 25 ppt. Both sites with the highest dioxin levels in whole fish came from rivers with upstream pulp and paper mill discharges. Pulp and paper mills had hitherto not been considered a source of dioxin. The chlorine bleaching process in paper mills that make white paper is thought to be the source of dioxin.

The levels of dioxin found in fish from Elevenmile Creek were 25.5 ppt in a whole carp and 4 ppt in a small large-mouth bass filet. While these levels are not above the FD guideline limit of 25 ppt for a filet, the whole fish levels are relatively high compared to published data from other sampling areas in the U.S. Champion only recently converted to a fully bleached system utilizing oxygen delignification as part of the bleaching process. Oxygen delignification is supposed to reduce the levels of dioxin produced. However, the change in process and technology is too recent to allow very many conclusions at this time. Presently, the EPA is testing all bleached mills, including Pensacola. What now?

At least three things need to be answered as quickly as possible. 1) Are the samples from Elevenmile Creek truly representative? 2) What is the level of dioxin in fish in Perdido Bay? 3) Is there an increased incidence of cancer in people who eat fish where dioxin has been found?

Brad Durling, a fisheries biologist and member of Friends of Perdido Bay, notes that

it is very likely that fish from Perdido Bay, especially the middle and lower parts, will have dramatically lower levels of dioxin than fish from Elevenmile Creek. Since dioxin, like many other contaminants, tends to accumulate in the fatty tissues, proper preparation of fish can reduce levels in the eaten portion. Use skinless fillets and remove the strip of dark colored meat from the lateral line area of the fillet."

4. Mr. Kriegel's letter - "Your letter to the News Journal concerning dioxins is one dealing with a very important and rapidly changing issue. I would suggest we meet to discuss these types of issues, rather than communicating thru the news media......Presently, item No. 18 in the Consent Order requires Champion to provide DER with timely reports on the EPA/Paper Industry dioxin studies. The Department and EPA will evaluate the data and take appropriate and timely action.

Champion plans extensive testing this summer in conjunction with the Florida Pulp and Paper Association. Working with EPA, they have retained consultants to test locally for dioxin levels in fish and shellfish. Testing should begin in June, 1989......

In addition to our concerns regarding the presence of dioxin, we are also very concerned about the presence of mercury in fish tested recently...Additional data will be forthcoming in the very near future regarding dioxin levels both in the Perdido Bay/Eleven Mile Creek area...."

5. As I began to write this book, I became convinced that we had not seen all the dioxin data which Champion and EPA obtained. On August 27, 2015, I made a "Freedom of Information Act" request for

dioxin values from Champion International Paper Company located in Cantonment Florida from 1986 to 1996. EPA responded saying they could find no records.

6. Pensacola News Journal, September 22, 1990

7. Jim Trapp. Letters to the Editor. *Amazed by letter sent by Champion.* Pensacola News Journal. May 14, 1990.

8. Federal Register. Environmental Protection Agency, 40 CFR Parts 63 and 430, Effluent Limitations Guidelines. Part II. December 17, 1993.

9. A good summary article of the dioxin argument can be found in a National Wildlife article online at https://www.nwf.org/News-and-Magazines/National-Wildlife/News-and-Views/Archives/1994/The-Truth-About-Dioxin.aspx

10. Pro Earth Times, "Commission says no!! to soft Dioxin Standard", April 1992

11. *EPA: Dioxins pose more risk than previously thought.* Pensacola News Journal from Associated Press. May 12, 1994

12. Ibid. 11

13. Ibid. 8

Chapter 8

1. http://www.dep.state.fl.us/water/watersheds/swim.htm

2. Dereliction of Duty; A profile of the Northwest District of the Florida Department of Environmental Protection. PEER White Paper, Number 18, August 1997.
3. State Archives of Florida on line. Record Group No.000550. Ecosystem Management Files 1992-1999.

4. Ibid. 2

5. *Perdido Ecosystem Management Strategies.* Department of Environmental Protection. July 1998 Page 2.

6. Perdido Bay Community Based Watershed Plan. The Nature Conservancy. December 2014.

Chapter 9
Howard R. Ernst, Chesapeake Bay Blues: Science, Politics, and the Struggle to Save the Bay. New York: Rowman & Littlefield, 2003.

2. The paper published from these studies - Jacqueline Lane, "The effect of variation in quality and quantity of periphyton on feeding rate and absorption efficiencies of the snail *Neritina reclivata* (Say)", J.Exp.Mar.Biol.Ecol. 150 (1991): 117-129.

3. "Changes in Submerged Vegetation in Perdido Bay, 1940-1987". Division of ecological services Panama City Field Office, U.S. Fish and Wildlife Services, Southeast Region, Atlanta, GA. December 1990. (Draft Report funded by 1988 EPA Cooperative Management Project.)

4. Ibid. 3.

5. Dolf Wijk and Thomas Hutchinson, 1995, "The Ecotoxicity of Chlorate to Aquatic Organisms: A Critical Review." Ecotoxicology and Environmental Safety 32, 244-253.

6. Arno Rosemarin, Karl-Johan Lehtinen and Mats Notini, 1990, "Effects of treated and untreated softwood pulp mill effluents on Baltic Sea algae and invertebrates in model ecosystems." Nordic Pulp and Paper Research Journal No.2, 83-87

7. Robert Livingston. *Perdido Project: Final Report River, Bay and Marsh Analyses.* December 2007.

8. Ibid. 1

9. From EPA data presented at a workshop from website: www.myfwc.com/media/3674454/Hagy-Workshops-Presentations-FlowandNutrients.pdf. James D. Hagy and Michael Morrell. Status

and Trends of Salinity, Water Clarity and Nutrients in Perdido and Pensacola, Bay

Chapter 10

1. Article by Charlotte Crane, Business Editor of Pensacola News Journal, " New owners face problems" Pensacola news Journal, June 11, 2000.

2. Robert Livingston, "Eutrophication Processes in Coastal Ecosystems. A report. August 2000.

3. *After protest, state to look again at paper mill pollution penalty.* Naples Daily News. July 29, 1999.

4. Ibid. 3

5. Scott Streater, *DEP puts teeth into enforcement.* Pensacola News Journal. June 28, 2000.

6. Anton Caputo, *Biologists optimistic om water plan*, Pensacola News Journal, August 16, 2000.

7. "Thinking Ecologically' proposes a framework for future environmental policy. Yale Bulletin and Calendar news Stories, Vol 26, Number 17. January 19 to January 26, 1998.

8. Marian M. Chertow and Daniel C. Esty. Editors, *Thinking Ecologically, The next generation of environmental policy (New Haven: Yale University Press, 1997)*

9. International Paper's Wastewater NPDES Permit Application; Water Quality Simulation for Effluent Wetlands by Nutter and Associates. July 2002.

10. Anton Caputo. *Sewage pipeline gets final O.K.* Pensacola News Journal. October 1, 2002.

11. Ibid. 10

12. Brendan Kirby, "Florida, IP say $84 million plan will clean Perdido Bay". Mobile Register, October 5, 2002.

13. "Pipeline Plan is model for the future", Pensacola News Journal editorial, October 2002.

14. Scott Streater, "ECUA denies bay pollution claim". Pensacola News Journal, July 20, 2003.

15. Dale Perkins, Letter to the Editor, Pelican newspaper, August 2003.

16. Gary Ghioto, *Wastewater project could harm Perdido.* Pensacola News Journal. September 26, 2003.

17. Elizabeth Bluemink. *Wastewater project draft nearly done.* Pensacola News Journal, October 3, 2003.

18. Anton Caputo, "Cantonment mill to cut 21 jobs". Pensacola News Journal, October 11, 2003.

19. Alisa LaPort. *"Environmentalists want say in IP's wastewater permit"* Pensacola News Journal. December 6, 2003.

20. Ibid. 19

21. Editorial in St. Petersburg Times. "Pulp Nonfiction" January 2004.

22. Sheila Ingram. "IP drafts permit for 10-mile pipeline." Pensacola news Journal September 3, 2004.

Chapter 12
1. Lynette Wilson. "Paper mill to cut more jobs". Pensacola News Journal, July 20, 2005.

2. Anne Thrower. "IP plans to produce less costly linerboard". Pensacola News Journal, January 28, 2007.

3. Nathan Crabbe. *U.S. Judge sets back pulp mill waste plan.* Gainesville Sun. January 15, 2007.
4. Anne Thrower. *Paper mill to switch production this spring.* Pensacola News Journal, January 10, 2007

Chapter 13

1. Paid ad in the Pensacola News Journal. May 9, 2008

2. IP discharge issues unresolved. Views Editorial. Pensacola News Journal. May 11, 2008

3. *IP Plan: Not the best.* Pensacola News Journal. May 18, 2008.

4. From 1999 EPA Toxic Release Inventory as cited in *Assessment of Environmental Pollution and Community Health in Northwest Florida.* Final Report September 30, 2009.

5. Robert J. Livingston. *Perdido project: Final Report River, Bay and March Analysis.* December 2007

6. Chris Read, Mill Manager. International Paper's Pensacola Mill. Environmental Policy. Proposed permitting documents. July 18, 2008. Page 244.

7. Ibid. 6 Page 242.

8. *Updated Summary of Operational Performance of the Pilot Constructed Treatment Wetlands at the Pensacola Mill.* CH2MHill. May 1998.

9. International Paper Company, Pensacola Mill. Revised Fact Sheet. Page 24 of 27. July 18, 2008.

10. Bram Canter. Recommended Order in DOAH Case No. 08-3922, 08-3923, Jacqueline Lane, Friends of Perdido Bay, Inc., and James Lane vs. International Paper Company and Department of Environmental Protection.

11. Decision First District Court of Appeals Case No. 1D07-4198, Friends of Perdido Bay, Inc., and James Lane v. Florida Department of Environmental Protection. September 22, 2010.

Chapter 14

1. Standard Methods for the Examination of Water and Wastewater, 20th Edition. 1998.

2. Carlton Proctor. *At long last, relief.* Pensacola News Journal. August 12, 2012.

3. Jeff Herrington. *St. Joe Co. sale of timberland to make Mormon Church Florida's biggest private landowner.* Tampa Bay Times. November 7, 2013

4. Lucy Morgan. *In Taj Mahal Tale, questions raised in judicial ruling.* Tampa Bay Times. October 8, 2010.

5. Christopher Scinta. *International Paper Sets Sales of Timberland for $6.1 billion.* Wall Street Journal. April 5, 2006

6. Meeting announcement from the Mobile Bay Sierra Club. *Securing the Future of Our Southern Forests*, a presentation with a discussion by Emily Zucchino and Rita Frost of Dogwood Alliance. March 1, 2016

7. Personal e-mail from DEP personnel to J. Lane. November 5, 2014.

8. Nutter and Associates, 2015 Annual Monitoring Report, Combined Effluent Distribution System. International Paper, Pensacola, FL January 2016

9. Personnel communication (e-mail) between DEP personnel and J. Lane. March 7, 2016.

Chapter 15

1. Testimony of Dr. Robert Livingston in Florida DOAH case Number 05-1610, Jacqueline Lane vs. Department of Environmental protection and International Paper Company.

2. A quote from Perdido Ecosystem Management Strategies. July 1998. Prepared by The Perdido Ecosystem Restoration Group and The Department of Environmental Protection. Page 8.

3. Chapter 99-223, Laws of Florida.

4. From Florida DEP website June 2016.
http://www.dep.state.fl.us/water/tmdl/background.htm#iwrdev.

5. Florida Administrative Code 62-303.100(5)

Chapter 16
1. Howard R. Ernst, Chesapeake Bay Blues: Science, Politics, and the Struggle to Save the Bay. New York: Rowman & Littlefield, 2003.

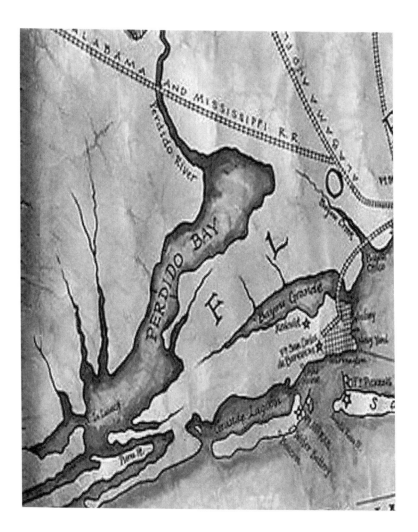

Perdido Bay

TIMELINE

October 1, 1986. Champion effluent routed to new aeration basin at 8:20 a.m. Sludge reached Perdido Bay 3 days later.

October 4, 1986. Massive fish and clam kill in Upper Perdido Bay. This event stoked an environmental outburst.

December 25, 1986. Date Champion converts mill to fully bleached. Historical exceedances of: nutrients, organic solids, BOD, transmissivity, toxicity and nuisances of odor, color, foam.

January 22, 1987. First meeting of Perdido Bay Environmental Association. Bill Kruczynski, an EPA scientist, said the bay was dead.

January 3, 1988. EPA's NPDES for Champion Permit expires. This is the permit which was issued in 1983

December 1, 1989. Florida's Temporary Operating Permit and Consent Order 87-1398 for Champion International goes into effect. Champion given 5 years to come into compliance with state standards.

August 7, 1990. EPA's NPDES permit goes into effect, except for several contested issues

November 9, 1992. Class action lawsuit against Champion filed in Baldwin County Alabama court by citizens on Perdido Bay for dioxin contamination

December 21, 1992. Champion applies for an air construction permit to make "improvements".

Spring 1993. Begin to see excessive blooms of drift algae at our beach due to excessive amounts of nutrients, mainly phosphorus.

April 1994. DEP announces they are going to give Champion an extension on their permit.

December 1, 1994. Champion's Temporary Operating Permit for Florida with variances and Consent Order expires.

Summer, 1995. Toxic algae, *Heterosigma,* appears in Perdido Bay.

October 2, 1995. Champion's federal NPDES permit transferred to the state of Florida.

April 22, 1996. Letter from DEP to Champion states their entire NPDES permit was rendered ineffective due to evidentiary hearing requests. NPDES permit issued in 1983 still in effect.

May 3, 1996. Five Million dollar settlement between class members on Perdido Bay and Champion approved by Alabama Judge.

May 27, 1997. Champion requests an additional year to look at feasibility of going into a neighboring Escambia River and Bay.

August, 1997. My field notes note increased sea grasses growing inshore at our beach.

Spring, 1998. Mike Papantonio, a local attorney with the Levin Papantonio Firm, starts running T.V. ads against Champion.

April 15, 1998. New performance rules (Cluster Rules) for the paper industry adopted and go into effect. By 2016 paper industry must achieve a "closed loop system".

February 2, 1999. Champion announces they have suspended their plans for going to Escambia River. They seek a permit to remain in Elevenmile Creek.

January 24, 2000. Announcement of legal action against Champion/IP, beginning of Ester's lawsuit

Spring, 2000. All life including plants and animals disappears from Upper Perdido Bay. International Paper takes over mill.

April 26, 2001. Impaired Waters Rule passed by Florida's Environmental Regulation Commission.

February 23, 2003. Dioxin of 33.3 Parts per Trillion (PPT) found in the sediments of Upper Bay.

January, 2004. David Struhs, Secretary of DEP, becomes IP's Vice President for Environment, Health, and Safety.

September 16, 2004. Hurricane Ivan, a category 3 hurricane hits Pensacola... Many Friends of Perdido Bay's homes flooded.

October 13, 2004. Meeting on DEP's draft permit to IP partnering with ECUA and go to wetlands surrounding Perdido Bay.

April 20, 2005. Friends of Perdido Bay, along with the Lanes, challenge NPDES permit issued by DEP to IP to build a 10-mile pipeline that would discharge to a wetland near Perdido Bay.

July 18, 2007, Escambia County Civil Court judge denies Class Certification in Ester's lawsuit. Lawsuit abandoned.

August 8, 2007. DEP Secretary denies permit for IP to go to a wetland discharge around Perdido Bay.

December, 2007. IP applies again for an NPDES permit to go to a wetland. IP still not meeting state standards, required to have a Consent Order.

March 15, 2010. IP wins second hearing. NPDES permit with a Consent Order goes into effect and is to expire five years later. IP must come into compliance within that time.

February 17, 2016. DEP sets specific numeric nutrient criteria for Perdido Bay. Limits for some nutrients are the highest in the state.

December, 2016. International Paper remains out of compliance with state laws. Perdido Bay is still badly degraded.

January 22, 2017. International Paper mill in Cantonment has an explosion. Mill is shut down.

GLOSSARY oF ACRONYMS and TERMS

ADOC   Alternative Dissolved Oxygen Criteria

ALJ   Administrative Law Judge

BAT   Best Available Technology Economically
               Achievable

BCT   Best Conventional Pollution Control
               Technology

BPT   Best Practical Control Technology

BOD   Biological or Biochemical Oxygen Demand

COD   Chemical Oxygen Demand

DER   Department of Environmental Regulation
               (changed in 1993 to **DEP** - Department of
               Environmental Protection)

ECUA   Emerald Coast Utilities Authority used to be
               Escambia County Utilities Authority

EPA   Environmental Protection Agency

ERC   Environmental Regulation Commission

FAWRCC   Florida Alabama Water Resource
               Coordinating Council

HAP	Hazardous Air Pollutants
IP	International Paper Company
MACT	Maximum Achievable Control Technology
MGD	Million Gallons Per Day
NPDES	National Pollution Discharge Elimination System (Federal Permit)
PBEA	Perdido Bay Environmental Association
PNJ	Pensacola News Journal
PPM	Parts per Million or milligrams per kilogram or micrograms per gram
PPT	Parts per thousand or milligrams per gram; if written ppt means parts per trillion
PPQ	Parts per Quadrillion
SSAC	Site Specific Alternative Criteria
SWIM plan)	Surface Water Improvement Management (a
TMDL	Total Maximum Daily Load
TOP	Temporary Operating Permit

TPD   Tons (usually dry) Per Day

TSS   Total Suspended Solids usually measured
dry weight

WQBEL   Water Quality Based Effluent Limitations

About the Author

With a PhD. in Marine Biology and publications in numerous scientific journals, Jacqueline Lane has applied her expertise and that of her colleagues to a passionate 30-year battle to preserve Perdido Bay. That ecological fight has been well-documented in numerous legal, political, and public relation forums over time, pointing to a larger problem in the United States. Dr. Lane is concerned that the health of native waters has reached an environmental tipping point.